WILD
HOPE

WILD HOPE

Marisa Bate

ONE PLACE. MANY STORIES

HQ
An imprint of HarperCollins*Publishers* Ltd
1 London Bridge Street
London SE1 9GF

www.harpercollins.co.uk

HarperCollins*Publishers*
Macken House, 39/40 Mayor Street Upper,
Dublin 1, D01 C9W8, Ireland

This edition 2023

1
First published in Great Britain by
HQ, an imprint of HarperCollins*Publishers* Ltd 2023

HB ISBN: 978-0-00-839241-3

This book is produced from independently certified FSC™ paper
to ensure responsible forest management.

For more information visit: www.harpercollins.co.uk/green

This book is set in 10.7/15.5 pt. Sabon by Type-it AS, Norway

Printed and Bound in the UK using 100% Renewable Electricity at
CPI Group (UK) Ltd, Croydon, CR0 4YY

For every woman whose story has gone untold

And mostly, for A – the greatest adventure of them all

'Never forget that it only takes one political,
economic or religious crisis for women's
rights to be put in jeopardy. Those rights
are never to be taken for granted; you must
remain vigilant throughout your life'

SIMONE DE BEAUVOIR

'Liberation is always in part a storytelling process:
breaking stories, breaking silences, making new
stories. A free person tells her own story. A valued
person lives in a society in which her story has a place'

REBECCA SOLNIT

'Young hearts run free'

CANDI STATON

CONTENTS

INTRODUCTION:

The polaroid

The polaroid is particularly small. Roughly about 7 x 7 cm. You have to bring the tiny square close to your face and squint, study it like a relic. Which is what I did when I first opened its paper packet. I took it out and held it to my face, breathing it in like I was breathing in the sunshine and wind on the waters of Lake Michigan that summer day.

In the picture it's 1974. My mother, Jacqui, aged 22, is visiting her Aunt June and her family in Omaha, Nebraska, bang in the middle of America. They'd taken a trip to the Great Lakes on the US–Canadian border. My mum is standing in front of the flat blue expanse next to her younger cousin, Vicky. Their smiles sparkle like the light on the water behind them.

That small, square picture is the story of my mother. The story of me. And the story of so many women. It is the story of us, of all our potential and promise, and the many ways in which this world tries to stand in our way. That picture is the story of how we, as women, in all our glorious multitudes, move through the world – and it is the story of how that world shapes, restricts, enrages and responds to us. It is the story of all the freedoms we deserve, how they are fought for and how they are taken away. It is the story of how those freedoms, and the struggle for them, make us who we are, to each other and to ourselves. It is the story of a daughter's pilgrimage to her mother. And it is the story of just how hard and just how miraculous it is to be a woman.

It is no coincidence that this small, square image was taken in the States. Many British people have a love affair with this nation which has long dazzled with its glamour and culture and vast natural expanse. It is ceaselessly transported to us through TV screens and cinemas and books. 'American landscape is *known*, like famous speeches in Shakespeare's plays or phrases in the King James bible are known,' wrote Jenny Diski,[1] a wonderful chronicler of the country. But America has a pull my family specifically cannot resist. It is the backdrop to our most dramatic and revealing tales – stories of crisis and rebirth, adventure and discovery, betrayal and forgiveness, beginnings and endings. My family is nothing but English: my mum is from Essex, my dad is from Bolton and I grew up in Woking. But it's the stories of America that tell me the most about who we are.

If you ask my mum about her visit to Omaha, Nebraska, the words come out of her mouth as one, *OmahaNebraska*, delivered with a smile and glint, like the sound of a ringing bell or as if she's about to start to sing. She says it in such a way that it always conjures something more mythical than Midwestern, or perhaps she makes the Midwest sound like a myth, all hot earth, thundering horse feet and wild Americana.

Growing up, whenever I heard my mum speak of that trip,

it was with awe and wonder. She'd left behind broken, grey 1970s Britain with a collapsed economy and energy strikes, and landed on big green lawns, bowled over by the wide porches and huge refrigerators, life in American technicolour. Nearly fifty years later, now retired, sitting on the sofa in her favourite sweats with some red wine in a small tumbler, she looks past me and says, as if to herself, that things were never the same again after her visit. It was like she'd seen too much. And what she had seen could not be unseen.

That day on the lake, she is wearing tiny cut-off denim shorts, a brown leather belt with a silver buckle, and a tiny brown halterneck crop top, two bits of thin white string holding the scrap of material on her slight, bronzed body. The outfit is indicative of the time: browns, denim and a deliberate affront to any traditional expectations of women. In the picture she looks, I think I can say objectively, magnificent – cool, beautiful, happy, a face full of freedom. It was her first time in the US and she was mesmerized by everything: the wide open space, the endless plains, the big cars, even the McDonalds – she'd never seen one before.

I found this photo a long time ago, when I was about 12 or 13, in my mum's old wooden school desk. The desk is slight, with a rectangular lifting lid and grooves for pencils. Inside are packs and packs of family photographs: Christmas gatherings, birthdays, cats, first days at school. From time to time, I'd open up the desk and rummage around. I'd sit on the floor with a lucky dip selection and inspect each photo. My chief motivation was to find evidence of the family we had once been. I was a baby when my father left. I needed proof he'd been there. But while I was looking for him, I stumbled across another version of her.

Surely it is one of the first markers of growing up: under-standing your parents had a purpose, a life – perhaps even a great one – before you. All we know of them is the stories they choose to tell us, but what about the ones they don't? This was something I understood from the get-go with my father. When a parent leaves and chooses another life, you know it in your bones somehow, even as a baby, long before language or reason can articulate what has happened. But I grew up in a whole other way when I set eyes on that small polaroid. I have always been incredibly close to my mum, but in that photo I saw her as someone else. And she was radiant.

It's not that I ever thought my mother wasn't radiant. She was my life, the love-giving source that made everything warm and bright, that sustained us in every way a human can. Her Muppet impressions left us in fits of giggles. She'd sew late into the night to make me what she couldn't afford to buy. She read every line of *Huckleberry Finn* out loud to me after a long commute home from a demanding job. She had a magical ability to guess the time exactly, sending us racing to the clock in the kitchen to marvel at how she'd got it right again. (Not a magic trick, it turns out, but a result of the military planning involved in being a working single parent.) Her love was fierce and protective, like a bear around cubs. She used to tell us that as long as the three of us – my brother and me and her – were on her paisley sofa, the one she bought with her first Christmas bonus when she was 27 and still has today, forty-three years later, we'd be OK, because all we needed was each other.

But something changed after I found that tiny picture. For the first time, I noticed the shadows on her face, shadows that weren't yet cast on that blustery summer day in 1974. I don't mean ageing, signs of time and wisdom that women have been taught to hate rather than love as signs of a great adventure. Something else.

I would come to understand that the face I knew was that of a full-time working single mother trying her very best in a world that was not set up for her, a world that told her she was a failure. I saw a tiredness that came from the 5.15 a.m. starts to make a daily three-hour round commute, but also from being responsible for everything – every unpaid bill, every logistic, every nightmare, every parent-teacher evening, every playground fight, every scraped knee, getting to every Saturday afternoon guitar lesson. I saw a weariness of disappointment – from her own father to my father: fathers who betray, fathers who do not stay, fathers who live with other people's children but not their own. I saw the sacrifices made. She'd had big career dreams. But when you are responsible for two small children and you need a secure paycheque, ambition has to bend to a new reality. Survival took precedence and so my brother and I became her dreams, the ones she fought for, day in and day out.

I saw the daily battle of her job. By anyone's standards, communications for London's Metropolitan police force – a particularly male and famously sexist institution – must be one of the toughest jobs around. The demanding late-night requests from newspaper journalists. The emergency calls into the office on the weekends. But I think the long hours were still easier than the male colleagues who weren't so sure about the woman, let alone a working mother, in their midst. Years later, her former colleague would tell me that she arrived at the office each morning slightly late, and there were phone calls to me and my brother after school. With her came a fluster, a whirlwind that didn't surround most of the men because they were just doing one difficult job while she was doing two.

Somehow, in that small, square image, I saw the absence of those things, like a colour-by-numbers not yet filled in, a blank, white space. The woman in the picture is blissfully unaware of the duty waiting in her future. It is a portrait of fresh hope that felt immune to the hurdles women faced, hurdles her generation were knocking down.

Only then did I properly recognize the implications of those dark shadows and what they stood for. The realization was like the wind slamming a door shut and jolting you awake. And so, I wanted to know, who is someone without all those things? Without disappointment, divorce, deception, discrimination for simply trying to do your very best each day. Who were you before sacrifices had to be made, before you knew you could have made incredible documentaries like your ex-husband did, but instead did the right and hard thing? Who was she before all of that?

What I knew of the before and after of that photo came to set a framework for how I saw not just my mother but women more generally. What happens to our hopes and dreams in a world that routinely makes things so difficult for us, lays traps, builds walls, closes doors? Working mothers are far more common now but many stubborn problems remain today, from the expensive headache of childcare, to the enduring expectation that the majority of care will fall to women, and all while they continue to be paid less, and are killed by men at a rate of two women a week. These challenges and attacks are only more common for women of colour and women with disabilities.

Why do we still not expect men to take equal responsibility for their children? Why does our economy make it easier for women to stay out of the workforce? Why does our working culture demand more of women while still calling them first over their male partner if their child is sick?

Why do cases of sexual harassment in the workplace happen every day in the UK? Why do women of colour still have to navigate micro-aggressions and racist discrimination? Why did things fall apart so quickly during the Covid-19 pandemic? A litany of broken promises to women's potential lay in its wake: pushed out of the workforce to look after children, denied proper PPE while making up as the majority of frontline workers, a deadly spike in domestic abuse incidents.

As I became older and began a career as a feminist journalist, the photo took on a further significance. When it was taken. The world was still feeling the tremors from a catalogue of political and social shockwaves that started in the 1960s. From Civil Rights and LBGTQ rights, to environmentalism, anti-war protest and a sexual revolution, young people had demanded a different type of society. This call for change had set cities ablaze, sparked new cultures, led to revolts against parents, drafts, governments. Young people spoke and moved and dressed and thought and lived in new ways. My mum was swept along in this current of change: she had just graduated from the University of East Anglia, one of the UK's new universities, the first in her family to get a degree, paid for by a full grant. Unthinkable things were happening: just as my mum returned to the UK, the Watergate scandal hit, resulting in the resignation of President Nixon.

My mum was part of a new wave of women who didn't have

to live as their mothers had, who could pursue careers and dreams independent from being a wife or a mother. In recent years in the UK, the pill had become available, abortion was legalized, divorce had become easier. In the US, Roe v. Wade, the constitutional right to abortion, had passed, putting an end to state-wide bans and restrictions, while the Stonewall riots of 1969 led to a period of transformation for gay rights. In 1971, in a basement in the London School of Economics, the first ever Gay Liberation Front meeting was held in the UK. On both sides of the Atlantic, those with disabilities were gaining new legal protections. The 1960s also saw the birth of the environmental movement. Many of these campaigns learning directly from the civil rights movement of the decade before. For my mum, and millions like her – although by no means all, notably women of colour and low income women – the horizon felt wide as the plains of the Midwest. The world, her world, was opening up.

On visits home long after I'd moved out, I continued to have a go at the family lucky dip in the old wooden school desk, now with a glass of wine, though still looking for the same things. During one of these visits in 2018, I looked at this photo for the millionth time, never not starry-eyed at my mother's 22-year-old self, her model looks, her record-cover cool. But this time, the sense of before and after felt stingingly pronounced. At this point, I was writing for a scrappy feminist website, bashing out hundreds of words each day on just how many hurdles women faced – some outrageously explicit, plenty pervasive – with the challenge to draw them into the light, putting a finger on what many women felt but couldn't find words for.

This work was taking place against the backdrop of Donald

Trump's presidency and Brett Kavanaugh's nomination to the Supreme Court, and the subsequent allegation by Christine Blasey Ford that Kavanaugh had sexually assaulted her when they were teenagers[2]. The Kavanaugh hearings, in which he was asked by members of Congress about his suitability to be a Supreme Court justice, came with extremely high stakes. Not only because it potentially meant a *second* Supreme Court justice who had been accused of sexual assault, following Anita Hill's allegations against Clarence Thomas in 1991[3], but because Kavanaugh's appointment would lead to a conservative majority court, providing Trump the opportunity to overrule abortion rights. If a case were to reach the Supreme Court, the precedent of Roe could be overturned, a position Republican strategists had long dreamed of. In time, I watched this nightmare become a reality.

The internet makes the world seem smaller; battles feel closer when we can watch them unfold live on our phones, even if they are across an ocean. Kavanaugh's appointment and allegation also came at the crescendo of the #MeToo movement, a global reckoning of men's abuse of power, and it enraged women the world over. We all had a stake because we all understood, on some level, what was playing out in front of us; far too many of us knew what it was to be violated, to be disbelieved and to not feel in control of decisions about our own lives. This American story on American soil about a defining issue in American politics and society drew global attention, like an American blockbuster. But more than this, it was simply about women and men and power – a timeless story without borders.

And so, as I looked again at my mum's smile dancing across her face, her short, cropped curls blowing in the wind, I asked yet again, where had the hope gone? Not just for my mother but for us all. A year before she had arrived in America, two young female lawyers from Texas, Sarah Weddington and Linda Coffee, had persuaded the Supreme Court in the case of Roe v. Wade that a woman's autonomy over her body was a matter of privacy, and therefore it was her right to have an abortion. Now, four decades on, as I sat with the polaroid and a glass of wine, very powerful men (and some women) looked likely to take that right away. When my mum arrived in Nebraska the world was opening up. How, as her daughter, a generation later, was I watching a world for women close down? What had happened?

I had so many questions: how can rights get undone? Why are we – our rights, our place and value in society – going backwards, not forwards? And how do we keep going in the face of difficulty and repeated, powerful resistance? How do we learn to push forward? Does that wild hope ever die? How can we discover it in seemingly hopeless times when we need it the most?

I write these words less than a week after the US Supreme Court took away a woman's constitutional right to an abortion, with outrage and horror still reverberating around the world. Now that small square is truly a relic from a bygone age – not just in terms of years, but in terms of women's freedom.

And these questions are certainly not just to be asked of America. Girls in Afghanistan are no longer being allowed to attend school; violence against women around the world continues to be as relentless as it is devastating; migrant women are denied human rights and access to basic healthcare; convictions of rape in the UK have reached an unprecedented low and violent pornography is more available than ever. Right-wing populist governments are enforcing sexist ideologies in countries such as Turkey, Russia, Poland, Malta and Argentina.

In these trying times, I want to understand what exactly constitutes hope and resilience – what are they? Where can we find them? How can we cultivate them when we unearth them? And I want to understand how they come together to march women forward, even as the tide tries to push them back. Just as they did in the 1960s and 1970s, when women, as well as many other groups, achieved, in no small way, the freedoms they demanded.

The Kavanaugh appointment was a reminder that the long-standing war on women is still raging. Those who heeded its warning were proven right, despite the inevitable claims of hysteria. It was a deeply impactful political moment for me. And it kept drawing me back to the polaroid, to the questions it brought up in me. Somehow they were part of the same story.

Sometimes, when you need to do something, that's all you know and that's enough. If this were an American movie, this would be the night I packed up my pick-up truck, handed in my notice and drove west. I knew I had to follow in my mum's footsteps, which was west, after all. I had to make the same journey she had made in 1974, on a Greyhound bus from New York City to Omaha, Nebraska. And so in the autumn of 2021, delayed slightly due to the pandemic, I would take the trip she told me about, sung like a hymn of discovery, and utilize the journalist in me to try to answer some of these questions. I would visit Aunt June – now living in Michigan – on the way and I would speak to a variety of women in different states, along the route my mum took decades before, to ask how they have kept hold to their hope, how they built their resilience, how they've witnessed women's rights ebb and flow like the tide, and how they still march on. I would use the stories of women, feminism's most powerful arsenal, to understand how the before became the after, what happens to all our dreams, ambitions and potential in a world systemically hostile to us, and how we navigate a world that repeatedly dashes hopes but never truly defeats. And I had my own hope too, a more personal one – that by retracing my mother's journey, not just across the Midwest but through the years, to explore how her life played out, I could cross the bridge between her before and after, too, understand better how she traversed those choppy waters, more often than not pushing her further away from where she wanted, and deserved, to be, but how she found the tenacity to keep going.

As I planned to understand my mother's story, and the wider story of women's rights, a silent, shy part of me longed to be bolder and braver, as my mother had once been when she took herself off to Nebraska, or to university, when she defied her mother's wishes and forged her own path. She had pushed at the boundaries of what was expected of her, as had many in her generation, and so many of my own feminist heroes. If I was to understand her, I would have to start by doing the same. I had to make this journey.

The decision to seek out answers in America also felt inevitable, a destiny I couldn't fight. I was being drawn to America – the place where every member of my family had discovered something life changing, something that had moved them to do something dramatic, something with repercussions that sent out ripples through time.

At the centre of this tangle of thoughts – my mother's life, what had changed for women in a generation, the regression of women's rights, and the need to understand hope and resilience – remained this tiny photo of my mother with a smile so bright that it could light a city. The warm wind of summer radiates so strongly you can feel it; her unapologetic, small body on display, the unknown possibilities ahead of her. In my search for her, I hoped to understand her better, how she and other women push through darker, harder times, how they keep going. I trusted that she would inspire me, as she always has, to find something greater than I ever imagined I could. As I booked a flight, packed a bag and planned an itinerary, I realized that it was her, 22-year-old Jacqui French from Chelmsford, Essex, hungry to see a world bigger than her own, who was leading me into a trip of a lifetime. One that would be as revelatory for me as it had been for her.

CHAPTER ONE

New York, New York: Hopeful beginnings

Arrivals
June, 1974

When Jacqui arrives at Newark airport, she is tired and hot. The flight had been marvellous. She was thrilled by the nine radio programmes and one film available on the plane. She'd felt dizzy with excitement as she listened to Maria Muldaur sing her big hit, *Midnight at the Oasis,* as they flew into the city. But she hadn't slept.

She wants to take a shower to wash off the jet lag before heading into the city. She takes her mother's heavy old brown suitcase into the cubicle with her, deciding a wet case is better than a stolen one, and lets out a sigh of relief as the cold water starts to run over her.

BANG! All of a sudden, she can hear someone hitting the cubicle doors. BANG! It's getting closer. BANG! Her shower door has been hit so hard it bursts the flimsy lock and the door is wide open; she is now standing naked in front of two male police officers, guns on their belts. She freezes, numbed by the fear and shock of what is happening. The officers take a look at her, say nothing and move on to the next cubicle. BANG! The noise continues and her small shoulders jump with every sound. She remains frozen until the banging stops and the men leave. She will never know what, or who, they were looking for.

After she's dried and dressed, she finds a drug store. Her head is thumping and she's still shaken by the incident in the shower. Waiting in line to ask the pharmacist for aspirin, she develops the creeping sensation that she's being watched. Two men are standing silently on either side of her, not moving. She can feel their eyes on her, boring into her, an invisible violation. She's too scared to take a look at them but can sense they are standing closer than they should be; an alarm bell goes off in her body that only she can hear. The racing of her heartbeat tells her any minute now something is about to happen. She stands rooted to the spot, frozen again, eyes ahead, sweating in her fresh change of clothes. 'Next!' yells the cashier. She steps forward and the men disappear.

Fuck, she thinks. *What have I done?*

She heads out of the terminal, looking for a taxi. Soon she is speeding down the highway and through the city streets to the Greyhound terminal in Midtown. She tips her head, straining to look out of the window at the skyscrapers. Her mouth hangs wide open, not quite believing what she is seeing. The World Trade Centre – the tallest buildings in the world – had been finished the year before. It was overwhelming. New York is fast and loud. All those cars and cabs and people. She feels small and very alone.

Fuck, she thinks, *what have I done?*

New York City was crime-ridden in the 1970s, a notoriously dangerous place. 'Brooklyn killing is 11th in 5 Days,' a headline from *The New York Times* barked the summer Jacqui arrived. But even her fear couldn't take the shine off the city. Joni Mitchell had just been through on her American tour, the Patti Smith Group had just formed and Bowie would soon play Madison Square Gardens. She was, albeit briefly, in the centre of the universe, and this lightning bolt of life was precisely what she'd been looking for.

Jacqui had been feeling restless, spending the last six months after graduating in London, working for a children's publisher in Lamb's Conduit Street. She'd always assumed she'd have a career in book publishing but she found it too slow-paced and she didn't like the people. She also wasn't sure if Tom, her hometown boyfriend, was for her anymore, either. Nothing seemed to sit right. She wanted something to happen to shake things up; she wanted something else. So when her grand-dad Harry gave her the £100 he'd be saving for each of his grandchildren after she turned 22, she knew exactly what she wanted to do. She didn't save the money or put it towards a deposit on a flat. She bought a flight to New York City and a Greyhound bus ticket to visit her dad's sister, Aunt June, out in the Midwest. She wanted to see June, of course, but she also wanted to break whatever this spell of discontent was slithering under her skin. And more than anything, she wanted to see America.

September 2021

I hadn't failed to notice that I would be arriving in New York on the twentieth anniversary of 9/11. Like the rest of the world, I had been stupified by the images I saw on TV that afternoon, for once watching the news and not MTV after school. A small part of me had questioned flying in on that day when I'd booked the tickets, but I'd come to think that starting my journey on 9/11 wasn't necessarily a bad omen. After all, I was trying to understand how our past shapes our future and there aren't many other dates in modern American history that have proven to be such a transformative line in the sand.

The day after I land in the city I will meet with my big brother, James, who now lives upstate. We'll be walking across Williamsburg Bridge, immersed in the heavy heat of the September sun, far too strong for our Bolton-Essex genes, listening to the rattling subway train below, the cars thundering past. We will be talking, excited to see each other, looking at the water beyond the large metal spikes. My brother will remind me that he was with our father on 9/11. They had been at the Tate Modern and my brother had found my father sitting on the steps outside. 'America is under attack,' he told him.

As he tells me this story, I will be struck by the cinematic nature of this moment: a plot point in history; my father's one-liner. I imagine the experience without smartphones, hearing this anecdote as Manhattan's unmistakable skyline curves in our peripheral view – those landmark buildings still startlingly absent. I will be struck by my brother and father, together, sharing such a moment in time.

But I'm not there quite yet. Right now, it's 11 September 2021, I'm flying into Newark Airport, I am a bag of nerves.

I write endless notes to burn through the energy and drink several cups of green tea as I practise what I will say to the always terrifying border control agents. I have every right to be entering the country but things feel strange after Covid; the rules are somewhat clear but not completely and I've heard horror stories of agents making it as tough as possible. American border control has always made me sweat – and I say that with the protection of being a white woman. I have been waiting for eighteen months, thanks to the pandemic. Now the men and women at immigration will be my final obstacle.

It is around 10 p.m. and the mostly empty plane had lowered its onboard lighting. The captain announces we are starting to descend and the air steward tells us that the National September 11 memorial can be seen from the left-side windows. I slip off my seatbelt and slide across to the other side of the plane to get a better view. As we circle over New Jersey, we hang above the edge of Manhattan, the city a grid of orange fairy lights below. In the place where the Twin Towers once stood, two endless beams of white light reach into the night sky, ghostly imitations of what had once been, stretching up past the height of the plane, far into the universe, a portal to the heavens. It is a breathtaking sight. In the dull noise of the cabin, suspended in the black sky, I feel shatteringly alone.

When we land, the terminal is empty. Thanks to Covid and the ominous date, it is the quickest I have ever passed through an airport. Clutching extensive bits of paper that pandemic travel demands, I wait behind a Black Bajan woman who I overhear has come to see family. She is being asked endless questions: her brother's name, has she got proof of a return flight, can she show this document, that document. My heart is thudding. Another agent becomes free and calls me over.

What is the purpose of your visit?

I can't say: *I'm on a literal and figurative journey to a woman in a polaroid who is my mother in the ultimate search for the source of women's resilience.* So instead I say: I'm visiting my brother.

'For how long?'

'Four weeks.'

He looks at me and hands me back my passport. Thanks, he says with a smile. Enjoy your trip. Inside I'm screaming with joy and relief and excitement, trying to hide my beaming face from other passengers.

As I turn the corner, I look behind me. The Bajan woman is still being questioned.

Like my mum nearly fifty years before me, I too get a taxi from Newark, but unlike her, I'm staying in the city for a few days, not merely passing through. I check into my hotel just after 11 p.m. (another miracle – no traffic into the city), text 'Made it' to my boyfriend, Ed, and when I enter my room on the twenty-second floor, I keep the lights off, drop my bags and head to the windows. The buildings are clambering over each other, as if trying to get somewhere, late for an appointment, in a city that has run out of space. They create an artificial constellation crowding up the night sky. It is the kind of view that makes you dizzy from the millions of lives in this world you'll never know.

New York was where it all started for my mother, in 1974. And so I know that it is where I have to start if I want to under-stand who she was, who she became, and how a three-week trip to suburban Nebraska, not obviously remarkable, nonetheless made her into a different person from who she was when she left. It will be a Russian doll of journeys. At the centre is a personal expedition to the most important woman in my life, a trail of discovery. Beyond that, I will be visiting one of the toughest battle grounds for reproductive rights, the Midwest, just as Roe takes its last gasps of breath and women everywhere try to figure out how we got here.

Revolutions

Adventure is in her blood. Her father was a staff sergeant in the British Army's intelligence core, which led to the family leaving Essex in the 1950s for a post in Tripoli, the Libyan capital on the coast of North Africa. Her memories of this time are incredibly strong, even though she was only three or four: playing with Arab kids on dusty streets, visiting stunning Roman ruins with the family on Sundays. These images are alive in her mind's eye today. Italian nuns, dressed all in white, gave her early morning lessons on the beach. She still has the jewellery her mother bought there: a thick gold cuff with coloured stones, earrings depicting tiny birds in tiny cages – a poignant motif worn by a woman trapped with my brutish grandfather, a bully with a violent temper. Sometimes when I'm dipping into the old school desk on visits home, I come across photographs of children in scraps of clothes running behind my grandfather's car in an excited delight. Since 2014, the Foreign Office has advised against all travel to Libya. These photos feel precious, like buried treasure.

When my mum was around 5 years old, her family was

stationed in Fontainebleau in northern France, the post-war headquarters for NATO air forces in Central Europe, where her father once pointed out General Eisenhower to her. She went to the international school, where, with a *Dad's Army* calamity, at lunchtime the kids would reenact the war, the Allied forces ganging up on the German kids, lobbing sticks and stones across the playground at each other. During the holidays, her parents would take her and her younger brother and sister on long, hot road trips across the border into Spain, one unrecognizable to the world now, tourist and resort free, and watch bull fighting with the locals.

It was in Europe that my mum fell in love with America. Her parents stayed away from army life as much as possible, eating in cafés and restaurants, speaking French with local friends. Yet to my mum, a big-eyed skinny kid, the American military base was a thing of absolute wonder, the shiniest coin she'd ever seen. Everything was slicker, newer, better than the European base they lived on. The American Navy, Army and Air Force Institutes (NAAFI) – the supermarket – was stocked with rows of enticing candy, shiny tins and comics like *Superman*. Even the American base's school bus was new, unlike the battered old army bus the British kids had to ride.

On Saturday mornings, she went to the flicks and lost her mind over American movie stars. When her and her little pals emerged from the cinema into the bright daylight, they'd immediately recreate everything they'd just seen. But she fell hardest for the white and navy lace-up leather shoes the American kids wore. The tap-tap-tapping they made as they walked by was to her the ultimate sound of glamour and she longed for a pair. Years later, at university, when she fell in love with F. Scott Fitzgerald, William Carlos Williams and Ernest Hemingway, and then in her job in television which took her to the Hollywood Hills, it was a different incarnation of those tap-tap-tapping shoes but still the same siren call, the same breathtaking wonder of Americana.

By the time my mum was 22, she'd travelled across Europe and lived in France – including time in Paris – and in North Africa, but had never been to the place she was itching to see most. And what better time for her dream of America to be realized. In the UK in 1974, there were miner's strikes, leading to an energy crisis, blackouts and the 'three-day week' – a state of emergency announced by Prime Minister Edward Heath to conserve electricity. My mum and her friends would roam from one place to another, searching for light and warmth. Failing that, she'd just 'hang out in the dark'. Her flat was damp and cold. The orange glow of America shone brighter than ever.

It wasn't just my mum being seduced by the need for something else. She had come of age in an unprecedented era of new beginnings, and young women like her – mostly white working- and middle-class girls – were watching the world change and responding to it. At the boarding school she attended after she passed her 11 plus, a group of young female teachers encouraged their girls to pursue education and careers, alongside mini-skirt competitions at lunchtime. Remarkably, the school took them to see the Rolling Stones, in Chelmsford, *twice,* once with support from Ike and Tina Turner. Both times, school uniforms were heartbreakingly mandatory. During these years, she and her friends spent money from part-time jobs on pieces of the new world – like Stones and Procol Harum records – while they looked on in awe at the demands of American feminists like Betty Friedan. When I was 13, Celine Dion was top of the charts singing the *Titanic* theme song. When my mum was 13, the Beatles were always claiming the number one spot. Girls went to their concerts and screamed from the pits of their lungs – a phenomenon often derided as teenage hysteria but which was in actuality a radical expression of a bold new sexuality. It wasn't just music that was remarkable. The same high-pitched shrieking had filled the corridors of her boarding school when news arrived that Kennedy had been shot in 1963, a few years earlier. She was 14 when civil rights leaders clashed with police, 15 when Elvis married Priscilla. When she was 16, Martin Luther King Jr was assassinated and the National Guard opened fire on anti-Vietnam war protesters at Kent State University, Ohio, killing four students. She was 17 when a man landed on the moon, the pill became available to unmarried women, the influential music show *The Old Grey Whistle Test* first aired on BBC 2 and the Divorce Reform Act of 1969 came into effect in the UK, seeing rates soar. A year later, as she prepared to leave school, the Ford sewing machinists went on strike, which would lead to the Equal Pay Act of 1970. She was in her early twenties when she wore a bin liner as a dress to a party because she thought it was punk, something I am devastated that there is no photographic evidence of.

In a remarkably short period of time the world changed, and an extraordinary number of women – although by no means all – were offered a new level of protection from the inevitability of a life defined by men, namely as a wife or a mother. By the mid-1970s, the Labour party had written this cultural shift into law. The Sex Discrimination Act, which created the first Equal Opportunities Commission to promote gender equality, was passed in 1975. That same year, the Social Security Pensions Act passed, giving wives full pension rights, recognizing their domestic contribution. Paid maternity leave was introduced as a statutory right. Albeit rarely enforced, women had legal support and workplace rights for the first time.

Women could have sex with who they wanted; they could have careers; they could control their fertility and, therefore, their own destinies. For young women like my mum, this was firelighter, ammunition to propel them far off into the distance. It's easy to imagine how much potential these changes had to create a gulf between the mothers who had been denied such liberation and daughters who took full advantage of it, within touching distance of each other, but worlds apart.

Once, my school friend Nicole and I asked my grandmother, my mum's mum, Margaret, what it was like to see the Beatles play in Paris in the 1960s, eagerly studying her face for a response, mesmerized she'd done something so impossibly cool.

'Oh very nice, girls. But have I told you about the time I saw Cliff Richard?'

Nicole spluttered out a laugh. If you talk to my mum about the Beatles, you'll get a similar diversion. At first, she'll tell you George was her favourite but it won't be long before she'll get to the important stuff: 'I was more of a Stones girl.'

My grandmother and mother sat on either side of a generational divide. My mum's parents often forbade her from playing her treasured Stones records. But my mother knew, like so many of her peers, that things didn't have to be as they were before. The times, they knew, were a-changin'. My mother did not want to do what her mother wanted her to do, which was not go to university but find a man who worked in the City of London and marry well. But my mum wasn't waiting for anyone to save her. She would do that all by herself, time and time again. She had given herself permission to want more than what was expected of her, allowing herself to believe everything was hers for the taking. And that was the revolution of her generation – granting yourself permission to do whatever it is you want to do, no matter if you were a working-class girl from Essex, your father was a bully and your mother thought smart girls got married to rich men.

And so in 1971, she became the first in the family to go to university.

In New York, I stay with James, my big brother, for a few nights, alongside his flatmate, Ben, and Ben's soppy and over-sized brown Labrador. The apartment is in a small commuter town along the Hudson, just over an hour from Grand Central Station. It is calmer here and chichi – organic health shops, an independent cinema – as those who can't afford the city decamp and push up prices.

I'm five feet and three inches. My brother is six feet four. I almost always forget his size until I'm confronted with it. He's not just tall, he's broad. And he's always the hippest person in the room. Jeans length is just so, shirt cut is just so. Growing up, with a few prompts from my equally hip mother, he developed achingly cool taste in music and film and TV, obsessing over Suede, watching *Twin Peaks*, taking the train to Soho on Saturdays to shop in the mod shops that are nearly all gone. I put an Elastica poster on my bedroom wall that once belonged to him. Not because I listened to the music but because James said it was cool. He's handsome, with a strong jaw and a long list of ex-girlfriends. I idolized my big brother.

When we first meet in the city on the corner of Essex and Delany, he looks well. James moved to the US over ten years ago after eloping with an American and getting married to his now ex-wife on a beach in Malibu at sunset with no one but the officiant present. Some families share a love of dogs, or a football team or *Monty Python*. For us, it's something closer to the American promise of reinvention and possibility, creating an undeniable magnetic pull that none of us seems to be able to resist.

My brother lives only fifty minutes from the small rural town that is home to Laura Kaplan, the first woman I'll meet on the trip before I embark on the Greyhound bus and start my journey across the Midwest. Laura was a member of the Chicago underground abortion group, Jane, that provided illegal abortions in the early 1970s before Roe came into effect. This group of women, some students, some mothers, and part of the women's lib movement, were highly organized and efficient, creating a system to help women of all ages and backgrounds safely terminate unwanted pregnancies. They were all feminist volunteers, each with a different role in the process of arranging, and eventually performing, abortions, and offering support. They didn't ask any questions, they were simply giving women choice, handing back an agency over their bodies the law at that time denied. A year before my mum arrived in New York in 1974, several members of the group narrowly avoided jail for their work.

The Uber driver drops me off on a single track road surrounded by woodland and a few other houses. As Laura had warned, there's no phone reception or 4G. Aside from the squarks and whistles of the birds, the air is silent. I take a deep breath and walk up a winding path, lined with greenery, to a small front door. I ring the bell and angry woofs shatter the calm. After a minute, the door creaks open and a small face peers around at me from behind tinted lenses: 'She heard the bell! She's going deaf but she damn well heard the bell!'

Small, in light blue jeans and a plain, short-sleeved T-shirt, 74-year-old Laura is trailed by her mostly deaf, ageing dog. Neither are unsteady on their feet, but perhaps not as steady as they'd once been. Although that shouldn't be misleading. Laura will prove she's as tough, sharp and sweary as I imagine she ever was. 'I'm just finishing the washing,' she says with a thick New York accent. 'Follow me.' She leads me to the back of the house, out onto a veranda and down some wooden stairs. Her garden unfolds in front of us, a lake of green lined with wildflowers, wrapping around the back of the property. Laura makes her way down to the far side of the garden and starts hanging sage green sheets on a line, reaching to peg the corners. As I wait, I look over at the remaining purples and pinks, the remnants of what must have been a spectacular riot of colour in the spring. We climb back up the stairs and into the house. The room we sit in is airy and light, with lots of open windows and a hammock hanging from the ceiling. She sits across from me at a wooden table.

'Coffee or tea?' she asks.

'Tea, please.'

'How very British,' she smiles, shuffling off to the kitchen.

When she comes back, she sits down, lights a roll up and rests her feet on a neighbouring chair. Laura's dog is now asleep on a rug next to us and a light breeze rattles the wind chimes. The snap of a lighter, the deep exhale of cigarette smoke and the light tinkle of metal will be the accompaniment to our afternoon.

Over the course of nearly three hours, Laura tells me the story of Jane. In 1969, a phone line was set up in a member's home. Women could call and ask for 'Jane' – a codeword for seeking an abortion. Signs were posted at colleges, in bathrooms and other places women met: 'Pregnant? Don't want to be? Call Jane: 643-3844'. Initially, the group worked with male practitioners before, incredibly, some decided that they needed to learn how to do the procedure themselves. Eventually, the office the group worked out of was raided and seven women were arrested and taken to jail. A trial was scheduled but just in the nick of time, Roe v. Wade passed, making abortion legal across the US. The charges were dropped. Over the four years the group existed, they facilitated around 11,000 abortions. As far as they know, no women suffered any ill-effects.

Jane was founded by campaigner and organizer Heather Booth and, like so much of the women's liberation movement, it was profoundly informed by the civil rights movement of the 1960s. Heather had been involved in the Mississippi Summer Project, the 1964 voter registration drive among African Americans. When she got back, a sister of a friend needed an abortion and Booth approached a doctor on the southside of Chicago who she had met in the south. Very soon, she was getting dozens of requests across the socioeconomic spectrum and was beginning to realize the scale of the problem. At the same time, Booth was part of the West Side Group, believed to be one of, if not the first, women's lib groups in the country.

Members of the group who were interested in issues of access to abortion began working to set up Jane. Booth would also approach women affiliated with different social movements and causes and ask if they were interested in doing something about the issue which was growing in both awareness and momentum. Yet there was always one condition: she was adamant that this was a political endeavour. And so a manifesto was written, and anyone involved had to get behind it. This wasn't just about healthcare, the manifesto said, it was about women's agency and empowerment, it was about women's liberation. Booth continued to organize in the years to come, eventually including for Bill Clinton and Elizabeth Warren.

Laura explained how she became involved with Jane after she'd graduated, newly awakened to the feminist movement. Her friend Alice, a good friend to this day, had an abortion with Jane and was 'bouncing off the walls' about how great the experience was, despite being blindfolded during the process to ensure the anonymity of the man doing the procedure. Laura signed up as a volunteer. Eventually, she would become part of the inner circle. She was learning to perform abortions herself when the group got raided. 'We were incredibly lucky we didn't kill anyone,' she says, blowing smoke to the ceiling. All women were counselled beforehand, they were informed of exactly what was going to happen, talked through the process – something that the medical profession (which was heavily male-dominated) simply was not doing at the time. It wasn't perceived as women's concern to know, or to be educated, about their own bodies.[4] 'I have to remind people that there were no books on women's health, there was no information about abortion, anyways, anywhere.'

As I sit in her home, the woodland all around us, I feel like I have found a feminist warrior, an elder who has retreated from the world to an idyllic resting place, finally living a life of much-deserved peace. I think of Rey finding Luke Skywalker in *Star Wars: The Last Jedi*, climbing a cliff overlooking the sea in some forgotten corner of the galaxy.

Laura will absolutely *hate* this analogy. I can hear her cursing as she reads the paragraph: 'Jesus, what is this bullshit?!' When we talk about the legacy of Jane, she waves her hand in a gesture like swatting a fly, with a look of impatience I've seen on my own mother's face, which asks, without words, why everyone is so fucking stupid.

'Oh, you were *so* brave,' she says mockingly when I put what I thought was a compliment to her. 'Bravery is only how it looks from the *outside*. Nobody sees *themselves* as brave!' She loathes it when outsiders turn members of Jane into 'warriors' or 'Amazonians' – and now Jedis. For Laura, the members of Jane weren't extraordinary, they were just young women doing what they had to do. 'The way we were raised in the 1950s, we were never the heroes. We were the damsels in distress who got rescued by the heroes. Through Jane, though, we could see ourselves as actors. Not passive, not waiting to be rescued, but rescuing ourselves.'

The folklore which has built up around Jane, and how problematic Laura finds it, is one of the reasons that she wanted to ensure the work of Jane was documented by someone from inside the group, and why she eventually wrote *The Story of Jane: The Legendary Underground Feminist Abortion Service* in 1995 to tell an honest account of what she and her fellow feminists were trying to achieve, without the sensationalism.

But she regrets selling the rights to her book. The Hollywood film company that has optioned it has suggested a 'Wonder Woman does abortions!' she scoffs. 'Please! I shouldn't be laughing but it's so stupid! It has nothing to do with reality!'

Now, half a century after Jane was raided, it seems very likely that we will see the return of safe but illegal abortions, led by the next generation of Laura Kaplans and Heather Booths. 'Women don't abandon women,' Laura says to me, a year before women's reproductive rights are overturned in the US by the Supreme Court. I will return to those words many times in the weeks ahead. And although it is by no means a universal truth, I will discover that when it is true, it's gospel.

As we start to hear the whoosh of the clocks going back on women's rights, learning from Laura couldn't feel any more timely. 'We created the world we wanted to live in,' she tells me. 'A feminist Wakanda . . . We didn't do this *to* women, we did it *with* them,' she says. The group was seminal for Laura and although she went on to do other feminist work – such as becoming a lay midwife, running a domestic abuse shelter with three other women – it was Jane that was 'the crucible. It changed how I saw myself in the world.'

I think of my grandmother and my mother, and the two sides of that divide. While there have always been bold and fearless women throughout history overturning the status quo, there is something remarkable about the revolution of damsel to hero on such a mass scale in a single generation. How intoxicating that must have been for young women like my mother, going to university, taking the pill, learning about women's lib for the first time, imagining their careers, rescuing themselves from lives they did not want.

'You hungry?' Laura disappears into the kitchen and comes back with a bowl of grapes, small, sweet and delicious, grown in her garden.

Would Laura break the law today to allow women access to safe abortions? 'I'm 74, not 24!' she laughs. The landscape is different now, too. Many women don't need to be sent to back alleys with con men trying to make a quick buck or demanding sex acts, when, in theory, they can simply receive abortion pills in the post, which are currently available and are harder – although not impossible – to monitor and police. Telemedicine also removes the 'theatre' of many anti-abortion groups, who choose to protest and harass women outside clinics. Abortion pills in the post – or smuggled over the border in jewellery boxes from Mexico, as recently reported in *The New Yorker* – don't offer them the same platform.

This is becoming the battleground of abortion rights, following the decisions of eight US states to ban abortion pills within hours of the Supreme Court's decision to reverse Roe v. Wade. However, they can still be accessed overseas. Aid Access, run by Dutch physician Dr Rebecca Gomperts, uses European doctors to offer telephone consultations and prescriptions. In light of the ruling, the organization has said it will continue to send pills to the US, even to states where they are now illegal. In December 2021, a group called Shout Your Abortion, led by Amelia Bonow, stood outside the Supreme Court and took the abortion pill Mifepristone in front of the press. In an interview afterwards, like an echo of Jane reverberating through the decades, Bonow said, 'Fuck this court, *we're doing it anyway.*'[5]

There is another shift now too, and that's one of greater awareness. For starters, there's a recognition of pregnant people, not just pregnant women, in an effort to make the pro-abortion movement as inclusive as possible. And there is also a broader understanding of women's lives, one that Laura and her mostly white and middle-class peers didn't have in the 1970s: many women have abortions, they are not rare, and terrible, terrible things happen to women and girls, routinely. 'It was the first time we'd met anyone who was in an abusive relationship. And then a dad comes with his 13-year-old daughter. I don't know if any of us made those connections because it was so foreign to us back then,' Laura remembered. Now Roe has been overturned, many states won't grant abortion access even in cases of rape or incest.

Laura isn't surprised by the reversal of the constitutional right to an abortion, or what she believes is the death rattle of democracy in the era of post-Trump America. But she's as furious as she ever was and the problems, to Laura, are the same as they ever were: 'It's the desperate cry of the white male. All this mythology around the foetus and life – BULLSHIT! They don't care about any of that; they care about controlling people.'

I'm in awe of how much Laura has given to other women. Her whole adult life has been about making the lives of women safer. But it is apparent that she has received something in return, too.

'I'm privileged. I have money, I'm white, I'm old. None of these issues directly affect me. I could just say, "I'm going to grow my flowers, vegetables and grapes and I'll be fine." Or I could leave. But, no, I'm not abandoning everybody else. I'm not doing that. You do what you can do. *To not do is a mistake.* I think part of it is being a post-Holocaust Jew in the United

States. I'm not going to be one of the people who did nothing. And this horrible turn of affairs in this country has given me the opportunity to be a person who does not do nothing.'

She gets up, rests her cigarette on the ashtray, disappears out of the room again. When she comes back, she's carrying a little plastic square, the size of her palm, that normally lives pinned on the fridge door.

'One year at high holidays, these were passed out. It's in Hebrew and English.' She reads it out loud to me: 'It's not up to you to finish the work. But neither are you free to give up.'

It's time for me to leave. Laura has a 3 p.m. Zoom on immigration laws; she's been volunteering to help local migrants receive Covid relief, still pushing the needle where she can. She walks me to my Uber. Standing next to her, I'm reminded of how small she is but what big stories she has. I wonder, how often, if ever, when we look at older women on the street, we take a moment to ask what incredible stories they could tell over grapes and cigarettes on a quiet September afternoon.

My conversation with Laura about her time in Jane has drummed home to me that during the years that the women's lib movement was beginning to take hold, and my mum was starting to explore the world on her own terms, (some) women made their own world, despite the limitations put upon them. This refusal to be defeated, or controlled, or denied agency was dynamite, blowing up a long-held idea of what women could and should expect out of life. In the cab ride back, I think of how empowering that must have been – to choose hope and action over despair and resignation, to believe that you could make your own world. It was an attitude shared across the social movements of the era, and a tactic my mum – and many others – would employ over and over again: to find power when others tell you you're powerless, to create your own hopeful beginning.

I'm back in the city, never bored of seeing the buildings brushing the clouds and the people and the noise and the electricity running through these streets, no matter how many times I find myself here. I don't have the fear that my mum had in 1974, just the thrill. Memories flood back of a previous trip as a newly single 20-something, with five girlfriends squeezed into a two-bed Airbnb on the Lower East Side, crossing Brooklyn bridge in a yellow taxi at 2 a.m. with a fresh post-break-up haircut, singing Rihanna at the top of our lungs. Being here reminds me of a different version of myself. And now I'm here yet again, searching for a different type of liberation, another form of self-discovery.

This trip, instead of late-night drinking dens and brownstone house parties, I'm particularly determined to seek out the spot of the Triangle Shirtwaist Strike, which took place in 1909 in the Lower East Side. Today, there's nothing to mark the location of the original factory where the young immigrant women, mostly aged between 16 and 23, who worked fourteen hours a day for $2 a day, started the uprising, except for a small plaque. Every day for eleven weeks, and empowered by the burgeoning labour movement, the young workers took their places on the picket line, despite facing severe police brutality. Eventually, 23-year-old Ukrainian Clara Lemlich led the strikes further, and they spread through the garment industry in Greenwich and across into the Lower East Side. Lemlich was arrested seventeen times and suffered six broken ribs. Over several days in a bitterly cold November, as many as 30,000 workers turned out to demand better pay and safer working conditions in what became known as the Uprising of the 20,000. According to reports, 90 per cent of strikers were Jewish and 70 per cent were women. While only some of the strikers' demands were met, one of the action's greatest successes was establishing women workers' rights to unionixe, and men accepting women as powerful union activists. By the end of the strikes, 85 per cent of all shirtwaist makers in New York had joined the International Ladies Garment Workers Union.[6]

But the story of women's progress never does run smoothly. Two years after the strike, a fire broke out in the factory. Doors were often locked to guard against unsanctioned toilet breaks. One hundred and forty-six workers died and it remains the deadliest industrial disaster in American history.

The strike is relatively unknown, despite the fact it had a huge global and cross-generational impact. We have all heard of International Women's Day. Today, even corporations and brands celebrate 8 March each year, hoping to be perceived as socially responsible and allegedly feminist, often despite internal working practices to the contrary.

A year after the strike, in 1910, German socialist Clara Zetkin suggested an international women's day at a women's conference, in no small part because of the Triangle Shirtwaist strikers. A similar day had already been created in the US, but Zetkin wanted to do something on a global scale. Her idea was a tribute to the American striking garment workers and designed to be an act of European solidarity.

Now, here on this journey, I also want to pay tribute to these young women. I want to visit the location of one of the first mass female strikes in American history – a new beginning of female resistance led by unspeakably brave young migrant women living in poverty (although I'm sure Kaplan would insist they didn't see themselves as such) and an important forerunner to the protest and organizing that would flourish later in the twentieth century. I can feel my mum guiding me here, too. The strains of socialism in her have always taught me to admire those who have the least but fight the hardest.

I decide to make the hour-long walk from my hotel to the spot in the early evening. The heat has cooled to a temperature that feels like bath water on my skin. The sky is an orange glow. I walk from Midtown, through Greenwich Village to Washington Square Park. I pass thin women in yoga gear, coffee shops that also sell pot plants, delivery guys, more thin women drinking martinis, police, tourists, old folks out for a stroll. After lockdown, watching the life of the sidewalks on a late summer evening in New York City feels intoxicating.

The site of the plaque commemorating the strikes is just off Washington Square Park, a place with its own radical history that, fittingly, will reverberate through the stories and events I will hear in the weeks ahead. The walk doesn't just lead me to the Triangle Shirtwaist strikers, either. It takes me past a particular former Methodist Church on the west side of the park. Since 2007, it's been 'Novare . . . a boutique condominium' of eight 'contemporary living' apartments, some with the original stained-glass windows still intact, with one recently on the market for just shy of $3,000,000. But for the previous 150 years, it was a place of worship and in the second half of the twentieth century, a shelter for progressive people and ideas. Between 1973 and 1984, the church was led by Reverend Paul M. Abels, America's first openly gay minister with a congregation in a major Christian denomination. The church also provided a meeting space to the country's oldest Black lesbian organization, the Salsa Soul Sisters, from 1976 to 1987. All around me in this city monuments to social change can be found from this era of progress. This walk, and discovering the church, is the first of many times on the trip that I will be reminded that where we are can tell us all sorts of stories about who we are.

It was also in that same church, in 1969, that a historical meeting on abortion was held. In response to a government committee on abortion reform, which was made up of 14 men and one woman (who was a nun), the Redstockings, a radical feminist group, held their own hearing, with their own 'experts'. Twelve women told stories of their illegal abortions. One of those was a young *New York Magazine* reporter called Gloria Steinem. Later on in my trip, when I'm miles away in a different state, Steinem, now in her late eighties, will appear at a Congressional committee on reproductive rights fighting the same fight. Back in 1969, lawmakers were making the case for why abortion needed to be legalized. Today, many make the case as to why it shouldn't be banned.

After passing the church, I enter the park from the northwest side. Immediately, a young boy of 13 or 14 stumbles towards me. His eyes are glazed, his clothes in tatters. Men playing chess on tables next to us don't look away from their boards. I step out of his way and the boy continues to tumble, unsteady and drifting, a small tree trunk about to fall.

I walk to the centre of the square and my eyes follow my

ears. From small speakers, classical music is blaring; a young woman is dancing on a large piece of paper, black paint on her bare feet, creating an image as she moves. Next to her, a salsa class of twenty or so people is taking place. 'Smile, ladies!' shouts a small woman with a Madonna-esque headset microphone. A few feet away, a group of college kids are blasting hip hop into a cloud of smoke. Opposite them, a band is playing and the bass player, with long white hair, looks like he's been there since the Redstockings days. Nearby on a bench, a young guy by himself presses buttons on a small black box and noises leak out of the big speaker next to him. It is a circus, almost ridiculous, defiantly joyous. It is the embodiment of Manhattan. It is New York.

I come out on the other side of the square and the noise softens. I start to look for the plaque. When I approach the corner of the street, I see a board up for building work. To my dismay, the plaque is covered. But still, I take a moment. The building that replaced the factory after the fire stands to my right. Washington Square Park is to my left. My mind starts excavating the layers of history, imagining the people and lives on these city streets, sketched out in the landscape – an urban geology of resistance and protest. But also built into the earth is the city's celebration of life, of diversity, its unifying hymn, the one I am literally hearing at this moment. I think of both the struggle and the joy of this city, and how they always dance around each other. I think of how interested my mum would be in the layers of history of this small city park, and I remember that as much as I watched her struggle, I always felt the joy.

*

It's 10 a.m. and Natalia has just finished handing out the newspaper she writes and publishes, *Feminist Revolution*, on the subway, which she starts doing every day at 5 a.m. She does this all year round, carrying copies in her backpack, regardless of the weather or how many people leave theirs in a trash can. She goes far and wide, always making sure she reaches the poorest communities, neighbourhoods like Harlem and the Bronx, and ensuring every edition is also printed in Spanish. Today, she's wearing a sweatshirt, a knee-length denim skirt and a baseball cap with the words 'The Future is Female', her dark hair falling just below her shoulders. She's sitting on a fold-up chair outside the Whole Foods we've agreed to meet at. We decide to find a spot in the shade in the square, Natalia on her chair, me on a bench, and neither of us paying any mind to the man who approaches us offering weed.

Natalia is a revolutionary, a transwoman, a lesbian, a poet, writer and political activist. She has worked, at various times, as a political and community organizer, teacher, paralegal, journalist, as well as in a variety of blue collar positions.

Born in Colorado at around the same time as my mum, Natalia's journey to where she is today began as a frustrated teen. As she watched police beating protestors at the 1968 Democratic Conference in Chicago on the family TV, it confirmed something that had been brewing inside her. It was the same thing that instinctively rejected her father's racism, that kept her wearing a peace sign round her neck at school even though it led to her expulsion, that made her protest against the war in Vietnam.

Natalia is part of the generation that believed the world could and should be better. She fought against war, for the liberation of women and for civil rights. She rallied against President Nixon and his conservatism. She raged against the Kent State shooting of May 1970, when Nixon sent the National Guard onto a university campus in Ohio to face anti-war protestors and the guardsmen shot four students dead. In the demand for change, Natalia was at the forefront – organizing, flyering, protesting, attending sit-ins and meetings, writing angry articles – and swept along with the currents of the moment, a youth-led revolution that questioned their elders and demanded a world that was more peaceful, more egalitarian. She says she was always influenced by impressive women. 'It was 1969, 1970, and there were some really powerful women in the women's movement at university. They really influenced me. I remember one day in May of 1971, one of the women walked over to me and she held up a feminist pin. She said, "Hey, would you wear this?" And I was like, "Yes, sure." So I guess it was my quote unquote, feminist beginning, being influenced by strong revolutionary women.' Next, Natalia moved to New York and joined a host of revolutionary groups, such as Weatherman, Yippies and the Students for Democratic Society.

The word 'radical' is easy to bandy about when talking about the late 1960s but I soon learn that Natalia wasn't messing around; she was committed to the struggle and remained so for the rest of her life. While many teens of the 1960s eventually moved on, cut their hair and got sensible jobs in industries they had sworn they would have nothing to do with, Natalia remained firmly in the counterculture, dedicating her life to the fight, attempting to liberate the groups she saw as oppressed – often by any means possible.

The first time she was arrested she was 15. Natalia has since been sent to federal prison twice, once for pleading guilty to conspiracy to receive and possess stolen explosives, serving ten months in the late 1970s. In 1999, she served six years for bank robberies. 'You may not think of bank robbery as being political but it all depends on why you do it and what the funds are to be used for. I robbed banks to pay the costs of publishing a Latino-oriented political newspaper,' she tells me matter-of-factly.

Natalia was radicalized all over again when, at the age of 60, she transitioned. She says she's still a 'newcomer' and 'transitioning is forever'. Soon afterwards, she began studying for a BA in Women and Gender Studies at New York City University and, while she'd always supported women's rights, something awoke inside her: to know what it is to exist as a woman in this world is to inherently understand the need for profound change.

'When I began transitioning, when I began to dress as a woman full time, all of a sudden, I started having this incredible level of male harassment.' She couldn't believe the affront, the audacity. 'I was here at Union Square one time and I sat down right over there on the steps. A man comes over to me and says, "Baby, you look like we need a date." When I was a man I never had women come over to me and say, "Hey dude, you look like we need a date."'

Her new experiences confirmed something she'd known before on a theoretical level but not in practice. 'I discovered that women are an oppressed class, just like I've been reading in all these books. Men think they have the right to control our lives, our activities, they think they run the streets. The process of transitioning was an eye-opener because all of a sudden,

I had to be careful where I waited for the bus. I had to be careful where I walked. I had to be careful how I dressed. I had to be careful on campus after dark because women are being raped.'

I see in Natalia, as I did in Laura, that same refusal to accept things as they are, matched with the determination to do whatever is needed to make them better – regardless of what the world around them tries to dictate. And as I learned from Laura: once a radical, always a radical.

I want to know what it's like to fight these fights for all these years and how Natalia has kept going in the face of such difficult times – the arrival of Ronald Reagan and the shift to the right in the 1980s, time spent in prison, transitioning.

'Maya Angelou says, "You may encounter many defeats, but you must not be defeated." Right now, we are suffering defeats. The Taliban taking over was a defeat. Losing legal abortion is a defeat. Having this right-wing trend in this country is a defeat. The vast majority of the housing evictions that are beginning all over America affect women of colour and working-class women.' Natalia raises an often under-reported but brutally unfair reality. Thanks to the economic impact of Covid, 30–40 million Americans are expected to face eviction. Women are nearly 16 per cent more likely to be evicted because, some suggest, the majority of single parents are mothers and their situations are particularly precarious. Things are even more unstable for Black women, with one study finding that, even before the pandemic, they were 36 per cent more likely to lose their home than Black men. 'These are defeats. But are we defeated? No. And we're gonna keep fighting.'

Natalia's own fight hasn't been straightforward. One women's group denied her entry because she is a transwoman.

Her eyes find the floor when she tells me her family no longer speak to her. 'I'd never even heard the word trans until I transitioned.' When it comes to trans rights, she says, 'There's still a long way to go.'

But she has found a home in the National Women's Liberation group. This acceptance and the purpose of her singular focus on feminism is having a noticeable impact on her. 'I'm in better shape than I've been in a decade. It's like my body is getting rejuvenated, as well as my spirit and my soul.'

I get the sense I'm speaking to a little piece of New York history – a radical, a product of a particular time, who believed she could change the world and put her freedom on the line for it, when the world really looked like it might be changing. I wonder how many people don't make eye contact when she hands them her newspaper on the subway, not bothering to look up and wonder who this woman is and why she's doing what she's doing. How many former radicals is this great city still harbouring? How many women with incredible stories to tell do we walk past on the street without giving a second look?

'There's a Cuban saying,' Natalia tells me, as she stands up, folding the chair, ready to leave. 'We carry the revolution in our rucksack.' And with that, she walks off back to the subway, her bag full feminist conviction slung over her shoulder, ready to get back to work.

It is a day of extremes. After my morning with a revolutionary feminist trying to reach women in the poorest boroughs of New York, I take the subway north to the Upper East Side, one of the richest parts of the city, to meet Susan Cullman, a former co-chair of Republican Coalition for Choice. Today, that sentence reads like an oxymoron but in the 1990s, at its peak, the group had an annual budget of $1 million to support pro-choice Republican candidates.[7] In 2018, in piece she wrote for *The New York Times*, (published five years to the day before the end of the Roe) Cullman resigned from the party, devastated and deeply offended by Donald Trump and the party's determination to end the right to legal abortion. Whereas Natalia and Laura believed changing the world for women had to happen outside the system, Susan placed herself firmly on the inside.

The lift in her building takes me to the penthouse and opens to a private hallway. Susan is elegant in a skirt suit and blouse, with perfectly neat white hair resting on her small shoulders. She offers me a warm smile and an ice water, and I make my way through the apartment, past a large wooden staircase spiralling upwards, through to the sitting room. Spectacular Manhattan views fill the many windows and I catch myself for a moment, suspended in the sky, intruding into an elite cloud-top world. The room is full of plush sofas that sit under naval paintings; family photos adorn tables and cabinets. The fireplace is covered with eighteenth-century blue and white Dutch Delft tiles.

I can safely say – and I'm sure she would agree – Susan Cullman is not a radical. She descends from an extremely wealthy cigar dynasty. But, as a 'Rockefeller Republican', known for their moderate views, she doesn't believe the state should interfere with someone's private health decisions and, as a fiscal conservative, she believes access to abortion 'reduces poverty, increases educational attainment and work competitiveness', as she wrote in *The New York Times*. Despite Susan's glaringly obvious levels of privilege, it's still easy to imagine that she is one hell of a fighter. Being a woman in the early 1980s pushing abortion rights on the type of men who told her 'not to worry her pretty little head', cannot have been easy. Susan was married to a senior economics advisor to Republican candidate Ronald Reagan. When a Planned Parenthood leaflet landed through their door and she casually remarked they should donate, her husband's hesitation told her something had changed. She knew he wasn't anti-abortion but he warned her that donating 'wouldn't look good for the party'. That was 1981. A year after Reagan was elected the fortieth president of the United States and the first one to make abortion an official party political issue – a key campaign pillar like access to guns or lower taxes. 'When the obituary for the Republican Party is written,' Susan wrote in her *New York Times* piece, 'the year 1980 will be cited as the beginning of the end.'

For younger generations, it's almost impossible to imagine a time when abortion wasn't a political ticking time bomb in America. But there was, and it wasn't that long ago. In the late 1960s and early 1970s Republicans, including Ronald Reagan, were openly pro-choice, signing state bills to legalize the procedure, reflecting that many, on both sides of the aisle, saw it as simply a healthcare issue. Yet very quickly, abortion would become politicized, a woman's right attacked and undermined for the sake of political capital, not because of any actual change in principle or belief. The campaign against abortion by the religious right was pure political scheming with life and death consequences, consequences those mounting the attack seemed to care very little about. (This change in position will also be true of Donald Trump, who once described himself as pro-choice but, in 2022, will take full credit for overturning Roe v. Wade, calling it the 'biggest win for life in a generation'.) A fascinating example of how times have changed can be found in the original Roe ruling. When the decision originally passed in the Supreme Court in 1973, the nine white male justices were a conservative court, much like today, with four Nixon appointees – an extremely conservative man himself who laid the groundwork for anti-abortion sentiment in the party.

But while there has always been religious opposition to abortion, particularly from the Catholic church, including Catholic Democrats, it was only *after* the passing of Roe in the early 1970s that abortion began to be deliberately shaped into a political firelighter. A significant advancement for the anti-abortion lobby was made in 1976 with the passing of the Hyde Amendment, named after its chief sponsor, Republican Congressman Henry J. Hyde of Illinois. Hyde blocked federal funding for abortions on Medicaid – the nation's public health insurance programme for people with low income. By doing so, the message was clear: abortion shouldn't be seen as healthcare everyone has a right to. Instead, Hyde targeted the most vulnerable, laying out the battle lines: a woman's access to abortion was a political and moral issue to be controlled by male lawmakers in order to win votes and promote an agenda. Strategists from the 1960s onwards, and particularly in the 1970s and 1980s, understood that this populist issue could unite a large, fractious right wing made up of mostly white conservatives, Catholics and Evangelicals, many of whom were threatened by the liberal laws and attitudes that had surfaced from the 1950s onwards, especially around the advent of civil rights. By capitalizing on that fear to drive the anti-abortion agenda in the name of 'traditional American values' – code for white Christian nationalism – a certain group in the Republican party believed they could pull the party to the right and put a right-wing president in the White House. And that's exactly what they did. By the time Susan was in Washington with her first husband, abortion had gone from a private matter between a woman and her doctor to a matter of national identity. The kicker, however, is that all through this period and right up until today, poll after poll shows that the majority of Americans believe some sort of abortion access should be available.

Women were the collateral damage as the scheming started to create pipelines to ensure the appointment of anti-abortion judges and access to senators and presidents. Emotive language, like 'life', 'family' and 'moral majority' proudly aligned anti-abortion sentiment with conservative ideals, whipping up religious frenzy – and, much more subtly, white supremacy. All defended, of course, by the shield of religious and moral righteousness. It set the electorate on fire – and has done ever since. That's why I'm keen to talk to Susan. Her forty-year fight for abortion rights within the Republican Party correlates with the right wing in America centring abortion as a political issue and successfully managing to deprive millions of women access to it. Susan had a front row seat from the very beginning.

Susan's husband's response – an ominous foreshadowing of what was to come – sparked something in her. 'You could hear a pin drop,' she says of trying to talk about abortion to other Republicans during those years, although she persisted. She brushed off the patronizing and sexist response from senators and congressmen who told her that it simply wasn't an issue and that she should leave 'the real' politics and the 'important' things like the economy to them. She ignored them and devoted her career to it.

Her first move was to contact Mary D. Crisp who had set up the lobby group Republican Majority for Choice and offer to help. Susan had been involved in activism before but not politics. 'I'm not a rabble rouser,' she smiles sheepishly. 'But there was a small group of very strong women across the country who gathered together to do their part.' The group insisted on the word 'majority' in their name to reflect that most Republicans supported some degree of abortion access. Their main aim was to help pro-choice Republican candidates get elected, working on their campaigns, raising money, garnering support from the party and from voters. One of these candidates was Senator Susan Collins of Maine who would, in 2018, the year Susan left the party, vote for Brett Kavanaugh as a Supreme Court justice, telling critics he had looked her in the eye and claimed Roe was 'settled law'. When Roe was overturned, Collins claimed she was 'shocked' Kavanaugh had lied.

Over time, as the abortion battle lines became fiercer and fiercer, the number committed to the group started to dwindle. There were fewer candidates who would come out as pro-abortion and less financial support for them. Meanwhile, due to the rise of Donald Trump, 'They lost faith in the party, they felt personally attacked,' Susan explains. Eventually 'they were disgusted, horrified.'

'It's not nice to lose,' Susan says, believing that she will see Roe overturned. It's easy to see her distress; she felt ousted from a party she'd given her working life to for her stance on abortion and she thoroughly rejected any form of Trumpism. She has watched progress reverse and women left with the same problem they thought they'd overcome fifty years ago, despite all she had committed to the fight. 'I'm afraid there's not much light at the end of the tunnel,' she says apologetically.

Susan Cullman and my mum are of a similar age. There are not many other obvious similarities. Their politics are widely different; my mum is far more of a swearing, chain-smoking Kaplan than a matching skirt suit Cullman. But I see something in Susan that I have seen in my mum. When people are in the throes of defeat or a feeling of failure, it is blinding, paralysing. They don't see their contributions, the small victories, their impact. Of course, when Roe is overturned, and Trumpian influence and ideology continues to have such a stronghold on her old party, it is easy to see why Susan might feel hopeless. But she fought tirelessly for women's access to abortion in a uniquely tough arena. I find that extremely inspiring – and it helps me to realize the fight itself is the inspiration.

Her despondency and sadness in the face of my admiration reminds me of the times my mother has doubted and questioned herself. Was I a bad mother, she'd ask me, washing the dishes after dinner in the kitchen. Did I leave you on your own too much? Did I work too much? Her face a picture of the same anguish, searching for a way things could have been different, even though they couldn't have been. What my mum has never really understood is that when she was filled with guilt for 'failing' me as society often told her she was, I was looking on, beaming with pride, at her important job in the big smoke. Susan Cullman can't really understand why I am interested in her, why I'd sought her out and come all this way to meet her.

She certainly doesn't think she had any hope to offer me. But as those fighting to make the world different in the 1970s knew, there was something distinctively hopeful in the struggle itself. If there is no hope, there will be no struggle.

Months after my trip, I will learn that Susan's sense of defeat was temporary. During the 2022 midterms, she organized women in New York and Connecticut to sponsor female candidates running for senate in North Carolina. Three of the four candidates they supported won. 'Needless to say,' she'll write to me in an email, 'these were pro-choice candidates, running in an anti-choice state.' It seems Susan couldn't stay away from the fight for very long. She had found the hope again, in order to get back in the struggle.

Susan has another appointment and I make my way down in the lift, heading back out into the bright sunshine and the heat, back on the dusty streets, with horns blaring from passing cabs and the life of the city rushing along like a river. I walk aimlessly for a while thinking about Susan, Natalia and Laura. They are very different women but, while facing resistance at all turns, had all tried to create the world they wanted. They weren't waiting for change, but instead had pushed for it, demanded it, created it.

My conversations also made me realize how we – the younger generations in search of change today – perhaps need to tell the women we admire that we see their struggle and are grateful for it. Not just the glory of what they achieved, or the drama of the defeat, but the fight, the slog of going out to battle, day in and day out. How do we tell them that they made all the difference because they gave us a blueprint, showed us a way forward, showed us what is possible?

And it dawns on me: have I told my mum how grateful I am? How I saw how hard it was, what she did for us? Does she realize that I know how hard she fought for me, that I saw how she paved a way so I could push forward?

Letting go

Since my arrival in New York, I have met women who were all at the start of something, who believed things could be different and fought for what they believed in. My 22-year-old mum shared that optimism in 1974. With a suitcase and £100 you could go in search of a dream, you could decide what type of life you wanted. It was enough to create your own hopeful new beginning – at least, for some in the seventies.

I too have the feeling of beginnings as my time in the city wraps up and my adventure into the Midwest is about to start. But it is not as straightforward as it was for my mum, that summer, forty-eight years ago. The city of New York isn't unknown to me, like it was to her. I've been here several times before and the memories create another landscape to navigate, their own city architecture, presenting themselves to me like the pages of a pop-up book.

The first time I ever visited I was 13 and my brother was 17. It was 1999 and my father had decided to take us to the city for a week before going west for a week in LA. It was the first time we'd been on holiday with him. There was a Yankees match, hot dogs from street vendors, climbing the Empire State building at dusk and being led around MoMA, my father imploring me to remember certain names: Hopper, Pollock and others I've long since forgotten. What I'll never forget, however, is the late-night viewing of a new scary movie that my father had heard a lot of buzz about. I'd never been to the cinema late at night before and I certainly wasn't used to watching horror movies. The cinema was empty and we were terrified. My brother used his jacket to shield my face. It turned out we were watching *The Blair Witch Project*.

Looking back, I see that the trip would have been a huge expense, as well as new terrain for my father. It was the longest he had ever looked after us both on his own. And it was, at times, emotionally fraught. He needed to smoke; I was too cold to sit outside. He wanted to watch *The Blair Witch Project*; I was only 13 (although, in his defence, somehow that movie was rated R). The friction of parenting seemed to burn us both. So often, my father gave us a glimpse into an exciting world – taking me to Notting Hill Carnival for the first time, showing us his work directing award-winning documentaries, bringing me to New York City and taking me up into the crown of the Statue of Liberty. Yet each time he revealed something new and exciting, the door quickly closed, leaving us behind once again.

Then there was the time I returned to the city with my mum. This was the first time she had been back to New York since she passed through in 1974. She was a mother now, and in her sixties. A lot of life had happened. On this occasion, we were there for my brother. New York was frightening to her yet again, but for very different reasons.

After James moved to America to be with his wife, they hopped from coast to coast, ending up in New York City.

Around 2013, my brother had hit a period of choppy waters in his life. We'd fly over in support – sometimes it helped, and sometimes it didn't. We spent Thanksgiving in an Airbnb in Williamsburg. As I cooked pasta to the sound of public radio, I'd watch the tensions between my brother and mother simmer until they eventually boiled over in an exchange of unpleasant words and raised voices. By the next morning, over coffee and bagels, looking across the water by the bridge, he'd tell us how grateful he was for us.

For all its glamour and excitement and beauty, I could see how relentless, how hostile that city could be. How it was so very easy to get lost in its current; how difficult it was to resist the pull of a place that seems as alive as any organism. And so, a freezing New York became part of those trips in my mind; as much as me, or my mother, or my brother.

I remember endlessly walking, sometimes behind him, sometimes without him. But always searching for him, wondering how to help. My big brother – tall, handsome, cool, creatively gifted. He was the sensible one. The neat, organized, tidy and reliable one. Until you're electrocuted with the realization that you don't know someone at all. It's like thinking you can see a full moon but you're just dazzled by the glow.

Each member of my family is etched out on these streets. New York is not just the scene of the start of my mother's big adventure; the men in my family have led me to this city, too, always on their terms, always with something difficult to traverse. Much like New York itself, their brilliance and creativity co-existed with something unforgiving and arduous, a challenging terrain my mum and I had no choice but to navigate.

For a long time, I felt that the stories of the men in my family weren't mine to tell. But isn't being a storyteller essentially a power grab in a situation in which you feel powerless? Isn't that what women have always used their voices to do?

And so, this time in the city, on my own, meeting strangers, I make my own hopeful new beginning. I have confronted memories of the past but I am letting them go. It is a cleansing, a balloon let loose in the wind, because I need to start this journey as I should, on my own terms. Surely you can't carry a revolution, or anything hopeful, in your backpack if it is weighted down with painful secrets. Storytelling may be a power grab but, as I will come to discover, it is also a liberation.

*

On my final night in the city, I have a glass of wine with a friend on the sidewalk. We talk about the Texas abortion ban which has just been announced and discuss what the inside of a penthouse near the park on the Upper East Side looks like. The buzz of one of the world's great cities is reverberating and I'm back in dreamy New York, the cliché-ridden one where you might find the love of your life or the next big opportunity just round the corner in the next bar. I'm sweaty and exhausted but riding the adrenaline with all the words of the women I've met running through my head.

It's a long way but I decide to walk back to my hotel, daylight turning to a soft dusk, the last of the day's glow bending around the tall buildings, spilling down the avenues as the city lights start blinking. Bars fill up and shops close. Pavement tables are cluttered with people, a chorus of worries and hopes and lives, untangling themselves after a long hot day. The percussion of the city sweeps me along: horns, engines, bells, shouts. I think of all the lives, injustices, dramas and victories of women's existence that this majestic place has borne witness to, from the strikers at the turn of the last century to the young women rallying to face the reversal of abortion rights one hundred years on. I think of all the ways this city has changed during this time – and all the ways it hasn't.

Dusk slips into darkness and I find myself in Times Square, remembering the time I came here with my friends in my twenties, and posed like Marilyn Monroe on a subway vent, wind blowing my skirt up, wearing a huge smile, hair newly cut to reflect my single status, recognizing the smallest taste of what my mum felt on her arrival in the US. *What now? What next?*

My stay in the city has reaffirmed to me that the world, in many ways, was a remarkable place when the Supreme Court ruled on the landmark Roe v. Wade case. And that world created some remarkable women. Women who saw the moment they were in and rose to the challenge. Women who infused the political with the personal. Women who centred women. Women, from different sides of the aisle, who found common ground and united in a cause, something almost unthinkable now. Feminists of the 1960s and 70s, known as the second wave, didn't get everything right; the movement has been criticized rightly for excluding women of colour and working-class women, and, often unfairly, for branding feminism as a man-hating exercise. But that doesn't mean we shouldn't learn from what they did get right, from the bravery and determination of those who paved a way for so many of us.

There were revolutions, big and small, as the 1960s gave way to the 1970s. And my mum was in the midst of her own transformation as she boarded a Greyhound and went looking for America.

CHAPTER TWO

Pittsburgh, Pennsylvania:
Testing the waters

A woman out in the world

The strip lighting, orange-tiled walls and windowless basement of the New York City Greyhound terminal hasn't changed much from when my mum was waiting in line to head west. She can't remember if classical music was playing from the tannoy when she was there as it does now, a strange symphony to the dim glow of the vending machines that two men are frantically raiding in an attempt to find spare change. When she did this journey, she bought a paper ticket. I have my app scanned. New York City is a much safer place today and I have the security of a smartphone, but the terminal is still an intimidating space; confined, low ceilings, crowded, barely any natural light. It doesn't feel dirty, exactly, just helpless to the grime baked in over decades.

It's just after 8 a.m. I'm standing in line for the bus from New York City to Pittsburgh, Pennsylvania, a journey of around nine hours and my first Greyhound ride. In the snaking queue, I'm sandwiched between a middle-aged man wearing a plaid shirt and brown cowboy boots, holding nothing but a stained yellow pillow and a bag of Reese's Pieces, and a young guy wearing red fleece pyjama trousers patterned with small bears in Santa Claus outfits. At the front of the line, a girl of about 16 grips her bubble gum pink acrylic nails round her luggage tightly. Her dad kisses her on the forehead goodbye.

The Greyhound is the largest intercity bus company in North America, with 123 routes across the continent. It is one of the cheaper ways to get around the States and is mainly used by those without cars – a stark marker of social class in America. On one journey, I will meet Eric, who is making a 20 hour trip to see his cousin. He has no car or ID, so he can't fly either. For many like Eric, bus journeys that take an entire day and night are the only option.

It is also perhaps the most notorious way to travel. Before I leave, a friend tells me someone was decapitated on a Greyhound (although that was in Canada). When I google the buses, countless threads discussing their safety are thrown up. On one travel forum, a nervous traveller asks: 'Greyhound, USA – safe or suicide?'

'Are you crazy?! The *bus*!' This is the reaction I typically get from Americans when I tell them I am making the trip on the Greyhound. Others look pained. 'That is *awful*,' one woman in St Louis will tell me solemnly. And some just look plain worried. My big brother tried to persuade me to take another provider – anything but the Greyhound, he said.

I, on the other hand, am excited. Here, in the bowels of the Port Authority in Midtown, is where the real adventure begins. I'd long associated the Greyhound with my mum's trip and was itching to see what she had seen. And aside from the low cost, the bus has another reputation, one I've indulged in. Greyhound buses find themselves in songs by Simon and Garfunkel and Eric Clapton. They are in the poetry of Allen Ginsberg and movies like *Midnight Cowboy*, starring Dustin Hoffman. They show up repeatedly in the mythology of Americana as a rite of passage for those searching for something, escaping. The bus has become a symbol of freedom, the ability to pack up, move on, get out of some godforsaken small town, reinvent – that implicit promise woven into the American dream, made possible by the never-ending road ahead of you. The fact that my bell bottom-wearing 22-year-old mother had ridden one in the 1970s only adds to the rose-tinted filter I see them through.

Leading up to the trip, I was gleefully gorging on American clichés, like a child allowed too many sweets. Simon and Garfunkel lyrics about Greyhound buses and Pittsburgh and Michigan and Cathy were on loop in my head, and I saw myself riding the bus as if filmed with a 35mm camera, square and grainy, from another time. But now I'm here, surrounded by strangers, I am nervous. Can I really do this? Am I brave enough? Do I have what my mum had decades ago, the ability to go headfirst into a situation that is unknown? Facing off against my own doubting voice, I can hear Lindsey. Lindsey is a war correspondent and an old friend of my father. As I stand in line, trying to look confident, I imagine her rolling her eyes at my fear of what to her would seem like the most pedestrian of trips. Lindsey likes to quote Clare Hollingworth, another war correspondent, on the importance of actually being somewhere, not behind a computer screen. 'I like to smell the breezes,' Hollingworth said. I was utterly romanced by this when I heard Lindsey say it, desperately in awe and intimidated by women who seemed so fearless and experienced so much. The phrase had been in my head when planning the trip. Now, as I swallow my nerves, I remind myself this is what I came for.

Right on schedule, Alfonso, our driver, appears at the terminal door – this is when the shouting begins. A Hispanic man in his sixties with a serious-looking moustache, Alfonso doesn't have time for anything, least of all passengers not following the rules. 'You must wear a mask! No mask, no ride! If you don't wear a mask over nose, I leave you on the highway. I will be sorry for you but I *will* leave you!' Alfonso is a man almost true to his word. Twice on our journey he slows the bus to a stopping point. The second time, there is a chink in his armour: 'I don't know why we play these games,' he sighs. Alfonso seems to soften considerably if you are smart enough to speak to him in Spanish. When I tell him in English my seat doesn't have a belt, he looks at me as if I've asked him to tie my shoelaces.

When my mum boarded the bus on her trip, a dishevelled looking woman slumped down next to her. Reeking of booze, her black make-up smudged round her tired eyes, she began talking incessantly. Politely, my mother told her to shut up. 'I'm very tired, I've just come from England, please stop talking,' she said, an unapologetic directness I recognize only too well. Very soon, the woman passed out. They spent the rest of the journey in silence. I am lucky enough to have a pair of seats to myself.

I too spend that leg of the journey in silence. Alfonso runs a tight ship and the yelling works. And once we pass the New Jersey turnpike, the fearmongering about the bus, my nerves and the sense of self-doubt fall behind me with the hundreds of miles we cross on endless highways. I start to spot enormous billboards that sit almost as high as the clouds and can be read for miles. 'AFTER YOU DIE, YOU WILL MEET GOD.

110% TRUTH'. 'JOE BIDEN: MAKING THE TALIBAN GREAT AGAIN!' with Joe Biden's beaming face superimposed on a man holding a machine gun and wearing a headscarf. Already, New York feels a long way behind.

Heading west might be a cliché but it feels thrilling and novel to me. Alone and anonymous on the bus, with nothing but an occasional glimpse of my own reflection in the passing fields, the sense of adventure is intoxicating. Here I am, testing the waters of my own sense of self, pushing at the boundaries of my self-belief. I am, at last, I think, smelling the breezes.

Another picture from my mum's old school desk: I'm 8 years old, sitting on the edge of the open boot of my mum's red Citroen. I'm wearing a black-and-white checked crop top, matching shorts and a cap. Sun yellow-blonde hair shows underneath. My skin is softly tanned. I look straight at the camera.

We've taken a pit stop on the drive down to the south of France during the summer holidays. My 12-year-old brother is the designated map reader, occupying the front seat. I sleep in the back. We stop at roadside services for a picnic of bread and ham, cheese and tomatoes. The warm air blows through open windows as we pass small French towns, listening to my mum's cassettes of Sam Cooke and Frank Sinatra and the Gypsy Kings on long motorways.

Other summers we'd take the train, sometimes to France, sometimes to Italy. I still don't know how my mum had the money for these trips. She shrugs if I ask her now – not because she doesn't know but because she'll never tell me how much she went without. On her fortieth, we stayed in bunk beds on a train and she woke us up as we passed through the Alps, her face a picture of wonder as we wound round mountain edges and snowy peaks loomed above. In the evening, the three of us would squeeze into one bunk and play 'tough toes', like thumb wars but for feet, giggling for hours.

There is something about the memory of three of us, in her secondhand car, zooming down French motorways, looking for adventure, heading towards the unknown, delighting in the journey, that comes back to me now as the bus snakes its way across the state line. And like the first smell of evening jasmine at the beginning of summer, it's somehow both excitingly unknown and deeply familiar.

The green light

When my mum arrived at the newly built University of East Anglia as a student in 1971, she hated it. She couldn't understand the middle-class kids just hanging around, having fun all the time. None of them seemed to have jobs. She was perplexed that their parents wired them money for no reason. After all, she would be the one sending money back to her mum. These people were spoiled, they didn't live in the real world, she thought. She was unnerved by their confidence, their accents, the way they'd try to dress and act like they didn't come from wealth even when they did. She didn't feel like one of them.

After her first term, she took the train back to Chelmsford for Christmas. She was relieved to be home and told her mum that she didn't want to go back. But Granny Margaret wouldn't hear of it and told her to give it another go. It was a moment of generosity, I think, considering my grandmother had previously made her feelings clear about my mum going to university.

She could have easily persuaded my mum that it was all a big mistake, that she should stay at home and help with the bills, focus on starting her own family. But she didn't. She told her to try again.

So my mum returned in the New Year. And slowly but surely, the outsider found her way in, starting to test the waters of middle-class life. She made friends with Marjorie and Claire, who remain her friends to this day, and the three would share a house in Norwich in their second and third years, eating spaghetti hoops on toast and cramming for exams together. She'd attend sit-ins (although what about she can't remember) and was surrounded by great minds, attending lectures with Malcom Bradbury and parties with Ian McEwan (when pushed, over a glass of wine or two, she will coyly suggest that they briefly and casually dated). She'd sit on the giant grey concrete stairs on campus, talking about the world, about boys and about the English tutor everyone fancied, who she once persuaded to climb in through her bedroom window when she'd locked herself out thinking that maybe this would be her chance (it wasn't). She'd go to the student union and talk about the world, about music and politics. She looked the part too: she wore bands of velvet ribbon round her forehead; she placed her head perilously close to an iron to force her natural curls straight and she made her flares even more flared by adding triangles of fabric.

Pretty quickly, she was all in: life was not just for earning money to send home to her mother, although she did that in the summer holidays – it was for living. Away from the worries of her financially struggling single mother, freed from the guilt of having this adventure on her own without responsibility, she rode the wave of what university life could offer. She revelled in exciting parties, interesting people, radical new ideas. In the summer, she even went hitchhiking with her friend Jane, first round Italy, where she briefly dated a guy who drove a Ferrari and claimed to be an Italian count, and then through Greece. The world was hers to discover, in no small part thanks to the full grant she'd received to cover her fees.

I've often come across little polaroids of her adventures at UEA – including the Italian count – in yet another dip into the wooden school desk. In the mythology of her life, university stories were some of the first I had ever heard. For a long time, I thought university had opened my mum's world and in many ways it did, providing a level of social mobility that is unimaginable today. But the more I dig into her story, the more I understand that trips around Greece in the 1970s were not so eye-opening for someone who had driven through a tourist-free Spain in the 1950s, who had lived in Tripoli as a child and remembers her little sister being born in a Parisian hospital. Perhaps I am guilty of assigning too much importance to her leaving her family behind and heading to university in order to find herself, because that is such a familiar narrative of how so many discover their place in the world. But I'm starting to see that her yearning to explore began with her family – as so much always does.

Then there was Gatsby. My mum read F. Scott Fitzgerald's *The Great Gatsby* in her first term and unknowingly began a domino effect that would change the course of her life. Maybe adventures just had a way of finding her. 'It seemed like a piece of magic,' she says of the book now, with its 'musical prose'. 'No other book has ever meant the same to me.' She immediately changed her degree from English to American Literature.

The book list enthralled her: William Carlos Williams, John Dos Passos, Gertrude Stein, Ernest Hemingway – these great chroniclers of the American condition. The excitement she'd felt reading comics like Superman and watching the shiny shoes of the American kids and the expensive Jeeps driving around the military base was here again. America glistened like Gatsby's green light across the bay and even Fitzgerald's tale of fraud, mirage and greed couldn't dissuade her that there was greatness there.

I have little doubt that the purpose of her trip to Nebraska, alongside seeing her beloved aunt, was to launch herself as far as possible into that idea of America, to get into the landscape itself, to try to understand what the glamour and shininess was made of. I can't help but think that for her, seeing the plains and huge space of the Midwest was a pilgrimage to the very notion of potential, ambition, a path to something better.

Unlike Gatsby, this mission didn't prove to be hollow. 'When I got out there and saw it all . . .' she didn't finish the sentence, as if language simply isn't up to the task of describing what she felt. 'It is such a phenomenal country. So young and so vigorous.' The very newness of it was the appeal, and it was the embodiment of the hope she carried in her. America represented all the potential she could find within herself.

Six years later, that same green light led her to Los Angeles. She'd got a job working as a picture researcher for the BBC and from here she landed her first documentary job as a researcher on a BAFTA-winning docu-series about Hollywood, in no small part because of her degree. Before she knew it, she was on a plane to LA, the only woman on the crew, and was sent to find Charlie Chaplin's octogenarian secretary who was still living in the hills. She set off to locate the little old lady. Now, not only had she seen America but she was deep in the thicket of one of its most famous cultural symbols. At 27, she was staying at the infamous Hyatt Riot on Sunset, ordering gin and tonics on room service. Would the little girl watching Saturday morning movies on the American army base have believed where she would end up?

My mum and dad met at the BBC in the late 1970s. In a sea of privately educated Oxbridgers, they were outsiders cut from similar cloth. My dad was born in Bolton. He escaped Granny Kitty and Grandad Eddy's tiny terrace house, heading for London aged 18. Kitty had gone into service aged 14; Eddy had worked in the mills. My father's adult life was a world away from theirs, travelling all over the world, directing documentaries.

My parents married in London on New Year's Eve of 1980. They didn't tell a soul and took witnesses off the street – even though I know how it ends, this still sounds romantic, exciting, once again pushing against expectations. When my brother was born two years later, they moved to Surrey, first to a cottage in Oxshott and then to a beautiful house in the woods near Cobham, my first home when I came along three years after that. It was my mother's dream home. Jack, the gardener, grew roses up the walls. My aunt would visit for long hot days in the garden with the paddling pool.

And here was my mother; she had a career in TV, a husband, a family and a beautiful home. The era had helped this ambitious and fiercely bright working-class girl from Essex choose her own path.

She'd made it.

The price we pay

America is big. Understanding that America is big, vast, *huge*, helps me start to understand why my mum found her trip out to Omaha so wondrous. For Europeans, it is hard to really get to grips with the size and scale of the country. Eleven states are bigger than the UK; Texas alone is about 2.8 times the size of England, Wales, Scotland and Northern Ireland put together. Overall, the United Kingdom could fit into the USA 40 times. This incomprehensible size is something I ran into repeatedly when planning the trip, especially as I would be travelling by bus.

Originally, I had planned to travel from New York City to Ohio. I would be making far more stops than my mum did and Ohio felt like an important place to visit because the once swing state had lurched to the right and is now particularly committed to making access to abortion as difficult as possible, not to mention introducing a bill with the completely wild demand that doctors should *reimplant ectopic pregnancies*, something that is medically impossible. And so I typed 'New York City to Ohio' into Google maps and hit the enter key. If I could drive, this journey would take about nine hours. But, depending on where I went in the state, the journey by bus is double that – and then add a few more hours. Unlike my mum, I wasn't 22 or broke. I didn't need to be on a bus for twenty-three hours. I needed a layover place, just for one night. And that's when I saw Pittsburgh, Pennsylvania, on the map.

Working out the logistics of my trip proved painstaking; minor details needed to be thought through and then thought through again. And as I tried to piece together an itinerary of bus timetables and Airbnb hosts, a recurring thought would linger: what would happen if a woman needed to leave the state to have an abortion? What if you had to take the bus because you didn't have a car but you didn't have twenty hours to spare? What if you and your abusive husband only had one car and because he beat you, you didn't want him to know you were pregnant, you couldn't tell him why you needed the car? What if there was no one to take your kids to school and pick them up while you were driving four, five, six hours across a state line? What if you couldn't afford the hotel room? Or the bus ticket?

Women across America have been asking themselves these questions every single day for years. Many of the women I will meet say Roe was never enough protection to begin with and, over the decades, different states have been able to introduce more and more restrictions, gradually eroding away this constitutional right and, in some places, transforming it into a series of impossibly high hoops to be jumped through at great economic and emotional cost, if at all. As I make my way across these states at the start of autumn 2021, during Roe's final days, for the majority of women who seek a legal abortion, it involves time off work, sorting childcare, finding money for gas, buses or planes, travelling long distances, especially if you live in a rural community, as well as facing family, community or social stigma. In some places, it involves mandatory counselling sessions, parental sign off, scans, multiple appointments, forcing women to bury or cremate surgically aborted foetuses. In Pennsylvania, where I'm headed, while there are relatively few restrictions, patients still have to wait twenty-four hours before the procedure – an enforced 'cooling off' period, designed to allow women time to change their mind. These 'mandatory waiting periods' have been condemned by the World Health

Organization for 'demeaning women as competent decision makers'. All of these things get increasingly complicated the further along a woman is, with fewer clinics able to help those needing late-term abortions. While fewer women are having abortions than thirty years ago, thanks to better contraceptive use and less teenage sex, this obstacle course is steepest for the most vulnerable: the young, the poor, people of colour, people with disabilities, those with an abusive partner.

In a post-Roe world, many, many more will find themselves battling these hurdles, especially if fears of a Republican attack on access to birth control are also realized. And even those who can find a way to travel will face legal abortion clinics completely overwhelmed with the out-of-state demand and dangerously, life-changingly long waiting lists. Senior Republican Mitch McConnell has already mentioned the potential of a future national ban. If that becomes a reality, women won't just be crossing state lines, they'll be crossing national borders. But, essentially, the same women will be asking the same question: *what if I can't afford the bus ticket?*

*

I arrive in Pittsburgh in the afternoon and the bus crosses one of the landmark yellow Three Sisters bridges which span the Allegheny River. The bridges are named after famous residents, including a shy Polish immigrant who later became known to the world as Andy Warhol. It's hard to imagine now, on this bright blue day, that at one time not so long ago, the city would have been a bustle of smoke plumes, black smog and mighty steel mills along the water.

When I saw Pittsburgh on the map as I was planning my

trip in the UK, it meant – crudely, simplistically, naively – Donald Trump. It meant white men who had lost jobs, industry long gone, ideas of masculinity threatened. I'd recently read *Janesville* by Amy Goldstein, a remarkable and journalistically rigorous portrait of Wisconsin walloped, along with other things, by globalization that led to factory closes, job losses and devastated families, as well as the chronic underinvestment in the communities left behind. Many American companies and their shareholders benefited hugely from the increased profit margins that globalization brought. But workers did not. And you can tell a similar version of the same story about West Virginia, or Michigan, or Pennsylvania, or other nearby Midwestern states.

However, as interested as I was in the city – in the wake of Trump's election I'd heard so much about it on everything from *The New York Times* podcast *The Daily* to Anthony Bourdain's *Parts Unknown* – I wasn't interested in asking white men about their voting habits. Too often, the plight of white men is seen as a profound indicator of society's health. My work as a feminist journalist, however, has led me to believe otherwise. As I have researched the history of the feminist movement and reported on life for women in the present, one thing has become apparent: if you really want to take the temperature of a country, have a close look at how well – or badly – it treats its women and girls. Which is why, when I began to research Pittsburgh a little ahead of the trip, I learned of, and was much more interested in, another story – one not of white men but of Black women who were vastly impacted but weren't making headlines.

In 2019, a report found that Pittsburgh was the most dangerous place for Black women and girls in America.[8] In the city, they suffered from higher rates of poverty, birth defects, unemployment and school arrests than anywhere else in the US. It's not surprising, therefore, that large numbers of Black women are leaving the city in hope of better opportunities elsewhere.

I meet Markeea Hart, or Keea, as she's known to her friends, a 31-year-old Black woman. Creative and ambitious, she was born in the city, studied and graduated from Edinboro University in north-west Pennsylvania, did a stint in Washington DC working in digital marketing and has only recently returned home. On her return, Keea launched *Girls Running Shit*, a podcast, community and network bringing together Black women and femmes with the aim to 'spread empowerment and positivity'.

If women like my mum were riding the swell of social change and mobility, fifty years later, Keea and other millennials (myself included) have been swimming against a tide of economic recessions, broken housing markets, pandemics, inflation, student debt, extreme wealth disparity and growing right-wing populism. Yet, remarkably, Keea's not letting any of that get in her way. 'In Pittsburgh, the culture is lacking here. Opportunities are lacking here. So we just took life by the balls and we did it ourselves,' she says, referring to *GRS*. 'No permission, no nothing. We just did it.'

One of the reasons Keea returned to Pittsburgh was the cost of living in the city. 'Where else are you going to get a two-bed apartment for $800?' she says. But financial independence comes at a price. She tells me, 'I'm able to maintain a lifestyle as a single Black woman here because of the affordability. And yet. There's a lot of racism, there's a lot of segregation in the city. Black women are not invested in, they're not even reported when they go missing. Damned if you do, damned if you don't.' Keea tells me she has felt excluded from local events and communities, a feeling she said she's had since high school for being tall, bigger and Black. 'I was just telling my boyfriend I get kind of upset when people are like, "I love your self-confidence, you're so unapologetic!" And I'm like, "What am I apologizing for? Are you amazed that we have confidence?" Growing up, I was literally told, women don't do that, you got to tone it down, you shouldn't be outspoken, you should dress this way, talk that way.'

And so it was imperative to create her own network, a community she felt herself in, one found mostly through the city's Black hair salons. In 2019, she told a local reporter: 'Black women . . . need to leave our imprint here. We must come together and start making territory again.'[9]

Keea gives me an insight into what some young Black women in America face today: cruel toss ups between affordable housing and racism, as they live with college debt and the cost of healthcare, with no savings for a deposit. She makes it plain how many obstacles there are between her and her dreams. For my mum's generation, the wind was behind them, doors were being opened. For Black women now, it's not even a case of doors being closed; they're barricaded off. My mum's story of social mobility and possibility was far easier to access if you were white. As feminist campaigner Audre Lorde pointed out, the women's lib movement, led by activists like Betty Freidan, centred on white women's liberation in the workplace, paying little mind to the Black women who had long been in the workforce, often in white women's homes. And while there were important Black leaders of the movement – like Dorothy Pitman Hughes, Barbara Smith and Toni Cade Bambara – they were overlooked. Gloria Steinem has said that despite her and Pitman Hughes being very much a double act, magazines and newspapers only ever wanted to take her photo.

Yet for Keea, it's been about making your own space entirely and, even with the challenges facing her, there is something undeniably hopeful about what she has created and the energy she brings to the cause. *Girls Running Shit* organizes events for Black women in the community to come together, to find like-minded people, to network with other professionals, to have a space to share issues that matter to them. There are networking evenings and an open mic night where women are invited to 'speak your truth'. The podcast aims to showcase local talent and give a platform to Black women's voices and concerns. Keea has also developed a non-profit wing of GRS, raising money to create 'care kits' for Black women and femmes in need. In the process, she is defying the narratives that have been set for her; while headlines warn of a mass exodus of Black women from the city, she's set on staying. She is prepared to have open conversations about mental health: 'We've all been through traumatic experiences and that's why we talk about mental health. We speak up because in the Black community, it's a taboo. It's a taboo that we all go to therapy, it's a taboo that we say that we're depressed.'

And GRS, like Keea, comes with a large dose of joy, too, something you don't see when you read about Black women in Pittsburgh in the national press. The GRS website is bold and bright with a beautiful picture of Keea with a group of women; her Instagram feed is impassioned and funny. 'With peace, love and power,' she writes on her site, '[Keea] continues to show that every woman/femme is a queen.' She has started a conversation in a place that has resisted one, and challenged what success looks like and where it can be found.

Keea also challenges me. As I listen to her talk about the hurdles Black women in her community face, she underlines the hurdles in my own mission: how do we celebrate the resilience and grit of women without erasing the reality of structural inequalities that no amount of resilience or grit can overcome? That no amount of American dreaming can transform? America's 'pull yourself up by your bootstraps' philosophy has made it easy to see poverty and hardship as a personal failing, ignoring the pitfalls of a racist, classist and sexist system designed to hold you back, often leading to layers of trauma passed down through generations. 'There are a lot of Black women here who are going to get evicted when certain things the laws change in a few weeks,' she tells me. 'But how can you thrive if the city will only invest in you when it's Black History Month, or you don't have nowhere to live?'

Keea does embody an American dream – a determination to succeed on her own terms, driven by self-belief. But she also makes it crystal clear that sometimes that simply isn't enough.

I pass through Pittsburgh quietly. The city feels deserted after Covid. My hotel is empty. At the Senator John Heinz History Center downtown, which is also empty, there is an exhibition called 'American Democracy: A Great Leap of Faith'. It feels extremely fitting for the moment and the location. Pennsylvania played a starring role in the story of American democracy: the

Declaration of Independence was drafted in the state and its governing framework formed the basis of the US constitution. It also held the first constitutional conventions that led to the American Revolution. Now, over two centuries later, an international think-tank has added the US to an annual list of 'backsliding' democracies for the first time, a difficult pill to swallow for a nation which proudly self-defines as a bastion of democratic idealism. Many Americans I speak to are still deeply shaken by the events at the Capitol of 6 January 2021 and Trump's 'big lie' that the 2020 election was stolen. The exhibition reminds me that America is still, by European standards at least, a new idea, an experiment, a leap of faith. 'The experiment hasn't worked!' Laura Kaplan had yelled in exasperation to me.

That night, I climb into bed, exhausted from a day of walking in the fierce heat. Next to me is a bag of M&Ms and my laptop. I put CNN on the TV. Soon I will learn the roster of the evening news hosts and journalist Chris Cuomo, for my sins, becomes my fast favourite as he monologues the day's news with the drama of a Greek tragedy in a Brooklyn-Italian accent. It is here, watching Cuomo, that I first hear the story of missing Gabby Petito, a 22-year-old woman on a road trip – about the same age as my mum had been on her trip. As my own trip progresses, my habit of M&Ms and an update on Gabby would become a nightly routine.

A story about a woman's safety out on the American road obviously piqued my interest. I was acutely aware of being a lone female traveller (LFT). Before I left, I had asked my friend Louise, who has spent the last few years living in Columbia and Mexico, for safety tips, trying to keep a lid on my anxiety, both to myself and those around me, like Ed and my mum. I feel my LFT status everywhere on the trip – when I arrive at bus terminals, when men hold open doors for me and I find myself looking over my shoulder to see if they are following me. I feel this when I'm walking down the street in the evening and I'm constantly clocking who is around, how many people are out and about. I'm interested in the story of Gabby because as a woman, I'm well trained in suppressing a familiar thought: *what if something awful happens to me?* Alone in big Midwestern cities, awake when most of the people I love in the world are sleeping on the other side of the Atlantic, I suppress this thought even further.

Gabby's pretty face, skinny, tanned limbs and blonde hair flash up on screen before Chris Cuomo starts ranting about Democrats not working together. In 2021, there were 257 missing women and girls in America, the vast majority under 21.[10] But, as Keea had said to me, it's only the blonde, white ones whose names we know. The Black women, the Native American women, the Latino women, the Asian women aren't looked for by police, tweeted about by concerned members of the public or discussed as part of nightly updates on CNN.

When I was a little girl, after my mum had read me a bedtime story, tucked me in, kissed me goodnight and turned off the light, I would open my mouth as wide as it would go. I was getting ready to scream in case of an intruder. And there were some good reasons for this. By the time I was six, we, as a family, had been victims of stalking, twice.

I don't remember the first instance but it became family

folklore, and I must have at least been conscious that my uncle was sitting in the garden all night with a baseball bat, even if I didn't understand why. My big brother, who was five when it started, can remember my mum picking up the phone and screaming 'Fuck off!' to the silence at the other end.

The house my parents bought together was down a wooded lane off the A3, buried in forest and behind an abandoned airfield. We had an idyllic childhood while we were there as the garden merged into the woodland around the house. My brother and I would ride our bikes to the airfield and in the evenings we'd go for walks to collect kindling for the fire.

Pictures from the old school desk show a white, wooden cottage with roses trailing up the front, a paddling pool in the garden and afternoons playing with Ben, the little boy next door. And that's what I remember, too. What I don't remember is the first time my mum heard knocking at the door to find no one there. Or the first time the phone rang and no one spoke on the other end. I don't remember the first time she saw a face wearing a balaclava at the window or the first time the police were called or when my mum decided she wasn't going to move or leave, or invite anyone to stay. I wasn't aware of the sheer balls of steel it must have taken to stay in a house in the woods with two small children while a man deliberately tried to frighten her into submission, and she flatly refused.

The stalking went on for three years, on and off. I'd guess that was by design: the fear of if and when he was coming back. When two plain clothes police officers attended our year six trip to the Isle of Wight, in my head they were protecting me from the stalker.

We never did discover who the stalker was. Though the second time we did.

This time we were on holiday in Italy. He appeared everywhere we went. One morning, while we were having breakfast at a hotel, I noticed a face, peering in at the window, staring straight at me. 'Look, Mummy,' I said. 'There's a man at the window.' When I looked again, he was gone but she had already spotted him and knew who I was talking about.

Italian detectives in blue jeans and cream linen blazers took my mother very seriously. They laid a trap – us. We were to take a walk one afternoon, to lure him out, and when we did, they arrested him.

You're never more than three feet away from a sex offender in Brixton, my mum would later tell me. Working for the Metropolitan police came with a frightening set of statistics, stories the public are shielded from, a daily, hourly reminder of things that happen to children, to women and girls.

Both her job and her life experiences made her incredibly tough. As did being a single parent. And being a single parent made her protective. But all of these things also made her fearful – fearful for us, for what could happen, what would happen. Fearful of the price some women pay.

And so, I went to sleep with my mouth open in case someone appeared at the window.

Because sometimes they do.

My father had been working away on a series for the BBC, which is where they met. She was the programme's academic consultant. I was 3 weeks old when my father told my mum he was leaving, some time before he actually did, seemingly chopping and changing his mind. Our nanny Helen remembers noticing that my parents were sleeping in different rooms. I've never heard a play-by-play account of what was said, how my mum felt. Who am I to pick at her wounds? As I got older, the realization of what he'd done became like my own bad memory – although I was too young to remember any of it. By osmosis, and through snippets I've been told, I see that time in my own mind's eye. It's a dark, cruel, lonely, agonizing time. I imagine the fighting. The anger. The hurt. The fear. The humiliation. The worry of being left alone with my brother and me. Becoming a single parent, like her mother had been.

My dad chose to play a peripheral role in the life of his children, a role that has ended, for now at least, through our choice. As I try to tell the story of my mother, mine her life for nuggets of insight and explanation, there is a stark contrast with my father. There are huge gaps in my knowledge about him but in many ways his absence has been as impactful as my mother's unwavering presence. It's important to say that there were moments of kindness, support and love, I suppose. But they were like beads slipping off string; I could never quite hold on to them.

Sometimes I think we should understand patriarchy as a public health issue, an emotional and psychological crisis passed down through generations.

My mother and grandmother both lived in worlds in which men earned more money and women were left holding the baby. A generation on, statistically, I still live in that world, although there has been progress: more dads at school gates, the introduction (although rarely adopted) of shared paternity leave and today, one in four households are run by female breadwinners. But we're 'backsliding' too: childcare in the UK is some of the most expensive in the world and the stigma of single mothers is alive and well. These problems are ones that our grandmothers knew, our mothers knew and now we know. Heartbreakingly, it's safe to assume that our daughters will know them too.

When my mum saw that happen to her own mother, when she escaped first to Norwich and then to Nebraska, London and LA, did she ever imagine the same fate would find her? Because she was part of a new moment in time, the rules had changed, women were winning rights, things were different. But just how different did they actually end up being after all? And despite all the pace and momentum and gusto my mum had rushed through life with to this point, the same invisible tripwires remained firmly in place: men are economically dominant, men are unlikely to give up their dream job for kids, men are expected to have careers and ambition. My mother suffered a social whiplash: for all her advancements, the same old problems threw her backwards. Yet when my dad left, he experienced a freedom she could only dream of. He was able to continue his successful and exciting career as a documentary maker, flying aboard Air Force One with presidents. For my mum, everything changed. Her story, the one where she was the heroine chasing her dreams, was on a massive diversion. There aren't statistics for how many women give up their career dreams after divorce compared to men but today, 90 per cent of single parents are women.[11] My mum and dad's divorce was, of course, a personal issue. But the landscape she had to navigate wasn't unique to her: the traps were laid for all women.

As for so many, the promise my mum had known in the early 1970s was met with a different, harsher reality a decade later. The hope that women had felt was bulldozed by a backlash. In the midst of this, my mum's own life had been transformed entirely. She was testing new waters again – a harsher, colder type of life she hadn't planned for. Now my mum had her own hurdles to cross, ones she never dreamed she would.

CHAPTER THREE

Cincinnati, Ohio: The hard work of hope

On the road

'I don't know how I made it out alive. Three people died. Someone was screaming, "Have mercy, have mercy!"'

The crowd around him is listening, and so am I. We're waiting for our bus at the Pittsburgh Greyhound terminal downtown. I had arrived early, bought a coffee from a nearby Starbucks and sat in the station with mostly sleeping men. Some Greyhound stations are open twenty-four hours and therefore become shelter to those with nowhere else to go. Our bus will go all the way to Los Angeles, on the other side of the country on the west coast, but I will get off at Columbus, Ohio, and then pick up another bus to take me to Cincinnati, Ohio. The journey should take around seven hours.

'That's why I take the bus. I ain't ever getting on another plane again'. The guy speaking is young, perhaps in his early twenties. His black hair is thickly gelled. He's wearing a black leather blazer, blue jeans and black loafers. He reminds me of the boys at school trying to get into Wetherspoons on a Saturday night, attempting to appear more grown-up than they actually were.

His attention is mostly focused on an elderly Black woman in a red baseball cap. A few minutes earlier, I'd watched her walk slowly to the front of the line, giving a friendly hello to all the passengers she was pushing in front of.

'I'm telling you, man, that shit was cray-ZEE! It changed my life. When we landed, half the plane was on fire. I'm going to see my boy but I ain't ever flying.'

'You think buses don't have crashes?' offers a young man in a navy tracksuit and short braids, standing on the edge of the group. 'There are more automobile crashes than plane crashes!'

And the floodgates open. Like a whistle has been blown, or a chequered flag waved, the dozen or so people waiting outside the door to our bus start telling their car accident horror stories – and all at once.

An older Jamaican man is particularly loud. Thick dread-locks run down his back and he is wearing a black trilby with a long white feather. He had been sitting on the edge of his suitcase but he rose to speak for the occasion. 'I was with my mother when we were in a crash. I thought I was going to DIE. They had to cut me out. Cut! Me! OUT!'

It is an interesting topic of conversation, considering we are all about to spend hours, for some days, on the road. In New York, a friend had told me that the Greyhound was 'the people's bus' and I'd laughed, writing it off as another example of classic American democratic idealism spilling over, so that even the buses belong to 'we, the people'. But today I can see what she meant; if you want to see a side of America that feels real, that feels utterly removed from the endless scripted reality TV shows and the Instagram filters and the dazzling white teeth and other lazy clichés then here it is.

In the din, my focus lands back on the young man in the leather blazer. He's moved closer to the old lady in the red baseball cap.

'She's a *gypsy*.' He spits the word out. 'My son's mother is a *gypsy*. I was earning $40,000 but couldn't get custody. She took off when she was four months pregnant. I hired a private investigator and tracked her down but she wouldn't put me on the birth certificate.' The old woman is shaking her head, enraptured by his storytelling. 'Then I got locked up. She put false bruises on the kid, said it was me.'

A hush has fallen over the crowd. Everyone is listening.

'She still calls me deadbeat dad and asks for money. My father calls me a victim. I've got to the point where I don't want to be in my son's life. I told myself, one day he'll come for me.'

While he's talking, I notice a woman, probably in her thirties, with pink hair and a long crochet cardigan shuffling through the terminal, pushing a metal walker and asking everyone for a cigarette. When I decline, she tells me to 'go fuck yourself'. Without warning, she picks up her walker, lifts it above her head and starts whacking the locked glass doors out to the buses with her minimal strength, yelling: 'Open the fuck up! Open the fuck up! Open the fuck up!'

A few of us stare in her direction. But no one says or does anything to suggest they think this is remotely out of the ordinary. Luckily, just at this moment, the driver appears, and his yelling begins, stopping hers. 'LOS ANGELES! THIS BUS IS FOR LOS ANGELES!' We start to file on – including the woman with the pink hair. Everyone takes a seat and when we pull out of the terminal, all is quiet.

Until it isn't. I can hear commotion coming from the back of the bus. I'd been warned to stay away from the back of the bus by every single person who I'd told I was making this journey. At school, this was where the troublesome boys hung out and the suggestion has been that it is the same on a Greyhound. The noise starts moving up the aisle. A young woman in a strap top, hair scraped back in a bun, gold hoops in her ears, is sighing as she walks past me.

'Come with me! I'm not doing it alone. Come with me!' An extremely nervous middle-aged Latino man follows her.

Heads swivel, following the pair as they move to the front of the bus. 'What's going on?' someone yells. 'Hey, what's happening?'

The young woman turns around. 'His wife has had an accident and he needs to get off the bus. He doesn't speak much English.'

The murmuring gets louder.

The young woman is now up by the driver, speaking into the Perspex screen that cordons him off.

'Excuse me, sir. This man needs to get off. His wife is in an accident . . . Sir? Excuse me? Sir . . . ? Driver . . . ? HELLO!'

The driver doesn't respond.

'Sir! It is an emergency! His wife has been in a car accident!'

Others are joining in. 'Yo, stop the bus, man! His wife's in trouble!'

I'm momentarily moved by the camaraderie. 'We'll pray for your wife, sir,' says the old lady in the baseball cap.

'See, man,' the young guy with the navy tracksuit says as he leans over the seat in front of him. 'I TOLD you there's more car crashes than plane crashes!'

'An hour!' yells the woman at the front. 'Driver says the next stop is an hour away. He won't stop until then.'

With this, the young woman walks back to her seat, and the bus soon hushes down.

But the show is not quite over yet. Pink Hair is now making her way down the aisle from her front seat, the walker nowhere to be seen. This time she's asking to use everyone's mobile phone. I write in my notes: *a five-foot shuffling live cannon on a bus with a mute driver.* This time, she doesn't tell me to go fuck myself when I decline to give her my phone, she just shuffles on by. A few minutes later, I hear her shuffling back up towards the front of the coach. And then I hear another woman.

'I gave you a cigarette, you ungrateful bitch!'

'Go fuck yourself!' Pink Hair yells over her shoulder.

I am starting to see that these buses aren't like those I am used to in London – mostly silent, private affairs, eyes to phones or looking out the window. They take on a small narrative of their own played out by a cast of characters, all so different, travelling for a host of reasons, confined to this small space for hours and hours, many clearly tackling low incomes and navigating daily struggles. On this ride, there is tragedy in the tale: the man who can't speak English, presumably new to America, an America filled with increasing anti-immigrant feeling, trying to reach his wife but hours away, helpless. Pink Hair is aggressive but there is something desperate about her; she has no phone, no money, she seems so very alone. She appears confused, asking over and over again where the bus was going and if she's got the right ticket.

The rest of the journey passes by in relative quiet and I start to wonder just what kind of American stories you could find if you rode these buses long enough.

*

We finally pull into Cincinnati and, after I've dragged my luggage out from the hold beneath the bus in the scrum of other passengers, I'm extremely glad to book an Uber to take me to my Airbnb. The driver who collects me is friendly and interested in my accent, so we start to chat. He tells me he's a geography teacher at a public school and fills me in on some of the city's history. I'm staying in Over-the-Rhine, a now gentrified corner of the city. This, he explains, was where German immigrants settled at the turn of the century. At that time, there was a canal separating it from the south side of the city, which is how it got its name. It broke my heart to learn that such a kind and enthusiastic teacher was working seven days a week, doing two jobs.

After battling with codes and keys and locks, plus four flights of stairs, I finally arrive at my home for the next few days. Just before dark, I pop out to a nearby supermarket, buying dinner and a bottle of wine. As I pour myself a glass, I collapse on the sofa and catch my breath. *I boarded a Greyhound in Pittsburgh*, I say to the empty apartment. Just like in the song.

The next morning is an achingly hot Sunday and after a walk around the neighbourhood to find coffee, I make my way back to my apartment, which is when I start to hear the music, gospel voices, slowly rising to a crescendo. The sound is everywhere, filling the air like summer wind. My eyes try to find the source as I make my way down the street and, as I stand on the sidewalk just in front of my building, they land on an elderly Black man, smartly dressed in a morning suit, and an elderly Black woman in a purple floral dress and matching wide-brim hat. They are both sitting at electronic keyboards on the sidewalk just a few metres ahead of me in the full glare of the sun. On the narrow sidewalk to their right, a few people sit on camping chairs under the shade of a tree.

It is a tiny congregation. The voices, soulful and big, eclipse the occasional car radio or passing siren. A woman watching rocks a little boy laid across her lap, defeated by the heat. I stand behind them all. While they are out on the street, it still feels intimate and private.

The scene feels stolen, snatched from a time before. Today, Over-the-Rhine looks like corners of New York, fire escapes, neat blocks, tree-lined streets, and street art on every corner. It also looks like corners of New York because of the expensive Italian restaurants and chichi coffee houses that sit across from hip boutiques that serve wealthy white women. But two decades ago, Over-the-Rhine was a different place, a mostly African American neighbourhood that was poverty stricken and dangerous. The Cincinnati Riots started here twenty years ago after an unarmed 19-year-old Black man named Timothy Thomas was shot dead by police. Today, the world knows George Floyd's name. The merry-go-round of history is hard to stomach.

As I make my stops in these Midwestern cities, I start to feel like I have brought a plastic spade for an archaeological dig. And although I'm not here to write about these places with any authority, and couldn't possibly do so, they are part of the story of women I will meet and become part of my story, too. And I'm struck again, as I was outside the Methodist church in Manhattan, that where we are will always tell us something about who we were, who we are and who we might still be.

Backlash

Just as my mum had come of age during an era of hope and social progression, the breakdown of her marriage and her entry into single parenthood arrived at another cultural and political turning point. But this time, things were moving in the wrong direction.

The 1970s may have been a hopeful time for the women's liberation movement but by now it was the mid-1980s, and, with newly elected conservative governments of Margaret Thatcher in the UK (1979) and Ronald Reagan in the US (1980), the feminist fight continued in new and old areas with hurdles aplenty whichever way women looked.

Susan Faludi's seminal book *Backlash: The Undeclared War Against Women*, first published in 1991, makes an extremely compelling case for how the media, advertising industry, popular culture and politics in the 1980s and early 1990s, on both sides of the Atlantic, successfully conspired to tell women that feminism was one big scam. The message of this era was that it had, in fact, been bad for women, leaving them miserable, unwell, single and childless. Women were being hurried out of the offices and advancement they'd just entered and back into homes and domesticity. This was because, as Faludi highlights, of a remarkable social shift that tipped the scales of power.

The early 1980s, she writes, was: 'a moment of symbolic crossover points for American men and women'. It was 'the first time white men became less than 50 per cent of the workforce, the first time no new manufacturing jobs were created, the first time more women enrolled in college, the first time more than 50 per cent of women worked, the first time more women with children than without children worked. Significantly, 1980 was the year the US census officially stopped defining the head of the household as the husband.' And it didn't go down so well. The backlash Faludi describes was to the very real change in the dynamics of men and women's power, brought about by the social movements of the 1960s and 1970s. A similar landscape was being redrawn in the UK. Writing in *The Sunday Times Magazine* in 1990, Neil Lyndon said, 'It is hard to think of one example of systemic and institutionalized discrimination against women today.' Instead, he thought that men were the new 'second-class citizens'. Worst of all, 'the penis is not taken seriously. It is treated as a crude mechanism . . . It is, in fact, the subject of institutionalized neglect.'

The messaging was loud and clear. In 1981, one cover of *New York Times Magazine* featured the words: 'The women's movement is over'. In 1986, a British women's magazine ran a feature called 'Goodbye to All That'. In the same year, *Newsweek* ran a story on the 'new problem with no name', referring to 'the emotional fallout of feminism' forcing women to 'make sacrifices'. In another feature, it declared single women were more likely to be killed by a terrorist than marry a man.

Instead, another image was surfaced – an older, more familiar one. In June 1990, *Esquire* dedicated an entire issue to 'The American Wife', which included a picture of a woman on her knees, scrubbing a toilet. That year, a *Daily Mail* headline announced, 'Why 90s Women Now Say No to Careers'. On the pages of magazines and newspaper lifestyle sections, feminism was being replaced with 'The New Abstinence', 'The New Femininity', 'The New High Monogamy', 'The New Mortality', 'The New Madonnas'. A former advertising exec, Faith Popcorn, christened 'cocooning' in 1986, telling the *Wall Street Journal* that 'We like to stay at home.' By 'we', of course, she meant women.

Both Reagan and Thatcher were also pushing the 'traditional wife' image, suggesting a woman's rightful place was looking after husband and children, while simultaneously punishing, with rhetoric and policy, single and unmarried mothers. Both Reagan and Thatcher promoted 'family' or 'traditional values', bywords for traditional gender roles, backed up by Christian right-wing groups in the US with names like Moral Majority. Women who did not fall in line, according to one of Reagan's top aides, 'were weakening the moral fibre of the nation'.[12] Thatcher wrote in her memoirs that most social problems could be fixed by 'strengthening the traditional family' and told journalist Jenni Murray that she did not want to see Britain turned into 'a crèche nation'. As the country's first female prime minister, she appointed just one female cabinet minister in eleven years in office.

The reality, according to the 1980s, was that working mothers were selfish, incompetent and wreaking havoc on their children's lives. The irony that she, the PM, was a working mother of two, seemed lost on her – Thatcher, it seemed, was granted unique immunity from her own narrative. On the other side of the pond, a spokesman for the New Right in the US, a coalition of conservatives, called day care 'the Thalidomide of the 80s'.[13] Independent and ambitious women were portrayed as lonely and desperate for a man. The press continued to push this agenda and the women's liberation movement was ridiculed as bra-burning, hairy and man-hating. It argued that singledom and the stress of being a working woman led to mental health problems, despite studies frequently showing that married women had greater mental health struggles, lower self-esteem and less regular sex. Singledom and stress of being a working woman also, apparently, caused infertility problems – as shown by infertility studies which, incidentally, routinely failed to include men. Endometriosis became known to some doctors as 'the career's woman's disease'.[14] Women who had been liberated by the social movements of the previous two decades and tried to live their promised ideals were targets of sexism and humiliation. Nora Ephron put it this way: 'Wives went out into the world free at last, single again and discovered the horrible truth; that they were sellers in a buyer's market and that the major concrete agreement of the women's movement in the 1970s was the Dutch treat.'[15]

In hindsight, the severity of the backlash proved just how much ground women *had* achieved. In Britain, at the end of the 1970s, there was one divorce for every three marriages.[16] In the US, around the same time, roughly 50 per cent of marriages ended in divorce and only 15 per cent of American families were composed of a father who worked and a mother who stayed at home – a figure that stood at over 50 per cent in the early 1950s.[17] But despite, or perhaps precisely because of this shift, the world was trying to suggest the women's liberation movement had been a moment of madness with a dangerous legacy, one that actually *harmed* women because they inevitably ended up alone, bitter, mentally unwell and infertile.

Women were accused of trying to 'have it all' – a backhanded dig at the audacity and greed of those with families who wanted to have a career, just like their husbands. And many conveniently overlooked that even if ambitions had soared, pay had not. In 1985, the year I was born, on average, women earned only 66 per cent of average male pay.[18] This was the landscape my newly single mother found herself in. Of course, that a single mother would dare to have a career seemed even more audacious to the mums at the school gates, to my teachers, to the men in the office. If working women with husbands were deemed selfish and irresponsible, it's easy to see what some made of my mum.

The world was disillusioned by revolutions that hadn't been transformative enough and a 1980s culture that liked to laugh off the 1970s as a bad trip that should be forgotten. The neoliberalism associated with Reagan and Thatcher was here to put an end to social movements. For my mum, the wild promise of hot Nebraska days must have felt a very long way away.

After my dad left, and insisted he wasn't able to pay maintenance, my mum needed secure work. She left TV behind and was fast-tracked in the civil service, taking a job with the Metropolitan police at New Scotland Yard. She was forced to sell our dream home in the woods and the three of us moved to a two-bedroom cottage in Woking. It was part of an old converted pub and, in time, when my brother and I became too old to share a room, the windowless basement cellar became my mum's bedroom. The staircase down there was extremely narrow, so a friend sawed her single bed in half, carried it down the slight, cramped cellar stairs and stuck it back together.

The cottage must have felt tiny to my mum but I loved it. I loved the stable-style split front door. In the summer, my mum would keep the top half open, as she had a glass of wine and a cigarette after work. I would run into the kitchen to meet her when she got home, as she placed her large, black work bag on the counter, pulling out a bar of chocolate for each of us.

At the time, my mum kept James and me well cocooned from the fallout of our father leaving, but when I became an adult, she told me stories that are hard to hear – of hunting down the back of the sofa for foreign coins that she might be able to exchange, of not taking the bus across the bridge each morning to save money, of making my school dresses instead of buying them. The kind postman would occasionally ask her if she 'wanted' her post that day, knowing that the bills might not be welcome, and sometimes he'd hold on to them for a couple of days so she could catch her breath. However difficult it must have been, I never saw her cry or despair or complain. If that happened, it never happened in front of us. Instead, she filled our lives with bedtime stories, Easter egg hunts, *Bugsy Malone* and dancing to ABBA.

Our nanny, Helen, started looking after James before I came along when she was just 18. She stayed with us during those difficult years and today she is like an aunt. I ask her now if she saw my mum struggle. 'No,' she tells me, 'never. I always thought she was such a strong woman. She never gave anything away.' I instantly recognize this ability to always – no matter what – put on a brave face and keep going. Some evenings, when she returned from work, she'd ask Helen to have a drink waiting for them both – my mum's a glass of wine, Helen's a gin and tonic. Was she lonely? 'Yes, I think she was.' There's a heavy feeling in my chest when I hear Helen say this, confirming something I've always suspected but have tried to brush off.

I discover some of these stories in unexpected moments. For years, my mum worked on London's Victoria Street. I must have walked up and down that street, either with her or going to meet her, a million times. New Scotland Yard was at one end of the street and in the summer holidays, James and I would spend the day at a play scheme there, subsidized by the civil service. But it wasn't until I was at least 30, when we were there again, this time headed for lunch, that for the first time she pointed out a pawn shop I'd never noticed in between the cafés and office blocks. She told me that she used to go in on her way to work to pawn any remaining bits of jewellery my dad had given her, that she hadn't already sold, to make it through the end of the month.

Times were never desperate or, at least, not that I know of. And James and I never went without anything, but money was obviously a worry, and yet my mum always managed somehow. As kids, we just never noticed. When the rain leaked through the hole in the roof of her Citroen 2CV I didn't realize she couldn't afford to mend it. I thought stuffing the hole with kitchen towel in panicked shrieks of laughter was just part of the fun.

Yet while I didn't notice the absence of money, I did notice the absence of time.

I was always aware of how tired she was. She could fall asleep anywhere – standing up on a packed commuter train first thing in the morning or slumped over a Blackberry on the way home. On her lunch breaks in the summer, she'd hurry down to St James' Park for a nap, asking a colleague to wake her with a phone call. Red wine would spill as her head jerked forward on the sofa at night. Cold tea bags sat in the fridge waiting to offer tired eyes relief.

Her alarm would go off at 5.15 a.m. A cup of tea always came first. She'd feed the cats and have some breakfast. Then she'd wake us, help with our school uniform, make sure we had breakfast. When we were much younger, she'd drop us at school before she dashed to the station. Later on, we were left to get the school bus. At one point, the heater stopped working in a car she'd bought off her niece. So each winter morning, while it was still dark and freezing, she'd feed an electric heater through a downstairs window out into the car to heat it up before the commute. She'd drive thirty minutes to the spot where she'd discovered free parking on a side street by a small station and then pick up the stopping train to Waterloo. On the train, she'd fire off emails on her Blackberry and then walk across the bridge, pass the Houses of Parliament and Westminster Abbey, across Parliament Square and down Victoria Street.

At work, after she'd swapped her Zara flats for one of the pairs that made up the mountains of heels under her desk, she'd field calls from journalists about the latest crisis, write press releases at lightning speed as stories broke, organize press conferences, brief officers before live interviews in front of camera crews, while getting to know the landscape of journalists and liaising with community leaders and the countless others in the Met's orbit. When she was on call, which was a regular part of the job, her phone would ring long after my brother and I were in bed or over the weekend. When a national emergency struck on a weekend, like the death of Princess Diana, she would drop us off at the childminders and rush into work.

She never stopped. She was always on. And not in an endearing, 'I don't know how she does it' way but in a bone-shattering, exhausted way. My memories of her busyness take particular form: endless Biros in the bottom of her handbag because any minute she could receive a phone call and need to take notes on a problem. 'I have to go, love,' is how she ended our after-school calls; she could never make summer fetes or sports days. When I had parent–teacher evenings, I'd have to make sure I got the teacher's final slot of the night, as this was the earliest she could attend. Later on in her career, I met her for lunch near her office. Ten minutes later, she was running out the door to manage another disaster. She was so busy one year she forgot to buy a turkey for Christmas and only remembered at 8 p.m. on Christmas Eve.

But I never, ever, saw any of this absence as neglect or chaos. Even when I was very little. One of my earliest memories is of sitting cross-legged on the floor of my classroom in St Matthews, my idyllic first school nestled away in a small Surrey village. My teacher is asking the class if we know what our parents do for a living. My hand shoots up, desperate to be picked. 'My mum works in London and she has three people working for her!'

Perhaps it was the way she dressed. Her big, heavy, black leather bag looked important. Her high heels and suit jackets made her look in charge. Perhaps it was because I knew she went to London every day, a thing that seemed significant. I had no idea what she did there but I'm sure I reasoned that whatever took her away from us was essential and necessary because why else would she do it? I was always immensely proud that my mum was doing what my friend's dads did.

After a string of different after-school childcare arrangements, we were both finally old enough to stay at home alone when I was 14. She'd ring at 4 p.m. and mediate fights from behind her desk in Westminster. She'd get home just as the *Archers* started, complaining that we hadn't drawn the curtains or turned on the lights. I'd be quiet for the fifteen minutes of the soap, bursting with all the things I needed to tell her about my day. Then she'd take off the armour of her work clothes, lay out tomorrow's battle dress and pour a glass of wine. Her phone and Blackberry would go on charge, but always in earshot, and she'd start the dinner, asking us about our homework, helping us with what we hadn't done, before she collapsed into bed and did it all over again the next day.

Recently, for my brother's fortieth, when he was visiting the UK, my mum and I stayed up after he'd gone to bed and blew up balloons and hung banners. As I stood huffing and puffing, and my stubborn 69-year-old mother balanced on a small step against my better advice, I thought of all the birthdays we've had over the years. All the birthdays where she stayed up the night before and blew up balloons and hung up banners. I thought of all the Christmases where she stayed up to wrap presents and stuff pillowcases full of toys, creeping into our rooms to put them at the bottom of the bed. I remembered the times she was up late when we had nightmares or when we were sick, soothing us. And her alarm would still go off before daylight. As I watched her untangle a happy birthday sign, one pair of glasses on her end of her nose, another pair on her head, I looked at her and saw it all – no matter how long the day had been, how tired she was after the commute, how worried she was about making it till the end of the month, she gave us everything she had. All the late nights, all the balloons, all the love.

Ordinary women

Seeing my mum work so hard while I was growing up has led me to believe that so-called ordinary women are extraordinary. Yet, as a society, we treat them as anything but. We barely pass comment on how much they juggle: children, jobs, older parents, domestic and emotional labour, not to mention the physical labour of periods, childbirth, the menopause, or the casual sexism of unequal pay, street harassment, being overlooked for promotions and opportunities, especially when intersected with race or disability or age. We don't ask them how they deal with the inequalities they face – or, at least, not genuinely because if we did, decades-old issues, such as the high cost of childcare, unequal pay or domestic violence, wouldn't still be such big problems. We certainly don't see their struggle as a state of the nation indicator or a problem impacting half of the population. We don't afford the issues that impact their lives with the gravity they deserve; we don't talk about childcare as infrastructure or domestic violence as homicide and terrorism. We don't talk about systemic racism and its link to poverty and how it intersects with sexism. We don't celebrate or support single mothers; we shame them. We have no patience or accommodation for anyone who doesn't fit into an ableist society. If we can't see her disability, we doubt her. If we can see it, we avoid her. And always, always, always, women's problems are for women – to talk about, to write about, to solve.

But on my journey, I wanted to meet women like my mum, extraordinary women who the world might label as ordinary. Not high-profile or famous women, not world-record holders or bestselling authors. Just those quietly getting on with the hard work of being extraordinary: putting in the hours, the unglamorous grunt work, the patience, the commitment. Women who I truly see as heroic, buried in the hard work of life, and often dedicating much of their time to making life better for others around them. These are, I believe, the women that can help us with difficult times ahead. It is these women we can learn from and who can help me understand what resilience is made of. I was lucky enough to watch my mother growing up but we're surrounded by women like her, if only we stop and notice.

One of the extraordinary but 'ordinary' women I meet in Cincinnati is 30-year-old Chelsie Walter. Chelsie is small and blonde. She's shy and incredibly polite. On first meeting, it would be easy to call her slight – both in her physique and her interaction with the world. But that would be wrong because she clearly has had a huge impact on her community. And she has a huge impact on me.

In a deeply divided nation, and in a state that will enforce some of the most extreme restrictions should the constitutional right to abortion be taken away, Chelsie believes in the power of storytelling as a tool for change. She does this through her web-site, Women of Cincy, to which she gives twenty hours a week on top of her two jobs, one as a designer for a monthly newspaper, the first specifically aimed at inspiring and empowering those currently incarcerated, and the other as a social media manager for a brewery. She's also raising her young daughter, Nora.

Chelsie has published 420 interviews with local women since 2017, at time of writing, reaching over 198,000 people, shining a light and amplifying the women's lives, work, community projects they are involved in and their hopes for the city. They are extensive and often moving portraits. The site has a particular focus on marginalized voices, to represent the diverse community that makes up Cincinnati. Chelsie transcribes the interviews verbatim, in an effort to 'truly give the interviewees their voice'.

The site began as an Instagram feed, started on the day of the International Women's March in 2017, before snowballing into an organization with charity status and a roster of fifty volunteers. After the election of Donald Trump, Chelsie wanted to find a way to fight back against the rise in racial tensions and the growing threat to voting rights, women's rights and LGBTQ rights. For Chelsie, storytelling is the most effective bridge to empathy and understanding of others. When I ask her about her motivations and the huge effort involved in running Women of Cincy, behind every answer is the same unspoken inference: *In a moment like this, how could you not?*

'It's been so hard,' she tells me. 'To be truly honest, we have almost quit 100 times. It really is a lot of work. We don't have employees. It's just everybody working their asses off. After they get off work from a long day and they put their kids to bed, women are sitting at computers typing and transcribing. I've also been through a lot these last two years; I have lost people close to me. And we've thought a lot about ending Women of Cincy. But it always comes back to if we *didn't* do this, think about all these stories that *wouldn't* be told – or the relationships that wouldn't have been created, connections that wouldn't have been made. You know, at this point, it feels like my purpose is to create this platform for other people to share their stories.' These stories feature grassroots activists, local authors and artists, biomedical engineers, councilwomen, mothers, teachers, businesswomen and non-profit executives. The site also includes a directory of women-led local businesses, as well as a mentorship programme for college students who can gain experience creating content for the website.

There are all sorts of stories on the site but some particularly stand out. Rosemary Oglesby-Henry runs Rosemary's Babies in the city, a non-profit supporting local teen mums. Rosemary became a mother at 17 and it shaped her life, meaning tough choices and sacrifices, as well as enduring sexual harassment and racism working at the post office to provide for her child. But for her, this was the only way. In her Women of Cincy interview she says, 'My daughter didn't have to walk past the neighbourhood drug dealer. My daughter doesn't know a life where her father is on drugs. My daughter doesn't know a life where her father is an alcoholic. She never had to see what I had to see. If I was able to shield my daughter from that by working a job for fifteen years that I hated, I would do it all over again.'

Similarly, Dr Zara Davis works with the local community because of her own experiences: 'I was a mental health therapist for twenty-plus years and ended up going to federal prison,' she told Women of Cincy. 'I received a twenty-four-month sentence, which was then reduced to eighteen months; in total, I was there for a year. That was just such a pivotal point in my life that inspired everything I do within the community today.' Dr Davis underscores much of Chelsie's ethos: 'When people meet me as Dr Zaria Davis and they don't know anything about my past, there's this shock factor when they find out I was sentenced, like, "No, not you!" Imagine how many other "No, not you!" people there are out there.'

Chelsie is from rural Ohio. Her father, who is from a long line of Kentucky coal miners, worked on the factory line making cars for thirty years. Her mother was born in the same small town as Chelsie, married her father right out of high school and had Chelsie young. She had a host of different jobs when Chelsie was growing up – in the grocery store, in the car factory, as a security guard, a secretary. Chelsie says where she grew up was very 'Christian and white'.

Until fairly recently, Ohio was an important swing state.

In 2008, Barack Obama and his team visited fifty times and spent $50,000 in advertising here, reflecting what an important a battleground it was. It worked: the state voted Democrat both in 2008 and again in 2012. But then things started to change. In both 2016 and 2020, Ohio voted for Donald Trump. In 2019, Governor Mike DeWine signed the so-called 'heartbeat bill', banning abortion after six weeks – a period of time in which many women don't yet realize they are pregnant – although it was later blocked by a federal judge. In response to the Uvalde shooting of nineteen school children in May 2022, DeWine introduced a bill making it easier for teachers to carry guns, with minimal training. And in the same year, an amendment was made to a bill that would see schoolgirls playing sports potentially subjected to invasive genitalia testing to confirm their sex, as part of the country's growing legislation targeting trans youth.

Chelsie wasn't engaged in politics at all when she lived at home, outside of the city. She was more interested in riding shotgun in her boyfriend's pick-up truck. 'Still got the boyfriend but we lost the truck,' she grins. Chelsie moved to Cincinnati to go to university. It was only a two-hour drive away but felt like a different world. Being exposed to different types of people from different communities was an enriching experience and soon Chelsie began to realize there were 'two Americas' – rural and city, divided 'by everything. Race, politics, wealth, class. Everything.'

'Where I grew up, people are conservative. They don't like change. It's a small community and it can feel quite cut off. In the city, it can feel like everyone is much more accepting of each other because they've been exposed to one another.' With so much of her family still in that same small town, Chelsie feels she has 'a foot in both worlds'. She says, 'I became convinced that if you guys just knew each other's story, maybe you wouldn't have these feelings towards people you've never met before?'

These divisions run through her own family. Before her daughter was born, she would fall out for months at a time with her Republican-voting father, unable to find common ground. When her daughter was born during the pandemic, she would only let relatives see her baby if they were vaccinated. 'I sent them the link to their nearest vaccination centre,' she laughs, happy to use her daughter as a way to persuade her family to bypass their anti-vax biases. The only relative who didn't protest was her 91-year-old great-grandmother who could remember the polio vaccine.

But Chelsie isn't here to persuade anyone on politics; she's here to persuade them on people. Women of Cincy is deliberately nonpartisan. For Chelsie, the work has to take place *before* the conversation turns to left or right. 'We're trying to meet people before they even make the decisions that get us to all these negative outcomes,' she tells me, referring to state abortion restrictions, voting suppression and racist re-districting efforts. 'Because all day long, you can throw facts and figures at somebody, you can stand outside their house with a sign, but till you truly touch their heart, they're going to put up walls.'

There are many reasons I think Chelsie is extraordinary: running an organization on top of two jobs and raising her baby daughter; choosing her own path even though it causes tension in her family; being proactive in creating the sort of community she wants for her family; elevating the stories of women, especially those stories that are most uncommonly lost or not celebrated; attempting to bridge a divide many are resigned to or stubbornly entrenched in. But perhaps mostly for truly believing that a story can make a difference. Shannon Watts, the incredible leader of Moms Demand Action, the largest grassroots group campaigning for gun control in the county, has said that 'it's relentless incrementalism that leads to revolution'. Story after story after story, Chelsie hopes, will lead to an avalanche of empathy. She is in this for the long game.

As I scroll through the Women of Cincy website, I'm left wondering how many extraordinary women in history have never had their story told, have been lost to time, discarded by a society that said they didn't matter. And I'm more convinced than ever that retracing my mum's footsteps and telling her story – and the stories of others – is a journey worth making.

The next day, continuing my whistlestop tour of extraordinary ordinary women, I meet Giovanna Alvarez. With glossy black hair and a smile like warm sunlight, her passion for her work is palatable.

Giovanna has been the director of the Su Casa Hispanic Center, supported by the Catholic Church, for twelve years. She leads a team that works with the Latino and Hispanic community, helping them with a range of needs, from learning English to accessing benefits and managing immigration status, connecting them to job opportunities, registering children for schools and organizing family reunification once children have crossed the border. Most recently, she has been a lifeline during the coronavirus pandemic, providing access to the vaccine as well as laptops and internet connections so children could continue learning in lockdown.

Giovanna rolls off the long list of work they do and it's clear what they are dealing with: people vulnerable to a hostile immigration system, exploitation and discrimination. I ask for examples of the cases she deals with. She paints a complicated and dangerous landscape. 'Children with complex medical needs and a mixed immigration documentation status. Or it could be a mom whose husband was deported and she never worked and she's now the sole provider for seven children and two of them have special needs. Or the lady who was not able to go to the doctor because she didn't have medical insurance. She was scared to go. Eventually, she got septicaemia and she had to have her left arm amputated because she didn't get the help she needed in time. In the past, we've had cases of human trafficking and for that we have to work with the FBI.' The centre deals with adults and children who have faced all kinds of trauma, including experiencing domestic violence. They help with housing, try to protect against wage theft – a very common problem, Giovanna says – and they work with local food banks.

Many of the stories about the reality of why immigrants are trying to reach America are similar. 'A lot of the problems [we encounter] are the same because we deal with poverty, and sometimes generational poverty, especially when people come from very remote areas. For example, there are a lot of clients from Guatemala, El Salvador, Nicaragua, Mexico, and they come from the most humble, most poverty-impacted areas. So you see those commonalities – poverty, a lack of the English language, coming here for better opportunities for themselves and their children. And sometimes we have seen that people here, in the US, don't understand why people migrate. But when you hear the stories, the push and pull factors of economics, when the corn in

Guatemala is more expensive than the corn in America, families starve. I have clients that said that when they were children, they had to search through the rubbish in order to eat.'

Giovanna also talks about the violence many immigrants face. 'Sometimes, people come who have been affected by the gangs. Children were trying to go to school but the gangs were pressuring them or beating them up to join and they didn't want to. Some people have had relatives killed by the gangs and they were threatened.'

The story she relays to me next, though, is the one I find most shocking. 'Sometimes, when mothers are sending 12-year-old children across the border, there is a high likelihood that the child might be raped, and so they give their daughters contraceptives.' The lives of immigrants call for an altogether different level of resilience.

But there are other stories too, ones full of hope despite the sadness and loss along the way. 'You can really make an impact if you invest in the education of these children. I've seen that first hand. When I started, I remember there was a family that came to the centre for help settling in the city. Shortly afterwards, the mom got sick and died of cancer. So her eldest daughter helped raise her younger siblings. And now, that girl is our intern, whilst studying social work at the university. When she walked in, I recognized her straight away. Now she's giving back. It's amazing.'

Giovanna is from Peru, where she was a lawyer. She came to the US, originally to Florida with her sister, married an American and had a daughter. Now she is divorced and a single working mother in a demanding job. She misses dancing and bars open till the early hours, and the colours and the life of it all. In Ohio, locals still regularly question her accent or her pronunciation, despite her speaking what sounds to me like perfect English. It's clear that Giovanna works in a tough landscape, continuously surrounded by heartbreaking stories – or 'strong stories' as she refers to them throughout our conversation – especially in an ever more divided America. She tells me discrimination and abuse have taken a sharp increase since the arrival of Trump on the political scene. I'm in awe not just of the service that Giovanna provides to her community, but of the passion and tenacity with which she does it.

Giovanna admits that hearing so many 'strong' stories can be difficult and that's why she's grateful for her team, a room of smiling women speaking a mix of Spanish and English, who she takes the time to introduce me to. 'But I also see the beauty of humankind,' she says, 'when people help each other.'

Crucially, there is one driving force for Givonna: 'I do it all for my daughter.' I recognize the struggle well and I am reminded that so often, our fight for what we believe in starts in our own home.

Mothers and daughters

Back at the Airbnb, I call my mum. Since I've been away, I've found it difficult to hear her worries for my safety. Before I left, she gave me a notebook like the one she'd taken with her on her trip. I was touched, but inside she'd written 'Keep eyes in the back of your head', as if my romantic road trip was going to turn into a mobster movie. I was trying to avoid being held hostage by fears of being a lone female traveller, especially with Gabby Petito still missing and the story dominating the media.

I was working hard to build courage against a world full of male threat, something I'd been aware of for far too long. I'd made a pact with myself that I'd push myself outside of my comfort zone at least once a day while out here. At some points on the journey I had already been so far out of it – riding buses and no one knew where I was; talking to strangers at restaurants, diners and bars; finding myself in women's homes asking them to tell me about their lives – I couldn't even see where the line was anymore. But I couldn't tell her that because she would worry. The Jacqui who seems so fearful today is so much at odds with the young woman in the photo I'm out here looking for.

So instead, on the phone, we talk about America. 'Isn't it big?' she laughs. 'Don't you just love the views?' she asks. 'How does a country that size vote for one man, love one film, watch one TV show?' I can hear the wonder in her voice, still, after all these years. 'Have you been safe?' she inevitably asks. I tell her I've figured out how to use the washer and dryer in the basement of the Airbnb. 'Have you had any trouble? Any shady characters?' No, I say. It's all been fine. There's half a beat's silence. 'You wouldn't tell me if you had, would you?'

If my mum has always pushed me forward into the world with one hand, the other one has cautiously hovered in front of me. She always let me know that she believed I could conquer the world, that I could do anything, and that I should be out there looking for whatever it was I wanted. Just like she had. But now, with the scars of time and life, that belief battles with the reality of me *actually* being out there, with all the associated dangers – real and imagined. The ones she was aware of through her job, from being a single parent, because of the threats she'd known in her own life. And now, I realize, her fear is something

I have inherited, like her small feet and profound love of Kermit the Frog. But is it fair to blame her for passing on that worry? Our mothers have lived in a world where the statistics were even worse, danger was even more commonplace and accepted, fewer women were believed, fewer people cared.

I can feel that inherent contradiction in myself as I make my way across the country. I can feel the drive, pushing me out further into unknown spaces, meeting a stream of fascinating people, trying to understand the lives of strangers. But I can also feel my fear. I wonder how much of that fear is a construct inherited and how much of it is justified – my evolutionary sensor keeping me safe in a world that is, unquestionably, with reams of evidence, dangerous for women. At times, I almost feel paralysed, not knowing my next move, caught between the reality of the statistics, my mum's worry and my determination to push on. Yet the more time I spend out in the world alone on this trip, the more the thrill of my journey refuses to wane and I begin to feel nauseating waves of regret that I haven't travelled alone before.

After we end the call, I try to shake the niggling thoughts of my safety or what my mum does and doesn't know. So I head out, in denim shorts, a black tank top, braless – a small and pathetic act of defiance against my own worries. It is early evening and the heat is tropical, suffocating almost. I walk only a couple blocks before I see a bar. *Why not?* I think. My adrenaline is still running from the day's conversations and it is nice to find somewhere cool. It's dark inside, not much other than a long wooden bar. A few TV screens are showing sports. I climb up on a stool. The barman comes over and raises his eyebrows in lieu of asking an actual question. A gin and tonic please, I say. With lime. He prepares my drink, drops in a small red straw and finally speaks when he asks for seven dollars.

A middle-aged couple on the other side of the bar smile at me when they hear my accent. 'Have you been to Oktoberfest?' the woman asks.

I shake my head.

'Where you from?'

'England,' I say.

'From England? Wow! On your own? Are you working here?'

'Just visiting,' I smile.

The couple have been to Oktoberfest and are, I suspect, more than a few beers down. They find a lone Englishwoman making her way through the Midwest fascinating. Becky, petite with straight brown hair, a lilac halterneck and straight leg jeans over cowboy boots, was particularly enamoured.

'I just think that's marvellous, honey! So cool! Let me buy you a drink. Cheers to you!'

She moves around to my side of the bar and directs the barman to get me another.

As I watch the silent barman pour me another gin and tonic, Becky's companion starts regaling us with stories of an inter-railing trip around Europe in the 1980s. He tells a story about being in 'downtown London' and being terrified in a Soho pub. I say I prefer New York to London any day of the week but, despite being only ninety minutes away on a plane, neither of them have been.

'You're getting the bus! Lord! Well good luck with that!' Becky shrieks. She says that her son takes the bus to college sometimes. She drops him off for the early ride at 4.30 a.m. I had him young, she says, like she might be preempting my next question. Her partner then starts telling me a different story about how he got a bus when he was in his twenties and was stuck on it for hours. 'Never again,' he laughs, shaking his head, 'never, ever again.'

'Anyway, let's take a selfie,' Becky says.

We pose for the picture, smiling, sweaty, excitable.

They wish me luck and head out. At the door, Becky turns around. Her smile morphs into something more sombre, 'Stay safe now, honey. Stay safe.'

The next morning, I am waiting in the reception area of the University of Cincinnati College of Law. An ornate wooden grandfather clock ticks loudly. A printer slowly spits out paper. Occasionally, students with large backpacks and water bottles rush past on their way to class. I'm about to meet Dean Verna Williams, the first African American to hold the position of dean of the law college, one of the oldest in the country. Previously, she spent eight years at the National Women's Law Center, a prestigious institution founded in 1972, and it was during her time there that she argued before the Supreme Court – and won – as lead counsel on Davis v. Monroe County Board of Education. Verna Williams' winning case established that educational institutions have a duty to address complaints of student-to-student sexual harassment.

Nearly a year after our meeting, Verna Williams will move to be CEO of Equal Justice Works, a non-profit that supports law students into fellowships at legal organizations in the name of public service. But today, Williams – a petite woman with cropped hair wearing glasses and a black N95 mask – opens the door and invites me into her office. We sit across a large table from one another. On the wall behind her is the familiar Shepard Fairey 'We the People' print of a woman wearing a hijab made of an American flag, one of a series created to protest the presidency of Trump. On a shelf by the door, I think I spy a framed picture of her and Michelle Obama and try not to stare. Dean Williams is one of Michelle Obama's close friends, having met her at Harvard Law School when they were students there. While Michelle Obama was first lady, Williams served as an oral historian, helping to record her time as First Lady of the United States (FLOTUS).

Dean Williams is now an academic but began her career as an ambitious young lawyer wanting to make a difference. Starting out, she was determined to focus on race: 'I always admired Thurgood Marshall and Pauli Murray and wanted to be like them, until' – she says with a faintest echo of Sojourner Truth – 'I learned I was a woman.'

Starting out at the Civil Rights Division of the Department of Justice in the early 1990s, Williams began to notice something: 'I had a hard time getting complex cases. I was assigned things that I could have done as a student. I saw senior women have cases taken away from them because, according to supervisors, they couldn't handle it, even though they had worked it up. I heard about complaints of sexual harassment. And I just thought, "My gosh, I'm in the *Civil Rights Division*."' So together with other women attorneys in the section, she organized and pushed the leadership to introduce sexual harassment training. 'And then,' she tells me, 'I got out.'

This was around the same time that a 35-year-old Black lawyer called Anita Hill alleged claims of sexual harassment against Supreme Court Justice Clarence Thomas during his nomination hearings.[19] I have read a lot about this and I was fascinated to ask Dean Williams what watching the Anita Hill story play out, in the moment, was like for a young Black female lawyer.

'I will never forget Justice Thomas saying it was a "high-tech lynching". I was so angry, horrified, that he would use that terminology, particularly when during the hearings he did everything possible to distance himself from being an African American. But when he was in trouble and his back was against the wall, he turned to that. I was dating somebody at the time and we would argue a lot about whether or not she was telling the truth. He kept saying stuff like, "Why did she stay in the role?" And I said, "There are all kinds of reasons she would stay; she's trying to keep her job." We had *really* big arguments. Needless to say, he's not the guy I married.'

The case led to what was known as the 'Year of the Woman' in 1992, when a record number of women ran for elected office, furious as they watched a senate judiciary committee of nine white men – led by Senator Joe Biden of Delaware – appoint Thomas and dismiss Hill. Just as the accusations of Anita Hill left a generation of women outraged, in no small part had I found myself in Dean Williams' office because of the hearings of Brett Kavanaugh, another Supreme Court Justice nominee accused of sexual assault during his nominations, nearly thirty years later. Here was the merry-go-round of history turning once more.

As Williams entered the world of work, she realized, 'There wasn't an issue that gender didn't touch.' But it took different positions for her to feel like she was making a difference – the thing she'd always wanted to do. In law school, she worked in a criminal defence clinic. 'I represented a low-income woman who had been charged with assault of her landlady. Because of that, she got kicked out and was homeless. While she was living in her van, her son got stabbed. I was crying about this case because I felt so bad.' Williams did what she could but the experience left her unsure. 'Her life was so complicated, there were so many issues, and I just felt at sea because I couldn't really help her. I wanted to go somewhere where I would have a better chance of making a difference.'

This is how she felt when she started working at the National Women's Law Center in Washington, DC, where she was the vice president and director of educational opportunities, focusing on gender equity in education. 'We helped people understand they were entitled to an income tax credit – the Child and Dependent Care Credit. We educated staff at childcare centres and then those people could educate parents. Likewise, in sexual harassment, I was in coalition with other groups, working with the Department of Education, on guidelines for schools. In both cases, we were advocating for a certain understanding of the law that could help people – and we were succeeding.' During this time, under the Clinton administration, Williams felt like the law was on her side. It is an interesting lesson to me in how we can all find the right way to be useful, to best fight our chosen battles.

Yet, as time has passed, the lens on what difference she made shifted. By the mid to late 1990s, Williams was doing important work on sexual harassment in universities, arguing her case in front of the Supreme Court and setting 'the standard' for practice by universities in America when handling allegations of sexual harassment. But today, in light of Kavanaugh, in light of #MeToo, she says, 'It feels like *now* the world is discovering sexual harassment? We were talking about this very topic thirty years ago. It felt like I was having an impact at the time, but . . .' she pauses and sighs. 'I guess we just have to keep at it.'

Sexual harassment isn't the only social issue that Williams believes 'we have to keep at'. To her mind, America is currently in a very dark place and the uphill battle towards a more just society can be exhausting.

She is disgusted by the events at the Capitol on 6 January 2021. 'I've never seen anything like it in my lifetime. It was absolutely horrifying and sickening. I'm old enough to have been around during the Civil Rights movement. Then there were smaller insurrections during the Second Reconstruction era;[20] that kind of stuff was happening all over the country – targeting Black communities and for lots of different reasons. But we never saw a major insurrection. And it was profoundly depressing. I mean, I had to go to bed the day I saw it. I just had to go to bed. It was so upsetting to me. And it made me think about the Reconstruction period because I thought this is what happened. It was horrifying.'

There's a stillness in her office as I listen to her. 'How much more violent is this backlash going to be? How willing are [Trump supporters] to completely deviate from the principles that they say this country was founded on?' she continues. 'It's hard. It's dispiriting – particularly as a woman and a Black woman whose life has been impacted by changes in law, and who believes in that – to see how easily it can go back. It's very frightening. I do remember thinking that the law expands and contracts. And we are in a severe contraction right now.

How does America find its way out of this darkness? One

way through, Dean Williams believes, is more robust social movements, activism by ordinary people wanting to make the change they want to see, like the Civil Rights movement that she can remember watching growing up – movements that aren't just enacted on social media but that can lead to a piece of legislation. 'Even here, some kids arrive not knowing how a bill becomes a law. They think activism is just being out in the street. That can be part of it but it has to be towards something *concrete*. People are not going to change just because you're out on the street. You need to come to them with what you want and then push to get that. And I worry that young people don't know what they want and they focus so much on the performative aspect. They are signifying on social media and they think that's activism. But it's not.'

Williams, however, is quick to see that there is good work happening, too. 'We talk about the "Trump bump" in law schools because after 2008, the great recession, applications were going down because there weren't lots of jobs in the big firm arena, but with Trump, and all those immigration bans, where you have lawyers going out to airports, helping people – every time I talk about it I get goose bumps – lawyers became heroes, right? And now there's a whole generation who saw that and they're raring to fight. Look at my daughter; she's going to go to law school. She wants to get in there, she wants to make a difference. And that's different from ten, fifteen, twenty years ago, when people were coming because law was an avenue to a really lucrative income. They're not looking for money, they're looking to make a difference.'

As with the shift in the 1980s following the women's liberation movement of the 1970s, Dean Williams says we're in another backlash: 'How do we go from Barack Obama to Donald Trump? It's a slap in the face to those of us who want the country to progress in another direction.'

'My parents also saw a backlash after the heady days of civil rights laws being enacted.' This was the late 1960s and early 1970s when Williams was growing up. The family lived in Washington DC and her parents were optimistic. On the drive to school, they'd pass civil rights marches. 'I was like kids who grew up under Obama and didn't know anything different.' But then things changed – the Kennedy assassination, the Martin Luther King assassination, the election of President Nixon. 'These were reactions to the country moving in a different direction. And just as you think, OK, we're making progress, people say, "No, we don't want to make that progress."'

For Williams, however, there is a slither of hope. 'With each wave of this, we move a little bit further forward.' She points out that she is better off than her mother, who wasn't allowed to work when pregnant and had to ask her husband's permission when she wanted her tubes tied. History is never quite repeating itself, she says, because, 'Where we are now is not the same as where we were before. The one thing we can't do is give up hope. Even in the darkest times, even during the Middle Passage and slavery, my people had hope. Civil rights attorney Sherrilyn Ifill, who runs the NAACP Legal Defense Fund, put it really well, when she said some words to the effect of "At no point in our story are the words, 'And then Black people gave up'." We don't give up. We just keep going. And it's not just us. Think about how long it took women to get the right to vote. Those women didn't give up either.'

In six months' time, I'll be in the UK clearing up after dinner.

The evening is cold and dark despite the flirtations of spring, and I have slippers and a big sweatshirt on. As I wipe the surfaces and stack the dishwasher, I watch hope take the form of Ketanji Brown Jackson from inside my iPhone propped up behind the hob. A district judge, she has been nominated by President Biden to join the Supreme Court and will become the first Black woman Justice on the Supreme Court. I will think back to my conversation with Dean Williams and her fury at Clarence Thomas, the injustice of Anita Hill, the law failing us in this moment – or, as she put it, 'in a state of extreme contraction'. I will watch Brown Jackson be questioned by the senate committee – not easy viewing, as white Republicans attack in the forms of both a deliberate racist dog-whistle to supporters and stoking America's highly toxic culture wars, the familiar theatrics of white men in the face of Black women challenging the status quo. When Anita Hill gave evidence in 1991, a senator from Utah waved around a copy of *The Exorcist*, suggesting Hill had stolen an accusation against Thomas from the 1971 novel. As Brown Jackson answers questions, Senator Ted Cruz of Texas reproduces pages of a children's book on race taught at a school Brown Jackson is on the board of. Both Hatch's and Cruz's clumsy spectacles were designed to belittle, humiliate and intimidate.

It is sadly predictable that this Black woman, born to public school teacher parents who grew up under Jim Crow segregation laws, who was the first Justice to have served as a public defender, is getting a mountain of shit from these moronic, frightened white men. But all that fades away in her closing remarks. Brown Jackson thanks her daughters – one of whom, when she was 11, wrote to President Obama asking him to nominate her mother to the court. She apologizes to them that she hasn't always got the balance of work and motherhood right. Behind, her parents beam with pride. Her husband is close by weeping, overcome by the moment.

Here it is. Here is the progress that sometimes it's so difficult to see, the result of the hard work of hope, years of being a Black woman striving for the top. Here is the mother apologizing to her daughters for the sacrifices she had to make to get here but hoping she has inspired them along the way. In the mess of it all, as this conservative Supreme Court looks to invite a litany of devastating changes to the law and, for the first time *restrict* not expand rights, we see the hope. The step forward. A line in the sand that can't be crossed. We are further forward that we had been before, just as Verna Williams had said.

Chelsie, Giovanna and Verna Williams all mention their daughters to me. As will many of the women I meet on the trip. They tell me their work is for their daughters, to give them more than they had or to create a better world for them, to show them there is another way. It is what many of them sacrifice for, get out of bed for, what pushes them on when the winds of resistance are blowing fiercely against them. To pass something on, to create something better, from mother to daughter. And it occurs to me that I am here in a mirror image. They are driven to make a better world for their daughters; I am driven to be better because of my mum.

The English term 'pilgrim' originally comes from the Latin *peregrino*, which means 'a foreigner, a stranger, someone on a journey, a temporary resident'. Over time, the word became linked with a religious goal. I am on a pilgrimage. I am a foreigner, a stranger on a journey, a temporary resident of the Midwest. And it feels like there is something sacred at the heart of it. Not religious but holy in its own way. The bond between a mother and her daughter can be, if you're lucky, as mysterious, powerful, sanctuary-giving and, occasionally, maddening, as any religion. For all these women working so hard, and to my own mother who worked so hard, I begin to see that I am that wild hope realized – a result of all the struggle, of all the hard work, of the extraordinary things done day in, day out, without fanfare or notice. And I am here to say: *thank you, thank you, thank you.*

Sacrifice

I once heard a podcast about a guy who visited all the twenty-two towns in the US named Lebanon. I remember thinking *What an interesting thing!* as we were driving down the M4. And then life does that weird thing where it throws you somewhere and you can't quite believe where you are. And here I was, in an Uber, on the Ronald Reagan highway, on my way to Lebanon, Ohio.

Since arriving in the US, I'd been reading about Lebanon, Ohio, because it had just become the first 'sanctuary city for the unborn' in the country outside of Texas. While much attention is paid to the southern states' crackdown on reproductive rights, for years now, as I was hearing first hand, the Midwest has also been building its legislative arsenal against a woman's bodily autonomy, even as a woman's constitutional right to an abortion remains in place.

A 'sanctuary city for the unborn' is a concept that was

initiated by a Texan pastor with the terminology borrowed from the Democrats' 'sanctuary city for undocumented immigrants' under Trump's regime. It effectively outlaws abortion and punishes anyone who has helped someone else access one. As a phrase, it's nauseating. As a concept, it is unconstitutional. And at the start of 2023, national and local pro-abortion organizations will win a legal challenge against the city for the violation, reversing the ban and the prosecution of those who aid another person obtaining an abortion. I suspect the city knew the challenge would come, even as similar ordinances began to spring up across the country. The ordinance – a local order without any real legal weight – was predominantly a piece of political theatre designed to whip up support and suggest political power. The interesting thing is that Lebanon, Ohio, didn't have an abortion clinic. It is a Republican stronghold. No one had suggested opening one, no one made an application. The nearest abortion clinic is sixty minutes away back in Cincinnati. But that wasn't the point. Not to the Trumpian fraction of the GOP ("Grand Old Party", a nickname for the Republican Party) who want to see the end of abortion, terrorizing whole communities with threat of criminalization. And not to the council members who want to use this issue as a ticket to launch their own political careers, like so many have over the last forty years, knowing full well that it brings record numbers out to vote in state-level elections.

I arrive in the small, affluent-looking town of Lebanon to see Krista Wyatt. We have arranged to meet in the local bookshop. It's actually closed that day but Krista is friends with the owner, a woman with a friendly smile wearing a 1970s style T-shirt emblazoned with 'reproductive rights', and she's opened it just for us.

Krista made headlines after she resigned from city council in May 2021, the spring before I meet her, over the abortion ordinance that created the sanctuary city status. Up until this point, Krista was the only Democrat on the council and, as much as Leslie Knope of *Parks and Recreation* loves Pawnee, Krista Wyatt loves Lebanon. It's her town. Even if her political views were in the minority. She knows a lot of people; a lot of people know her, and knew her parents before her. 'My mother's name went a long way in this town. I've had people tell me when she died, that if there was ever an angel, that was her.'

The arrival of Trump meant Krista experienced homophobia for the first time. 'I was 55 years old before being gay was an issue in this town,' she tells me. When she was running for council, a local radio station ran a segment asking if America could ever have a gay president and callers aired their bigotry. She recalls seeing a big sign in a park forty minutes up the road: 'LGBT: Liberty, Guns, Beer, Trump'. She worries for her wife and their children. 'What if our campervan broke down in front of a sign like that?'

A firefighter for most of her career, Krista ran for city council in 2018, two years after Donald Trump was elected to the White House. She enjoyed serving the town she loved, but things had begun to feel different. 'This is my town. I didn't want to leave. I wanted to be a public servant. That's all I want to do. That's what my parents taught me to do. But they took that away from me.' By 'they', she means the Trump-emboldened Republicans changing Lebanon. 'The far-right Evangelicals have been gaining ground, they've been really changing things in this town. Before the abortion ordinance, they introduced the right to carry concealed weapons into a city building that acts as a municipal court during city meetings. We've been invaded by people thumping their bibles. Stable minded, professional people have become radicalized,' she says. 'Since Trump, you can't have a conversation with them.'

As with Pawnee's fictional city council in Indiana, the next state along, Krista's work on Lebanon's council involved the routine and, as she would admit herself, the mundane: assigning budgets to fix potholes, occasionally buying a new ambulance. 'I'm embarrassed,' she tells me. 'I mean, why did you have to find me? You should have never even known my name. But my resignation got your attention. That shouldn't have to happen. We should not have to make decisions about women's bodies at the forefront of our local government. Our local council was supposed to work on infrastructure, or city budget, or parks or public safety. Future planning, developments. That's what the city council is supposed to do. Not this sort of stuff.'

The majority anti-abortion council rushed through the ordinance, voting for the local ban to go into effect immediately, demonstrating a Trumpian bullishness, a disregard for law and order. Enough was enough. Krista knew what was coming and resigned three hours before that meeting took place. 'I could not have my name attached to that,' Krista says simply. 'If I have a young lady who lives next door to me and says, "Can you drive me to the abortion clinic? I need help," and I do that, then I'm a criminal. If I loaned her money, I can be charged with a crime. If she calls her pastor, and says, "What do I do?" and the pastor mentions abortion, he or she could be charged with a crime. That's what really upset me more than anything.'

She called a press conference and resigned on 25 May 2021, three years into the position. The city council should never be, as she said in her speech in front of a wall of local reporters, 'a moral compass'.

Previously, Krista had spent some years as a paramedic. 'I bet you those men on city council have never held the hand of a dead 17-year-old whose life you watched slip away in front of you because she used a coat hanger.'

But her resignation wasn't just about her own principles or beliefs. 'I did it to wake the city up – to open their eyes to what was happening right under their noses.' It was a personal sacrifice made to raise the alarm. 'Many have stopped me – in the supermarket, in the hardware store – to thank me. A man came up to me and said, "You know, you're the most tolerant person I think I've ever met. For you to resign tells me I need to be paying more attention to what's going on."' It clearly wasn't an easy decision. Krista used the word 'heartbreaking' in her statement and in the short time I spent with her, I could see that it was.

Krista is full of life and energy; she talks at speed with a passion and enthusiasm for her community. And while she says she'll be 'working behind the scenes' to try to restore Lebanon to the place she once knew it to be, her concern for the future is evident. I sense her anguish at the people running her town, the fear for local women who will need abortions, the fear she has for herself and her family as a gay woman.

After abortion, Krista believes the same faction will be after LGBTQ rights. This is already happening in places like Florida with the so-called 'Don't Say Gay' bill which bans public school teachers from encouraging discussion about sexual orientation or gender identity in primary grade levels. In Dobbs v. Jackson Women's Health Organization – the Supreme Court case that led to the reversal of Roe v. Wade – Justice Clarence Thomas' written opinion suggested that the ruling, and the undermining of the right to privacy inherent to Roe, potentially opened a door that would allow the reversal of other rights, including same-sex marriage.

After our conversation, I take a walk around the town and notice the American flags hanging on the porches. In twee shops selling overpriced kitchenware, bible verses carved into wood hang in windows. I feel uncomfortable when blonde women with bright white teeth smile at me, as if something sinister lies just beneath their glossy surfaces.

Small, seemingly sleepy Lebanon, Ohio, is not the only town in the US lurching to the right and introducing 'sanctuary cities for the unborn'. These ordinances have been voted for in Texas, Louisiana, Florida and California, among other places. In time, when Roe is repealed and abortion rights are handed over to the individual state, the status will become unnecessary if the state outlaws abortion entirely. (After Roe fell, a law that banned abortion after six weeks was triggered in the state of Ohio, however, it is currently being challenged in the courts and is not yet in effect.) Whatever the future of abortion, the sanctuary city status is a deeply troubling tactic that seeks to isolate those who need abortion care and penalize a community that wants to help them. Yet, in this bleak picture there are still slivers of hope.

Back in the UK, I will talk on the phone with a young

local reporter called Erin Glynn. Erin tells me that Mason, a slightly bigger and more diverse town nearby, also voted for the anti-abortion ordinance that Krista resigned over. But then something interesting happened. Six months later, the city council repealed their decision. This was because residents voted off four council members, replacing them with two Democrats and two Republicans, all who believed, like Krista, they weren't the city's moral compass and they shouldn't defy state and federal law. Not only did this demonstrate the power and importance of hyperlocal politics but also that resistance can work. In Mason, the resistance had – at least while Roe still stood – won a battle. Perhaps hope was closer than I realized.

I have only ever seen the women in my life make sacrifices, never the men. My grandmother was left alone with three children, and then my mother sacrificed her career in TV and her sense of self to devote everything to my brother and me. I begin to understand that on the path of resilience there is an acceptance of sacrifice, that something must be given up in order to keep moving forward, that future gains will come from current losses – and it is normally women who pay that price. It is, I imagine, somewhere deep within our DNA. We all come from generations who knew they would have to sacrifice something: their health for childbirth, their ambition for marriage, their independence for motherhood, their happiness for convention and expectation, and, in some cases, their freedom for their lives. Krista showed that sacrifice can be a strong statement of intent. There is often a generosity and nobility associated with it. But at its heart is a loss, a quiet mourning of the fact that this world won't allow us to be all that we could be.

The women I'd met in Cincinnati all had something in

common: they didn't shoot out of state to a town where the laws and lawmakers were more to their liking. Instead, they stuck around for the hard graft, the long game; they rolled up their sleeves and got on with it. These women make me realize that one of the most dangerous habits of our era is thinking that posting on social media is a form of action when, in actuality, it gets millions off the hook of actually doing the hard work because it gives the appearance of caring without the labour of real change. When we look at what has changed over the last fifty years, we have to look at ourselves, too. Maybe we have greater awareness now but do we act less, do we do less of the hard work of hope?

The women in Cincinnati also made me realize that resistance against a backlash or finding a path through adversity isn't easy or quick. Change is a process. The erosion of rights doesn't happen overnight but neither does the defence of them. The road is long and often it will back up on itself. We will get lost, side-tracked, knocked over. We will face more backlashes. In 2022, I will watch the mockery, bullying and dehumanization of Amber Heard during her US defamation case brought by her ex Johnny Depp in horror. It is cited by numerous prominent feminists as a backlash to the #MeToo movement.

The women I met in Cincinnati knew what they were up against and still they pushed on. To do, as Laura Kaplan had said, is better than not to do. These women live in a state where they face nationalist and racist populism, divided communities, hostile treatment of immigrants and ambitious men happy to throw women's bodily autonomy under the bus if they think it might get them closer to Washington or closer to God. They do the work of defending women's rights though it is slow and arduous and hard. Though it requires sacrifices. But that's the gig. That's how we make a change. Perhaps those of us who found feminism in the fourth wave have been brainwashed into thinking our hypersanitized efforts behind a smartphone in a slogan sweatshirt, or our attendance of a march for a set of great pictures for Instagram, is enough. It is absolutely not. The evangelical, far-right anti-abortion movement is famously strategic, committed, multifaceted and dedicated to the long game, showing up time and time again, fighting on every front. And look who is winning.

I now understood that you don't start fixing a leak in the roof when the water has already poured through; you maintain your house, as you live in it, routinely, as each small crack appears. This is what I saw with Chelsie, Verna Williams, Giovanna and Krista. Their work was day by day: one interview at a time, one case at a time, one conversation at a time. Not just when an alarm is being sounded but on the quiet days too, when everyone is looking elsewhere.

CHAPTER FOUR

Detroit, Michigan: To know our history, part I

Bingo with June and Betty

I'm back on the Greyhound again, this time for a five-hour journey. I'm headed to a town an hour north of Detroit, Michigan, where Aunt June and her family moved to from Omaha, Nebraska, on account of her husband's job with General Motors, which is based in the city. June is my great-aunt, my mum's aunt, her dad's sister. I always think of Aunt June as an American; it's where she has spent most of her life. Now just shy of her nineties, she left Chelmsford, Essex, for the US in 1956, at just 23. But her pride in her homeland never left her: she refused to take up American citizenship because she didn't want to lose her British identity. When I arrive, there's a small Union Jack outside her flat for sheltered accommodation in my honour. One of her cats is called Barney Rubble, a nod to cockney rhyming slang.

Aunt June married Bob, who was then serving in the US Air Force, and took her back to the States. They'd met at a dance on an army base in Essex. She remembers now, 'I was terrified when I arrived; it was like a different planet. And

Bob didn't even meet me at the airport; his mother did!' Bob was a devout Catholic and June and Bob went on to have ten children. 'I used to hate going to church, getting all those kids ready first thing on a Sunday by myself!' she laughs. Today, June has seventeen grandkids and fourteen great grandkids, and is beloved by them all.

Growing up, I heard a lot about June and her family, and occasionally saw June when she visited the UK or at family weddings in Europe – though these memories are distant and hazy. I always knew, however, how fond my mum is of her and I heard endless stories of this sprawling extended family of mine somewhere in the Midwest. And here was my chance to meet them, alongside, of course, spending time with June and, crucially, asking June what she remembers of my mum during that visit nearly fifty years ago. What did June make of her wide-eyed niece when she arrived as a 22-year-old ready to see more of the world?

On my trip, I have been asking women I've never met about their memories and their experiences, trying to build a picture of lives I don't know. But it feels just as important to be having these conversations with women in my own life – especially the ones who could help me see further into that little square polaroid.

June remembers my mum's legs. 'She had such short shorts on!' she laughs. 'Your mother was beautiful, all the boys were looking at her.' She shows me photo albums with pictures from the trip, pictures neither I nor my mum have ever seen. June's right: her shorts are short, her tops are cropped, her legs are long and slim and there's always a cigarette between her thin fingers. She looks cool and confident with who she is – a steady, unflinching gaze meets the camera, or sometimes a broad, relaxed smile. And that's how June remembers her from that time: a confident young woman who she enjoyed having there. They laughed together, they drank together, they talked for hours on end. There was an ease to her stay, as June's family showed her local attractions and taught her how to play pool. I get the impression that June saw in my mum what I had always seen in that picture: a young, hopeful person, ready to make their mark on the world.

I stay with June for four days and we laugh a lot. While she moves slowly on her walker and is reluctant to take her medication, she is as hilarious and wry and sarcastic as my mum always described. When June's daughter-in-law took her on an initial visit to the sheltered accommodation in which she now lives, a member of staff asked June what she liked doing. In her slow, soft voice, with a poker face, June replied: 'Robbin' banks.'

Here all the staff know and love her. The younger ones especially. The kids who help out in the on-site restaurant are her biggest fans. There's a picture of a crowd of them, with June in the middle, all holding up their middle fingers, or 'flipping the bird', as Americans say. One of them has recently taught her the phrase 'lit as fuck' and she says it all the time, including to a young man who helps us with breakfast. He blushes and looks at me apologetically, while June's heavy, full laugh rolls out across the room.

As we wander around the building, she points out other old ladies as if she isn't really supposed to be among them, like any minute now, she'll bust out of this place, and her ageing body, and return to a time before. Sometimes, she says, she attends the residents' Q&A meetings just to laugh at the banality of the questions, mostly around lunch options, and occasionally heckle. When we walk past a room where an elderly man is getting a sports massage, June starts making innuendos, as much for herself as for anyone else's entertainment, laughing away. When we get to happy hour, where residents are allowed no more than two drinks, she asks one of the staff to slip another shot into hers. One of my favourite moments is when she takes me to bingo with her 96-year-old pal Betty, who keeps her plastic chips in a pill cup. The vibe is serious and June lambasts her opponents with allegations of cheating, offering me a sly smile, always inviting me in on the joke.

While I had come to June with questions about my mum, what I wasn't prepared for is how much she's like my mum. There's the same silliness, the playfulness, the constant giggling. Everyone can be laughed at, no one is off limits, including themselves. There's the same cynicism, the same recognition of the absurdity and stupidity of many things, particularly men. There's even the same sneakiness. I remember my mum loading me and my brother with cutlery off a plane once, to take to our holiday villa. While I stay with June, she slips one of the glass tealights off the table into her walker and tells me to take it home as a souvenir. There's a devil-may-care wildness to them both, matched with a knowingness and wisdom. And there's always a punchline, too.

Seeing my mum in my great-aunt is surprisingly reassuring – I could place her somewhere, understand where she came from in a way I hadn't before. When I was young, my mum so often felt like an anomaly to me. She was the only single mum I knew, working in a way I saw friends' dads work, with a single-mindedness to pursue a life she wanted and a political worldview that felt different to the Surrey housewife mothers of my school friends. She felt very different from her own mother in lots of ways – her ambition, her priorities, her independence.

But in June, I saw a familiarity that located my mum somewhere, set her within a context. She doesn't look like June but they have the same dark skin that belies their Essex roots. There are the same dark eyes, dark hair. And there's the same glint of something in their eye, a private joke, a suppressed giggle.

Not only does spending time with June help me understand my mum; I see something of myself in these two women. I start to reflect that I take great pride in making Ed laugh. He's always said that my sense of humour is silly, slapstick, *Carry On* – just like my mum's, something I'd never really given much thought to before. Often, when I put down the phone to my mum, he'll ask what we've been laughing at. Or when she stays for dinner, the three of us will find ourselves laughing as she's inevitably scathingly rude and creatively insulting about a Tory MP, sly, outrageous and sarcastic – just like June. And now I know there's something there, something intangible, something that links me, my mum and June.

During this trip, I've thought so much about the hardships and obstacles that connect and unite women, especially in terms of how difficult things were for my mum as a single parent. But in this moment, I can see the joy – the magic of laughter, little moments of liberation from all else that befell us. I remember the fun we had, the happiness that was so evidently there too. I have found a piece of my mum, here in June, here in Michigan, here in America.

While I'm there, the family do the bidding of the matriarch and all June's children who live nearby make an effort to see me, introducing me to their kids and grandkids. Her 20-something granddaughter Brooke – tall, slim and blonde, a former cheerleader – is particularly kind, taking me out in Detroit with her friend, playing Taylor Swift in the car, batting off the constant attention of men as we bar hop in the gentrified corners of the city. We laugh together when, in a hip bar, a woman from Texas, visiting her son, hears my accent and asks me if I've met Prince Harry. I see June's generosity and kindness in Brooke as she shows me around. I'd heard a lot about Midwestern hospitality before I arrived and it is abundantly clear in all of June's family, as they treat me like I am one of them. Or maybe it's just what June has taught them.

But family isn't always so straightforward. Some of June's kids want to know if I know Mark. Who is Mark? I ask. Mark, I learn, is my mother's half-brother, my half-uncle. When my grandfather left my grandmother for another woman, they had a family, something I'd only ever vaguely heard about, and so infrequently I'd almost forgotten. They are all fans of Mark, they tell me. June, especially, encourages me to meet with him back in the UK where he lives. What stories do they know? I wonder. Or what don't they know? What does Mark know? But I think of my mum and I know it's not my place to find out, and so a Facebook friend request from him remains unanswered. On this journey of collecting stories, it becomes obvious that even though they are the closest to hand, family stories can be the ones buried the deepest, hardest to reach. And as they overlap across generations, who they belong to becomes less and less clear.

While I'm there, June points out a picture of my grandfather – her brother, my mother's father, Mark's father – on her wall. It is the first time I've seen his face. My mum stopped speaking to him decades before he died. Once, my cousin showed me photos of my grandparents dancing; it looked like some time in the 1950s or 60s. My grandfather was twirling my grandmother around on the dance floor, her glamorous smile and painted lips full of excitement. But in the series of pictures, his face had been cut out. Now I see him, finally, it's not how I have imagined him; he has a thin face, pinched, stern. It is more like discovering a document in an archive, a date on a letter – just the evidence of a fact, no emotional tug. The stories of violence, bullying and adultery will always keep this man a stranger to me.

Yet, our fathers play a role in our lives, even if we don't like it or understand it or want it. As I and my mother before me know only too well. This isn't a story about men, about fathers, but I have to give them a cameo because, whether I like it or not, the actions of men have long shaped the lives of women. Although my father and grandfather are very different, they share some similarities, not least their first name, and, through choices they made long ago, they left my mum and me in the same spot; estranged and isolated from them. Many times on this trip already, I have felt the dizzying merry-go-round of history, making me nauseous with its repetition. And now, here it is, in my own story. But whatever we think of our fathers, they have made us who we are, inadvertently, accidentally. And it strikes me as an uncomfortable inevitability that on this trip to learn more about my mother, I have, for the very first time, seen my grandfather's face.

There's a strange contradiction to my time with June. In all the laughter and the talk of my mother, there's another narrative. One that runs concurrently, the ominous current in a stream that you can't see on the surface. June keeps Fox News on every night. She falls asleep in front of the TV and it's still on in the morning. And every morning I'm there, I wake to the sound of a story of violence. A man has shot his girlfriend dead. A toddler has accidentally shot themselves after getting hold of a gun. We don't comment on this news; it just hangs, like heavy air before a storm.

When June is showing me the photo albums we go past the pictures of my mum and she shows me pictures of her children and their children and their partners. As she talks, the story of violence against women hangs between us again. Someone's partner is in prison for domestic violence. Someone's ex-girlfriend came home to find her mother and little brother had been shot dead by her stepdad before he set their home alight. I hadn't come to June looking for stories of violence against women but here they were, weaved into the same photo album that held the pictures of my mother. And that's the thing about stories: the ones you hear might not be the ones you were expecting. But when you take a step back, when you start to join the dots, you see that some stories are always there, playing out somewhere, if only you listen closely enough, if only you look beneath the surface.

My time with June is brief; I'm packing up for my next stop. As I say goodbye to the cats, I realize that from June, I've perhaps learned less about 22-year-old Jacqui in the photo and more about the Jacqui I've known – the mother who, regardless of the challenges she faced, was always laughing. June's life as a young mother with ten kids and persistent homesickness wasn't always easy. My mum's life as a single mother with a demanding job wasn't easy. Was it on her trip to visit June that my mum learned that laughter is a survival tactic, a type of resilience in itself? And was my mum doing what we've done for so many generations, what I am doing right now – looking to the women behind us to understand how we move forward?

CHAPTER FIVE

Chicago, Illinois: To know our history, part II

We don't live single issue lives

In the vast desert of Midwestern trigger laws (bills waiting in the wings should Roe be overturned), abortion restrictions and senators who would rather pray for dead children than pass gun laws that could save their lives, Chicago is a liberal oasis. It has a rich feminist history of suffrage, grassroots women-led movements (like Jane) and supporting access to abortion, which continues today. It is also a city that feels like an injection of adrenaline from the moment I arrive.

Chicago is the third largest city in the country, a city of the Industrial Revolution, built around rail and river. The cityscape of Art Deco buildings and modern skyscrapers sets my pulse racing. There's a distant echo of New York, all the energy and life, but it is still distinctly itself, with its own spark. I immediately love it. There are many famous people from this city: Al Capone, Barack Obama, Oprah Winfrey, Bill Murray. But I take a small, private delight in knowing it is also home to Alicia Florrick of *The Good Wife*, a TV show full of strong, impressive, flawed and fierce women, including Alicia – a working mother with two kids and a taste for red wine. After checking into my hotel, sitting at the sports bar next door with a hamburger and a glass of wine, I feel a static from this city jolting me awake, despite the late hour. When my mum passed through Chicago on her trip, the bus tipped them out at the terminal to go to a nearby diner for some food. When she got to the front of the line, the server was English. She was relieved to hear a little bit of home late at night in this strange city. I, however, felt electrified by being here on my own. An English accent, I'm sure, would break the spell the city instantly cast upon me.

The spell only intensifies when I start to talk to some of the residents, not least Megan Jeyifo, the executive director of Chicago Abortion Fund (CAF). I meet Megan at Carver 47, a café celebrating Dr George Washington Carver, one of the most prominent Black scientists of the twentieth century, an environmentalist who was born into slavery. The café is in Bronzeville on the southside of the city, a neighbourhood known as the 'Black metropolis'.

Often overshadowed in the media by nationwide abortion providers such as Planned Parenthood, local abortion funds are the frontline of abortion access in the US. These small non-profit organizations do the very hard and real work of getting a person an abortion who wants or needs one but who does not have the means to do so by themselves. Megan and her team (and almost every other team across these non-profits) raise the money for the terminations. They figure out the logistics, which are often extremely complicated. The clinic an individual can go to will depend on several things, such how many weeks pregnant she is and what state stipulations she must meet in order to access the abortion – the number of visits to a doctor, need for a screening or the requirement for mandatory counselling. On top of all this are practical details, such as train and bus schedules, a place for a woman to stay overnight if she needs it. Megan tells me of a recent *Mission Impossible*-level story of sneaking a woman into a hospital after hours in another state just to get a sonogram so she could figure out how far gone she was. 'Luckily, I knew the right people,' she says. CAF has been dealing with the same issues that the post-Roe world will bring for thirty years – moving women across state lines to access abortions they can't afford. The challenge, if the Supreme Court overturns the right to legal abortion, she says, will be the numbers.

Abortion funds are often the first point of contact for many women in need and that's why Megan believes, in an echo of Jane, that they offer more than just practical advice. 'People will call, distraught, crying, saying, "How did I let this happen? What have I done?" but we explain it's not their fault; they are not the problem.' The problem, she says, is an unjust and hostile society. Her job is to let them know there's someone on their side: 'I'll say, if you want to talk about your feelings, I will listen to you. But you don't need to justify it, you don't need to tell me. "I already have four kids, I'm working part-time, I'm getting sick because I'm pregnant and they're going to fire me if I miss another day . . ." You don't have to tell me that. Your decision is your decision. I'm here to support you, no matter what.'

Megan's work is driven by her belief in reproductive justice. Not healthcare or rights, but *justice*. To understand what this means and why it's so significant, we have to go back to 1994. In June of that year, activists attended a conference in a Chicago hotel to hear President Clinton's plans for women's healthcare reforms. However, soon many of the Black women present realized these plans did not take into consideration income, housing or the criminal justice system – all areas that negatively and disproportionately affected Black women. And so they formed a breakaway group. Twelve Black women – including academic Loretta Ross, seen by some as one of the most vital and influential voices on the issue in the country – took themselves to their own room. Together, they discussed the need for a framework that recognized how issues of women's healthcare, including abortion, intersects with racism, economics and social justice. Together, they developed the term 'reproductive justice'. The group would eventually call themselves Women of African Descent for Reproductive Justice.

Ever since that meeting, 'reproductive justice' has equated to the right to freely choose to have or not have a family, despite the issues facing the most marginalized and disadvantaged. Such as the reality of having a child in a country where 20 per cent of Black women do not have health insurance and four times as many Black women die in childbirth, regardless of income or education. Or the fact that in the US, Black women are four times more likely to have an abortion than white women and more likely to live in areas where it's harder to access contraception.[21] Abortion access impacts Black and Brown women disproportionately, yet it has historically been a movement predominantly led by white women.

'When I first learned about reproductive justice,' Megan tells me, 'and about how much the framework also includes supporting people who decide to parent and supporting parents who need access to things so that their kids can live full and healthy and thriving lives, I was like, *Oh my God*, this is so great. And then to learn that it was Black feminists, here in Chicago, twenty-five years ago, who coined the term, and what that has meant for the wider movement, it was just mind-blowing.' Her understanding of reproductive justice motivated her to start volunteering at CAF, leading eventually to her running the organization.

When Megan wanted to start a family, she needed IVF. 'But we can't create the families that we want if we don't have the money.' At the time, Megan had health insurance through her job, working at the University of Chicago. This helped significantly when she needed a Caesarean and had extra bills to pay. 'I realized this was all about my autonomy potentially being limited because of money.' She says she was lucky and didn't go into debt, but it drummed home what was at stake for so many. 'It's like Audre Lorde says, "We don't live single issue lives."'

The cost of having the abortions she has needed in the past and the family she wanted for her future is behind much of her work and a big reason why she is so passionate about reproductive justice: 'It's super personal to me. And does keep me up at night. Because I know what denying someone an abortion means. I know what that looks like. You're four times as likely to fall into poverty if you're denied an abortion, and people are already struggling. I've talked to hundreds of people during my time on our helpline who have needed care and I bring that with me to everything I do, everything.'

Megan was also part of an organization called We Testify,

a network of diverse people who tell their abortion stories with the aim of shifting the way the media understands and reports on, according to the organization's website, the 'context and complexity of accessing abortion care'. There is a particular focus on women of colour, queer identities and those in conservative and rural communities. But even for Megan, taking that step to share her own abortion experiences has been a challenge. 'I could talk about my abortion but for the longest time, I just couldn't talk about the fact I'd had two. If I told my full story, I'd pretend it was someone else and use a pseudonym.'

It's unsurprising that women experience shame and stigma around abortion in a culture that shames and stigmatizes them about so many things. The anti-abortion movement is loud and aggressive, but even those who claim to support abortion can add to the problem through the language they choose – or choose not to use. Biden's administration is repeatedly criticized for putting out statements on the need to defend the ruling of Roe v. Wade but failing to mention the word abortion. 'A woman's right to choose' is rarely qualified with what she is actually choosing. Hillary Clinton's directive that abortion should be 'safe, legal and rare' in her 2008 campaign – an echo of her husband from the early 1990s – went some way to suggesting that it shouldn't really happen, despite the fact that the Guttmacher Institute, a research and policy institute focused on sexual and reproductive health and rights, has suggested that one in four American women will have an abortion before they are 45. All this opaqueness helps perpetuate the shame, to the point that even the most vocal abortion advocates can also feel the stigma. Like Megan did. And like her mother before her did.

'I knew my mom was a clinic escort,' Megan tells me, helping patients safely access an abortion clinic in the face of anti-abortion protestors who, at best pray and sing outside, or at worst intimidate, yell, attempt to change a woman's mind, block her way, display images of dead foetuses and harass anyone entering the building. 'But I didn't know she had an abortion until after she died. My dad told me after she passed.' Megan's mum was a fierce advocate for abortion access. 'She sent me to a Catholic school with a seventh-grade paper on the pro-choice movement.' Word got round and, the next day, one of her classmate's dads found her and showed her a picture of a foetus. But even she didn't tell me her story. Megan reminds me how hard storytelling can become when we are telling those closest to us.

Now she is trying to break the cycle of shame. The true line of progress, surely, is in jumping off the merry-go-round of history. 'If you've had an abortion tell your children, tell your grandchildren, talk about it, make it not be this hush-hush thing,' she says. On an episode of *Pod Save America*, Megan recently revealed she heard one of her twins say to the other, 'Mom had an abortion before she had us.'

The ultimate goal of Megan, CAF and the reproductive justice movement more widely is to support the people who are most impacted by bans and restrictions to become leaders themselves. The movement has to look like the people it serves, Megan insists. 'We need to build people's organizing capacity, their leadership capacity, their abilities to advocate for themselves versus a giant reproductive health behemoth. Because that's not what the abortion movement looks like currently. It should centre people who have had abortions, women, trans and gender nonconforming people, Black and Brown people, people of colour, young people, people in rural communities, young parents. That is what we think the future of this movement looks like. And we need to provide the resources to make sure those are the voices that are centred and those people have the chance to lead their movement.'

As we talk, I think of my conversation with Laura Kaplan and her awareness that in the 1970s, Jane was mostly middle-class white students on the other side of the city counselling Black mothers from the southside. And although Jane did educate and inform the women they helped, speaking to Megan and understanding the reproductive justice movement, it feels like the long overdue next step is the empowerment of all women, especially the most marginalized, to advocate for themselves, to execute their agency, to secure their own liberation. Indeed, Megan's own story from a volunteer who has had an abortion to executive director is a direct example of that road to empowerment.

The next day, I'm in the waiting room of Chicago's Women's Health Center (CWHC). In this small space, people are waiting quietly. An elderly woman with glasses and a stick sits next to her husband. A young woman in ripped jeans turns a page of her book. And all around them is a riot of colour. Framed protest posters cover the walls: 'Equal Pay for Comparable work'. 'Stop Sterilization Abuse'. 'Working Women Unite'. 'No Buy Offs, Sellouts or Trade Offs'. 'All of Us Or None of Us'. A giant Black Lives Matter banner hangs above the reception desk. This mini archive of women's activist art is more than just a wall display; it speaks to the centre's radical roots. The CWHC is a direct descendant of Jane. When seven members of Jane were arrested in 1974, bail money was raised but then the case was dropped. Some money went into the Emma Goldman Clinic[22] and the rest went to the CWHC. That was nearly fifty years ago.

So much of women's liberation was focused on the female body – sexual liberation, liberation from fertility, physical liberation in a new form of dressing. It was – and is – a central battleground. Therefore, understanding how it works and how to care for it became a deeply political act. As Laura Kaplan had pointed out to me, ever since healthcare was institutionalized by men and taken out of the hands of local women, be it family or members of the community, women hadn't been able to access basic health information – the medical establishment simply didn't see it as their concern. The CWHC was an antidote to that.

The CWHC was set up in 1975 by women who wanted women to have greater agency and knowledge of their own bodies, who saw the confirmation of women's right to an abortion as the beginning of something, the ticket to even greater liberation and autonomy. They centred women's instincts, voices and experiences, empowering them to make their own choices by giving them knowledge. And they continued to push at boundaries. In the early 1980s, they were one of the first clinics to provide fertility treatment to single women and lesbian and queer families. Lisa Schergen, the executive director, and Terry Kapsalis, a member of CWHC's Clinical Services Committee, tell me that is still the case today – in fact, other than an increased level of care for trans and non-binary patients, the clinic very much operates how it always has. Women in consciousness-raising circles in the 1960s were using a speculum, mirror and a flashlight to see their cervixes for the first time, to understand their anatomy and feel in control of their bodies. In 2021, patients at CWHC are still offered the same tools to do the very same thing for the very same reasons – just to take a look at what is there. For many people, it will still be the first time they've been offered the chance to see this part of their body. CWHC believes women familiarizing themselves with their own bodies is a type of empowerment. The act has become symbolic of the centre's guiding principle – that patients have the right to self-determine their healthcare and have free access to it. Terry has even described it as 'magical'. So central is this notion to CWHC's philosophy that their podcast is called *Mirror and a Flashlight*.

Unlike most contemporary healthcare, all patients are allotted thirty to sixty minutes slots to discuss all their issues, in detail and holistically. If a sexual abuse survivor needs an examination, the clinic staff will work with the on-site counselling team. Patients pay what they can to ensure everyone can access treatment. There is a deliberate effort to break down traditional dynamics of provider and client, which were historically based on male anatomical knowledge and women deliberately being kept in the dark. 'We see the patients as much as experts as we are and we ask for their expertise on their own bodies,' says Terry. The idea is that, while strictly adhering to medical expertise, an individual's understanding of their own body and how it works is seen as valuable information, and a patient should at all times feel informed and in control. Again, I hear echoes of Laura Kaplan and it feels like a little slice of the women's lib movement is still alive and operating in this corner of the city, somehow resistant to the intervening five decades. In a country without universal healthcare and with the greatest wealth disparity in the world, perhaps the revolution worked here. They created the feminist world they wanted after all.

Though, while that feminist agenda is still at the core of the CWHC mission, today there are broader objectives: 'As times have changed, our understanding of what feminism means has changed,' Terry tells me. 'In this organization right now, we do describe ourselves as a feminist health clinic. And I think the word "feminist" describes our approaches to care and health education. But we also talk all the time about capitalism, racism and intersectionality.'

I'm incredibly moved by the endeavour. So are many of their clients. Lisa wells up when she tells me of the feedback they get. 'People say, "You have saved my life" or "I didn't know care like this was possible" or "I've never had anyone respect me this way before".' They have clients who are three generations of the same family. 'I'm getting emotional,' Lisa laughs. Terry passes her a box of tissues.

Terry and Lisa share many of the fears for the nation I've heard from others on my trip: fear of growing hate, discrimination, division. All of these things have a knock-on impact on mental health, which they see in their patients, with increasing symptoms of anxiety and depression. And this makes their work even more vital. As access to legal abortion comes under greater and greater threat, should it be such a surprise that some of the feminist practices and philosophies that have their beginnings in the 1960s once again feel urgent and relevant?

Both Megan and CAF, and Terry and Lisa at CWHC are carrying on the work of those before them. Their communities' histories built the foundations on which they are standing on today. They recognize that, they learn from it and they continue to practise those early lessons. In the frightening times ahead, as women's healthcare becomes even more trapped in a web of misogynistic politics, the lesson here is clear: we must look back to the women before us. If they have a road map for us, we must use it. Or, at the very least, study it, adapt it. In Laura Kaplan's book on the story of Jane, she quotes from a 1973 book called *Witches, Midwives and Nurses: A History of Women Healers*. In it, authors Barbara Ehrenreich and Deirdre English write, 'To know our history is to begin to know how to take up the struggle again.'

We must look back to the twelve Black women in a hotel room in Chicago who helped lay bare the social and political dynamics of abortion in a much more meaningful, just and liberating way for the most marginalized. We must remember our mothers, and their decisions, their shames, and take that knowledge with us. We must learn from the organizing of the past – like the feminist healthcare movement – and understand what they got right, but also what they got wrong. We must remember that we've nearly always been here before and if we want to move forward, we must understand all that was achieved before us.

The exercise in looking back to learn what we can from those who have been fighting and resisting far longer than we have feels more important than ever as women's rights are being stripped back. To take that wisdom, to utilize it and build on it. Looking back is essential work in the pursuit of moving forward. Rebecca Solnit writes: 'Together we are very powerful, and we have a seldom-told, seldom-remembered history of victories and transformations that can give us confidence that, yes, we can change the world because we have many times before . . . you row forward looking back.'[23]

Dinner for one

I have a couple days left in Chicago before I catch the next bus and I let the city carry me along. I have dinner for one in the Italian candle-lit restaurant where Frank Sinatra held his fourth wedding reception. Afterwards, I take the subway to a suburb north of the city and head to a blues bar. I'm there early, hours early in fact, in a spectacularly uncool way. Two women sit at the empty bar and talk about a bank robbery that day in the city, resulting in a car chase the wrong way down the highway which climaxed with the shooting of a cop in the head. I'm hovering nearby. 'Does that kind of thing happen a lot in Chicago?' I ask. A young mixed race woman called Angel, with tight ringlets and a beautiful face, turns on her bar-stool to look at me. 'Don't go getting any ideas, OK? There's more to us than just that shit. Don't think you know about us.'

Slowly musicians arrive and the music begins, and I feel every beat as if it's all taking place inside my own chest. On their breaks, the members of the band unexpectedly come to sit with me, intrigued, maybe, by the blonde on her own at the front, from England. I meet the singer, the drummer and the bassist. They tell me about the tour they've just been on, where they'll play later, that time they came to London. Soon, a white-haired man with a beard down to his stomach sits next to me. He's wearing white snakeskin cowboy boots and a Canadian tuxedo. He says hello and offers me a kind smile, as if perhaps we might have met before. My interaction with these strangers feels relaxed. They are all men but there is no threat or fear. It's easy and friendly. That feels rare and for that reason incredibly welcome. I could have stayed for longer but at 1 a.m. I say my goodbyes.

I spend the remaining few days walking, neck propelled back by the Art Deco buildings that hold their own next to the flashy corporate towers. I take an architectural boat tour, and the city seems to be humming with its history, stories and ambition. I crane my head at the Tiffany glass dome ceiling in the Chicago Cultural Center and I go in search of Hemingway's typewriter in the American Writers Museum. Later, back in the sports bar, watching Monday night football, I scribble down everything I've seen and done and thought. And it's all such a thrill, like walking on a tightrope and knowing I'll make it across. I think of a Sylvia Plath quote about all the things she longs to do but can't because she is a woman. 'I am a girl, a female, always in danger of assault and battery.'[24] And yes, some days the existence of male violence is all consuming, and yes, violence has been a constant hum, a reality I can't escape when talking to and thinking about women on this trip. But then there are days, or perhaps more accurately moments, when it all slips off my shoulders, a coat left behind on the floor. And maybe it's a product of the naivety of being somewhere I don't know, or the excitement of being in this city, or taking this journey on my own, a journey towards a version of me I'm coaxing out, but today it is one of those days. 'God, I want to talk to everybody as deeply as I can,' Plath continued in the same diary entry. 'I want to sleep in an open field. I want to travel west, to walk freely at night.' Sitting on a bar-stool, halfway through my journey, these words come back to me, illuminated by the truth I see in them. I still can't walk freely at night, not truly in a world where male violence still prowls the streets, but I am travelling west. And I have a level of freedom that Plath could only wistfully, romantically, dream of.

I find the dive bar I'm desperate to visit, the one that I'd seen on *Anthony Bourdain's Parts Unknown*, his magical travel and food show. Erotic art plasters the walls under dim light and above a long bar where patrons play chess. There's a picture of a naked Sarah Palin and the rug made of a polar bear. There's a picture of Trump's head between a woman's legs. Bourdain had said it gets going in the early hours but I went in the early evening – a compromise Plath would have understood. Sitting in a corner, with a gin and tonic, in the softness of the lamp light, I took a moment to appreciate that I was there. I took a moment to appreciate that I was there with a drink that hit the back of my throat like fire. I took a moment to appreciate that, best of all, I was there alone, I was having this adventure.

CHAPTER SIX

Indianapolis, Indiana: Holding on to faith

The heartland

It's just past 6 a.m. I'm jumping in an Uber to head back to the Greyhound terminal. 'Going to the airport?' the driver asks as he puts my luggage in the car.

'No, the bus terminal,' I say slowly, confused by his confusion. 'Like I requested in the app.' He looks surprised.

When we arrive at the terminal, a few men are asleep on the pavement by the door. 'Is it open?' the driver asks, catching my eye in the rearview mirror. He sounds worried. I can see the lights on inside. I get out and walk to the door, pulling on the handle. 'It's open,' I say.

The driver is standing by the boot of the car with my case, scanning the terminal building. 'I'll wait with you,' he says. This is a first. In London, Uber drivers would throw you out of their car into a burning inferno if that's what the app told them to do. I thank him for his concern but insist I'll be fine.

I drag my case past the homeless men sleeping in the doorway and push against the heavy glass door. Inside, the now familiar strip lighting and low music are there yet again. Each bus terminal seems separate to the laws of time and space, just a continuum of eternal waiting, a purgatory with vending machines. On benches, more men sleep. I take a seat and wait.

Soon a young woman arrives wearing beige sweats and a hoodie. She parks her luggage on the bench next to mine and then makes her way over to the small kiosk on the other side of the terminal. She orders some breakfast and heats it up in the microwave provided at the end of the counter. When she comes to sit back down, she places some of the food on her seat and then takes something wrapped in paper, hot out the microwave, and a bottle of orange juice, over to a man sleeping on the chairs nearby us. She gently wakes him up by tapping his shoulder. He startles, looking confused. She smiles and hands him the food. He sits up slowly, taking in the items, and quietly says thank you. In this tired place, a small moment of kindness shines brightly.

She and I are on our way to Indianapolis, Indiana. A Republican state famous for corn, it is also home to Pete Buttigieg – the first openly gay man to run for presidential nomination in a major party. And former governor and vice president Mike Pence, who is calling for a national ban on abortion. It is here too where Conservative Supreme Court Justice Amy Coney Barrett, and self-declared constitutional originalist – someone who believes the US constitution should be interpreted in the context of the time it was written, a time when women didn't have the vote or many rights – was previously a federal prosecutor and academic.

The journey to Indianapolis is a particularly glorious ride. We snake through the city while it's still dark but as we head towards the interstate, the sun starts to rise. A warm, white light begins to illuminate the view outside my window, picking up the golden yellows of the fields. Electric lights in homes, shops and gas stations can't compete with the burgeoning day and start to fade. Now the sky is a palette of smudged blues and oranges and pinks. I'm tired from the early start and my eyes are heavy but I resist. This is the Greyhound magic I'd been looking for.

It probably comes as no great surprise that I've ended up with a man who has visited twenty-two American states. When we met, we realized we shared an American dream. Ed loves the majestic national parks, the barbecue, the music, the wilderness. It was Ed who suggested I stay in a B&B. He'd stayed in a few in the southern states and had stories of larger-than-life hosts cooking all sorts of local wonders for breakfast. You'll meet some interesting people, he said.

Ted's B&B, just north of downtown Indianapolis, came highly recommended online, but it was pictures of the fun, lavish decor that convinced me to book. The room I went for is covered in French Art Nouveau-style lamps and prints, with a stained-glass window above the bed and large mirror with an etching in the glass of a flapper girl, which sits over the fireplace. There is a hot tub in the room. The walls are pink and lined with fake flowers in ornate vases. On the website, Ted describes how guests can borrow any of his 3,000 DVDs and treat themselves to the freshly baked cookies on hand. I was sold.

When I arrive, Ted, now in his eighties, trim and athletic

looking, is wearing a navy T-shirt tucked into navy shorts with white ankle socks and white trainers. Bright-eyed and friendly, he helps me with my case and shows me around, pointing out the highlights of the DVD collection, including every single musical ever made. He offers a warm welcome, like I'm a guest in his home.

My room lives up to my expectations. I dump my stuff and while I'm trying to figure out how to turn on the hot tub, I notice a laminated five-page magazine profile about Ted left on the bed. His smiling face is on the cover of the local publication and the article, with the headline 'Renaissance Man', covers his time as a musical theatre star, when he ran for local office and the jewellery business he currently owns with his son. He's described as a 'world traveller with national political interests and a love of his local roots'. I'm instantly intrigued and a little bit excited by this local celebrity. But I am even more fascinated when I explore the rest of the B&B, especially after I wander into the living room.

The stars and stripes hang in the corner next to soft-looking sofas. Books and design magazines are piled high on the coffee table. Almost immediately, a bronze bust catches my eye. It's Ronald Reagan. Next to it is a copy of *Newsweek* magazine with Reagan on the cover from 1980 and a hardback book, *Images of Greatness*, a collection of portraits of Reagan during his time in the White House. In front of the bust there is a picture of Ted with Mike Pence, signed and addressed 'To my best friend Ted!'. And then another, this time with their wives.

And that's when I realize: I am behind enemy lines.

In the ebb and flow of women's rights in America, Ronald Reagan and Mike Pence are two considerable dams, standing in the way of progress. Reagan, following the path initially laid by President Nixon in an effort to attract Catholic voters, was the first president to centre abortion as a key party issue, as I had discussed with Susan Cullman in New York, bringing the growing anti-abortion politics of the Republican fringes into the White House.

Mike Pence once admitted he wouldn't have dinner alone with a woman who wasn't his wife and that he liked to call his wife 'Mother'.[25] A former Catholic from a family of Democrats, during his college years he turned to Evangelicalism – and the Republican Party. The shift in faith would determine his politics. As governor, Pence repeatedly led the call to defund Planned Parenthood and signed every abortion restriction bill put forward by the legislature, including one that banned seeking an abortion due to foetal genetic abnormalities. In 2016, Pence signed a bill that required the remains of miscarried or aborted foetuses to have a funeral: they were to be buried or cremated. With a prayer.

I looked around the place some more – there's a picture of Ted with screen legend Ginger Rogers, Republican Ben Carson and billionaire Elon Musk.

Ed was right, you sure do meet some people in a B&B.

Finding faith

So much of the crusade against women's bodily autonomy in the US is done in the name of faith, either by true believers who claim life starts at conception, or individuals and groups, who, over the last forty years, have found whipping up religious fervour a convenient cover for more cynical political ambitions

– namely, controlling women and keeping the same white men in charge.

Kandiss Taylor, who ran for governor in Georgia in 2022 had a slogan on the side of her campaign bus which put those ambitions in plain sight: 'Guns, Babies, Jesus'. This slogan neatly surmises the holy trinity of American religious conservatism. One which is, crucially, united under a banner of white supremacy. The role of racism in the anti-abortion movement, thinly veiled by religion, is nothing new. In fact, many would say that the modern anti-abortion movement has its roots in the racist backlash to civil rights.

Attacking abortion was, many have argued, a highly charged response to the end of racial segregation in schools, which was first decided by the Supreme Court case of Brown v. Board of Education in 1954. As a result, independent, so-called 'segregation academies' led by the fundamentalist preacher Jerry Falwell were set up in the south from the early 1960s for white kids only (with some versions and variations still existing today[26]) and were granted tax-exempt status as 'charitable' education organizations. But in 1968, a group of Black parents in Mississippi brought a suit against the academies, arguing the schools' discrimination shouldn't be tax free. This led to then president Richard Nixon revoking the exemption.[27]

The move did not go down well with Falwell, the infamous Baptist pastor, televangelist and founder of Moral Majority, an organization set up to politicize disgruntled Southern white evangelicals who resisted the era of change. As the civil rights movement was winning victories in dismantling pockets of white supremacy, Falwell and others like him looked around for an issue to galvanize potential voters, pull the Republican

Party to the religious right and attempt to hang on to a racial power and privilege they were so accustomed to. Thanks in no small part to a religious conservative strategist called Paul Weyrich, abortion became that issue.[28]

With no concern for the reality of what it would mean for women's lives, in the late 1970s, Falwell became a significant architect in transforming abortion from a private matter (that Evangelicals had hitherto shown little interest in) between a woman and her doctor to a political hand grenade. In fact, a decade earlier, today's Bible Belt in the south had some of the loosest laws in the country. At that time, Alabama offered women greater unrestricted access to abortion than New York.

Falwell, by his own admission, did not preach his first anti-abortion sermon until 1978, five years after the passing of Roe. 'So what changed?' writes Ilyse Houge, the former president of NARAL Pro-Choice America, a reproductive rights lobbying and advocacy group. 'A conservative movement built on maintaining white privilege began to lose steam and went looking for a new bogeyman to keep its people engaged . . . What came next is not so much a story of true believers as it is about a group of people dedicated to preserving the status quo in a changing world. Religion and philosophy were contorted to give a moral sheen to their agenda, but their real power came from inflaming a targeted group of Americans who were terrified of losing economic and social status in an increasingly diverse and tolerant country. They were mainstreaming bigotry.'[29]

But as I spend time in Indiana, I start to see another side to American faith, especially around abortion. Americans talk about faith much more casually and often than we do in the

UK – especially, or so it feels, in the Midwest. I notice that it comes up in most of the conversations I have. When I spend time with a relative in Detroit, I meet one of her friends, a young doctor working in psychiatry at an ER in Flint. I ask her how she copes with such a tough job and she simply replies: 'Jesus.'

I begin to see faith not just as a loud, political weapon, shaming and blaming vulnerable individuals – though it can be that – but also, sometimes, as a quiet personal stoicism, a source of resilience. I am still appalled by the Christians who intimidate people outside of clinics with prayer circles, offensive banners and completely meaningless offers of 'help' in states that provide no welfare support to families – not to mention the Machiavellian and hate-fuelled scheming of the likes of pastors such as Jerry Falwell. But even as a firm atheist, sometimes I am almost envious of the type of faith the women I meet have, that seems like an inner compass keeping them going, no matter what.

One of these people is Sue Ellen Braunlin, a retired doctor, a fierce advocate for abortion access and a Christian, who has been embroiled in two of the country's most high-profile abortion cases of the last twenty years. Sue is the co-president of the Indiana Religious Coalition for Reproductive Choice (RCRC) and when I meet her, she has joined the board of the National RCRC, where she will be elected chairperson, before resigning in June 2022. Sue didn't come up through the women's movement or the pro-choice movement. She began her activism in church, running sex and relationships education programmes for Sunday schools.

Sue is softly spoken and exudes a genuine warmth. We're sitting on her garden patio in a suburb of the city, taking shelter in the shade from the hot September sun, while her daughter's frustrated yet adorable puppy watches us from the other side of the French windows. Sue invited me into her home even though she had flown back late from a conference the day before. There is a generosity to her that is immediately obvious and which may go some way to answering my first question: how did she find herself involved in two of America's biggest abortion stories of the last two decades?

Sue was a fierce advocate for both 36-year-old Bei Bei Shuai and 33-year-old Purvi Patel, two women at the heart of cases that made headlines across the globe. Both were imprisoned for foeticide – the murder of the foetus – by the state of Indiana. (Foeticide was first passed in law in Indiana in 1979 to prosecute a person who knowingly or intentionally kills a viable foetus. Thirty-eight states have foeticide laws but Indiana was turning the law on women – and would become the first state to use the law to prosecute a woman for having an alleged self-induced abortion.) 'I couldn't believe this could happen in our country,' Sue says. 'Right before our eyes and hardly anybody around here even knew about it. It was such a wake-up call.'

In 2010, an eight-month pregnant Bei Bei Shuai swallowed rat poison in a suicide attempt. She survived and three days after she gave birth, her daughter died.[30] Bei Bei was charged with murder and attempted foeticide. She faced forty-five years to life in prison. But not long after her conviction, in a surprise plea agreement, the charges were dropped, with Bei Bei pleading guilty to 'criminal recklessness' and serving 178 days in prison.

Sue found Bei Bei accidentally. 'I was just researching images of protests for a presentation I was putting together when I stumbled across pictures of people holding "Free Bei

Bei" signs in Indiana. I thought, "Why have I never heard this?" It turns out the people in the picture were from a gender studies class at Butler University. A professor had told her students about Bei Bei's case, how she was in jail, and two of her students had gone down and protested outside. Then the defence attorney hired an intern from Butler, who started a social media account. They did not have much following but it said that there was a trial hearing to dispute the findings.' The prosecution was accusing Bei Bei of homicide. 'And that's when we realized what was happening and me and three other women from church decided to go down.' It was believed to be the first time in the state's 200-year history in which a woman was being prosecuted for murder over suicide while pregnant. 'It was just a punch to the gut that this was happening. That it *could* happen.' Was it radicalizing, I ask? 'Yes, it really was.'

Sue, in her role at Indiana Religious Coalition for Reproductive Choice, reached out to Bei Bei, who remains a friend to this day, and promised to do what she could. 'I began calling the prosecutor's office to try to understand why she was doing this. I liaised with the defence attorney, spoke to the press, organized and attended rallies, sometimes speaking at them, and worked with other local groups to raise money and awareness. Doing whatever was needed.'

She was so stunned by the law that Sue created a Google Alert for 'foeticide Indiana' so she could track how many women faced these horrifying charges. 'That's how I found Purvi.'

Thirty-three-year-old Purvi Patel was the first woman in the US to go to prison for allegedly inducing her own abortion. In 2013, the year Mike Pence was sworn in as governor, Patel miscarried. After she arrived at the hospital bleeding profusely, she was arrested, accused of inducing an abortion and having a baby she allowed to die. In 2015, she was sentenced to twenty years for child neglect and foeticide. I was 30 at the time, around the same age, and saw the pictures of Purvi in handcuffs on the TV – her long black hair, her downcast, frightened face in the courtroom, broadcast to millions the world over. I remember thinking how strange and cruel parts of America must be.

Despite an initial assessment by a pro-life doctor, the hospital had found no evidence of abortifacients in Purvi's blood. Yet Purvi still served eighteen months for child neglect and foeticide before a successful appeal saw a judge order her release. 'I knew from Bei Bei's case that the only thing you can do is hit it early and hard,' Sue says. She explains that resistance to a case such as this has to be quick; a lot of noise must be made as it could potentially have some sway if the case makes it to trial. 'It's a matter of prosecutorial discretion that they're choosing a case like this. It's not required or expected that a prosecutor go after women in this way. But all you need is just one prosecutor, one hospital, one detective and this thing can take off like a runaway train.'

The threat of life imprisonment was overturned successfully for both women but the ordeal was far from over. Purvi has since moved to another part of the country. Sue says, 'The community continued to hound her family till they managed to drive them out of business. It was like a whispering circle.' Sue is quick to point out that, '100 per cent of women accused of foeticide in the state of Indiana are Asian American women who represent 2 per cent of the population. There have been so many mistakes made in siloing the reproductive rights movement and in completely overlooking racism and poverty.' Later in our conversation, Sue remarks on the racist history of the state. 'When the Klan was big in Indiana in around 1925, it was very, very big. At least one-tenth of the people, and some people say a third of the people, including around a tenth of the women in Indiana, were with the Klan.'

It's easy to see how these particular women – Bei Bei and Purvi, marginalized on all fronts for their ethnicity, immigration status and gender, making them some of the most vulnerable in the community – were used as test cases for lawmakers to see just how far they could control women and their bodies, how far an agenda could be pushed, reducing them in the eyes of many to mere political ends. When Bei Bei was prosecuted, she immediately had her citizenship revoked, proving the persecution of her was directed at the multitudes of her identity. It is frightening to consider how these situations could so easily happen again today in Indiana as abortion rights are eradicated, and racism and white supremacy simultaneously push further and further into mainstream politics.

The link between racism and anti-abortionism remains today. After the Buffalo, New York, shootings in 2022, when a white gunman shot dead ten Black people in a supermarket, the world learned about the 'Great Replacement' theory, which the killer had referenced in ramblings he'd published on the internet ahead of the massacre. This is an idea held by white supremacists that powerful liberals are 'replacing' the white race with migrants whose votes they can control. Republican senators and pundits on Fox News have legitimized this theory, employing certain language, often emphasizing the word 'replace' in broadcasts, interviews and at their own mainstream political events as a dog-whistle to those who subscribe to the twisted ideology.

The fear that white people are being replaced is, no doubt, in part born from a reality that estimates the white majority American population is shrinking. It's this insecurity among a certain group that some political scientists believe led to Trump's 2016 victory.[31] If you believe that your tribe's grip on power and dominance is slipping, logic follows that you will also believe that in order to preserve your race, white women should not be allowed to abort white babies. (And, of course, this thinking is laced with the patriarchal assumption that women's primary purpose is child rearing.) In doing so, you insist on weaponizing women's bodies for your own hateful, fearful agenda. Just as lawmakers did to Bei Bei and Purvi, just as Jerry Falwell did.

Sue trained as a doctor in a Catholic hospital where, I was surprised to hear, she was taught the life of the mother was always the priority – something, she says, that 'stopped after the Clintons arrived in the White House. Hillary made a bid to reform healthcare and political lines were drawn in the sand.' Sue tells me that before the 1990s, official Catholic healthcare policy, drawn up by the US Conference of Catholic Bishops, emphasized dignity for non-paying patients and holistic medicine. But, 'In the 1990s, the Catholic Health Association shifted focus to Catholic identity in healthcare.' It is well documented that, although Clinton's healthcare reform failed, it planned to include greater access to abortion. When working on the reform, Clinton met with Catholic leaders who said while they supported the need for better affordable healthcare for

Americans, it would be a 'a moral tragedy' to 'burden' the package with abortion costs coverage. By the 1990s, abortion was a fraught political topic, increasingly casting the issue as a black and white one. You were for or against – even in hospitals.

Sue married a fellow doctor, a Jewish one, and they have successfully navigated an interfaith marriage in which they share two children (who both work in the same Catholic hospital that Sue and her husband did) and a strong belief in religious choice. Despite her commitment to her faith, she is not at all blind to its pitfalls. She calls religion 'a vector for racism'. 'And,' she says, 'we wonder, as religious people, why secular people don't want to work with us? I think historically, religious people have gone into secular movements and said, "Hey, we're here to be the moral authority for you." And people have already figured out that arrogance. So now it's really hard to build alliances if you're coming in as the moral authority of religion to people who have long seen the hypocrisy in the ways religion works, even in progressive denominations.'

Sue also reflects on how dangerous the church has been for women. In the late 1980s and early 1990s, she witnessed 'the powerful alliance between Catholics and Evangelicals in the growing pro-life movement that was just like gasoline.'

While the Catholic church had always voiced opposition to abortion, the additional support of the Evangelical movement, which proved to be, at times, far more extreme, was explosive. Part of the landscape that Sue is referring to is the violent anti-abortion group Operation Rescue, founded in 1987 and led by an Evangelist called Randall Terry, a former car salesman who did his best to rain terror over abortion providers to stop what he called 'the murder industry'. The group's name came from Proverbs 24:11: 'Rescue those unjustly sentenced to die.' Jerry Falwell called Terry 'the Martin Luther King of the pro-life movement', while an article from *Rolling Stone* in 1989 said Terry had 'walked straight out of a Ronald Reagan daydream'.[32]

In 1991, Terry went up against Faye Wattleton, then CEO of Planned Parenthood, on the *Phil Donahue Show*. Wattleton was the first African American and youngest woman to hold the position. When I watch the interview now,[33] there is something startlingly familiar about it. Terry, a white man, is flustered, dramatic, theatrical. He accuses Wattleton of 'black genocide' as he flaps his arms and barely keeps still in his seat. By contrast, Wattleton remains calm and composed, and does her best to politely intervene as Terry yells over her, an incessant adult toddler. Here it is again, just as with Anita Hill and Ketanji Brown Jackson: the apparent threat of a Black woman in a position of power causing a white man to become hysterical, dramatic, lose composure – everything that women are so often accused of. It's the same scene, the same dynamic playing out over and over again.

A year later, Wattleton led the organization during the biggest attack on the right to legal abortion since 1973 in Planned Parenthood v. Casey. A Republican governor from Pennsylvania had passed an Act placing greater restrictions on abortion access – including the demand for a husband's written consent if the patient was married. Planned Parenthood declared this unconstitutional. The Supreme Court ultimately sided with Planned Parenthood's assertion that the right to privacy allows women to access abortion, keeping Roe in place. However, the court also ruled that states could impose their own restrictions, as long as these restrictions didn't place an 'undue burden' on the person seeking an abortion – a term that's been problematic ever since. Undoubtedly, it was a significant gutting of women's rights but the constitutional right to abortion remained and states could not ban it. And, just as in 1973, it was upheld by a conservative majority court.

Despite, or perhaps because of, the Supreme Court upholding Roe, the religious anti-abortion lobby lurched to the extreme. In 1993, Dr George Tiller, a physician from Wichita, Kansas, who performed late-term abortions was shot in both of his arms. This came after numerous death threats and a clinic bombing. Dr Tiller had already been forced to hire bodyguards and wear a bulletproof vest. A target throughout his career, in 2009, he died when he was shot in the head at point blank range while at church on a Sunday morning. Arson attacks, threats and clinic members wearing bulletproof vests were common in red states during this period and have continued, albeit less regularly, in some areas ever since. The *Huffington Post* reported in 2022 that, 'In the last forty-three years, anti-abortion activists have committed at least eleven murders, twenty-six attempted murders, 956 known threats of harm or death, 614 stalking incidents and four kidnappings, according to the National Abortion Federation. The supposedly "pro-life" movement has bombed forty-two abortion clinics, set fire to 194 and made 667 bomb threats.'[34] There is something chillingly apt in how Sue describes the development of the anti-abortion movement in these years 'like gasoline'.

It's hard to see this strain of the Christian church and its leaders as much other than radical violent extremism and domestic terrorism targeting women's autonomy on behalf of a religion whose major tenets are, supposedly, love and forgiveness, all in a country whose constitution purports religious and personal freedom.

Before meeting Sue, I viewed her faith and her activism at odds, which is one of the reasons I was keen to talk with her. But now I see clearly that this isn't the case. In fact, it is the opposite: they are in sync. As she has said, 'Evidence-based, cost-effective, brilliant public health policy is truly pro-life. This is the position of reproductive justice.'

Sue's faith motivates her to take up the cases of others but it doesn't blind her to the rights of a woman to make a choice about her own life and her own body. Together, science, ethics *and* faith led her to advocate on behalf of some of the most vulnerable – and at personal cost. 'Some of my neighbours no longer speak with me. I've lost friends over all this. I will say my social circles are getting smaller and smaller.' But, she adds, 'It can also intensify some friendships.' I realize that Sue believes in social justice just as strongly as I do; I had just long disassociated it from any denomination of American Christianity. Which is telling. As I had learned from Laura Kaplan, there is a history of the church *supporting* abortion: it was Protestant ministers in New York, along with some rabbis, who began the Clergy Consultation Service – the first public abortion service in the country, when abortion was still illegal in the 1960s. The first abortion clinic in the US was opened in New York in July 1971 by the city's ministers.

To understand the full picture of the abortion movement in the US is to understand the role of the church – how it has hindered and how it has helped. But as I am learning, for many of the women I have now met and admire, faith is also central to their own personal fight – it is the fuel to their resilience in tough times.

I'm talking to Dr Sharon McLennon-Wier over Zoom. She's just four months into her new role as the CEO of Center for Independence of the Disabled, New York (CIDNY), a non-profit that started in 1978 to provide a range of free services to support those with disabilities in the city and enable them to live independent, self-determined lives. She's a New Yorker born and bred but her schedule was full when I passed through the city. Still, I was determined to speak with her. I knew she'd be able to give me unique insight into women's resilience.

Dr McLennon-Wier knows a thing or two about resilience. For starters, she is a licensed mental health counsellor with a doctoral degree in counselling psychology and an adjunct professor of psychology. 'Resilience is a great psychological phenomenon,' she tells me, which, 'not everybody has, although, there are ways to cultivate it with some patients.' And she understands resilience better than most. Dr McLennon-Wier is a blind, Black woman living in America. She once fell from the subway platform onto the tracks. Luckily, two men were quick to help and saved her life. 'It's not been easy,' she explains, 'on multiple fronts.'

It certainly wasn't easy throughout her education. In the 1990s, Dr McLennon-Wier studied biology. She had to spend time figuring out how she'd get from one place to another across campus and there was very limited technology available, other than a tape recorder to help her learn. It hasn't been easy following her ambition, either. She wasn't permitted into medical school because of her disability and so couldn't become a psychiatrist, as she'd dreamed of. Instead, she took the route of counselling and psychology. And, today, still it's not easy as a Black woman. 'Even as an educated Black woman running an organization, you're still not at that point where you get the respect. And that's really hard. I just think that the systemic fibre of racism is really embedded in our society. I don't know how to fix that. But I know it's very present.' Despite all of those challenges, she perseveres – and she achieves.

Dr McLennon-Wier's determination to follow her dreams and have a successful career despite the obstacles came, in part, from her mother: 'She raised me to do everything that my older sister could do, even though I don't have vision.' This, she believes, helped develop her inner sense of resilience. 'It really helped to understand that, yes, it's going to take you longer to do stuff, but you can still do it.'

Hearing how much McLennon-Wier has had to overcome to get where she is today is staggering. 'I have to apply to fifty jobs just to hear back from one. I have been rejected time and time again. I have been told I can't do things even though I know I can,' she explains. Have the many obstacles ever got the better of you and made you want to quit, I ask? 'Oh, yes. Every step of the way. When it takes you two or three times longer to do things, when you have people who say you can't do it – there's no way you're going to get into that programme or there's no way you're going to be able to travel to that place – of course you want to stop. It has felt lonely. It's felt like you're beating your head against the wall and you want to try but don't know if you're going make it because there's so many obstacles in your way.'

Some things have gotten easier over time, she says, for her and for others with disabilities. 'Thanks to the passing of the Americans with Disabilities Act of 1990, and amendments made in 2008, I'm able to have the job I have here at CIDNY. We have curb cuts [lowered curbs for easier access] that everyone gets to enjoy; you can get on a train and they announce the stops. You can go into a Starbucks and if you're using a wheelchair, you can roll up to the counter and are able to make your order. There are accessible restrooms. I can independently go to an ATM machine and get my money out. At home, I'm able to turn on my TV and talk to the remote control and tell it to go to on demand or get whatever movie I want. That wasn't always around.'

To speak with Dr McLennon-Wier reminds me of the layers of resilience some people require just to get through their day, tackling multiple discriminations, from ableism to racism and sexism, and still finding the energy to keep moving forward. When I press Dr McLennon-Wier for how she does that, she tells me what I've been hearing a lot lately: it's her faith.

Raised a Roman Catholic, today she is Baptist. 'During the bad times, when you want to cry, the times you didn't get something, when you feel like you're a failure, to have that inner spiritual faith and prayer has really pushed me on. It has been seminal for me. And if you talk to a lot of different groups that have been marginalized, you'll learn they need something, that kind of hope, that belief in something else bigger than themselves, or the hope that is going to get better, so that they can also propel themselves through those difficult times. It's about that conviction or belief in something, the belief that you are here for a reason. That you can change your life. That you can make a difference in the world.'

I've always been interested in the faith of others. The devotion to something that can't be proven is easy to doubt and mock, which I've heard happen at London dinner parties. But for those who organize their lives around something mystical or spiritual in some way, I wonder what process might take place internally for that to happen and what can be gained from it. I'm fascinated by a private source of strength, an unwavering voice that says everything will be OK, that it's meant to be like this.

America's religious fundamentalism seemed especially pronounced in popular culture when I was growing up – put under a microscope by the likes of Louis Theroux or the incredible Harrison Ford movie, *Witness*. And, more recently, the stunning memoir *Educated* by Tara Westover – the story of her survivalist Mormon family. America always perplexes as much as it enthrals, a place that seems so familiar and yet so alien. And that is true when it comes to faith.

But my interest in the idea, the problems and the tangle of faith, comes from my mum. I've never really seen her practise her faith but she's said it is there. Occasionally, she'd take me to church on Easter Sunday but I went to a Church of England school and thought sitting in church was just something you did, whether or not you believed. Over the years, she has alluded to it being there, subtly, very occasionally. It's a part of her I don't know and I'm sure I never will, one she keeps guarded, out of sight. And it seems contradictory to the parts of her I do know. When I saw Frances McDormand's character in the film *Three Billboards Outside Ebbing, Missouri*, a no-nonsense, foul-mouthed mother happy to tell a Catholic priest precisely what she thought of the church harbouring paedophiles, I called my mum, laughing: 'That's *you*! She's just like *you*!' But underneath my mum's rage at religion and the crime and corruption it has historically committed is a private faith. As I talk with Sue, and Dr McLennon-Wier, I think of my mother, and how, in certain moments, faith looks like clinging to a sturdy tree trunk in a storm, keeping you rooted through the hardest of times, reminding you there is a way forward, even in the moments when it feels like there isn't, reminding you that all this hardship and all this struggle might be for a reason, a lesson worth learning.

Keeping the faith

My mum kept her faith in herself and us throughout the 1990s, even if those around us didn't have any. The first time I realized there was a problem was when I was at Friday club in the local village hall when I was still in junior school. A small girl called Caroline, with a pointy face and beady black eyes who squawked and pecked like a bird, told me that I was a bastard, laughing as she hopped away. I didn't understand. As far as I knew, bastards were boys. But then another kid pointed out that bastard was the name for people with no dads.

Over time, my mum's role as a single parent came with a background noise, a radio left on in a different room. I couldn't quite catch what was being said but I knew the mumbling wasn't kind. Friends' parents asked what time my mum got home from work, a look of concern stretching across their brow. Teachers tutted and rolled their eyes when I wasn't able to attend something, get a lift somewhere or prepare something for class because, just this once, she didn't have time to glue/bake/drop me off. Once, as a little girl, when I fell off the end of a shopping trolley and cut my head open, the doctors in the hospital asked my mum if she was a lone parent. When she said yes, they asked if she was responsible for my injury. The assumption, always lurking, was that single mothers are bad mothers.

In an interview with Victoria Benson, the CEO of the UK's largest single parent charity, Gingerbread, for an article I was writing, she confirmed that the stigma and shame my mother faced is still there now, with single parents all but forgotten during the pandemic as supermarkets announced shoppers couldn't take children in, assuming another parent was on hand. Ahead of my trip, I researched the history of single motherhood and discovered just how forgotten, ignored and penalized by the state lone mothers have been for so many years – in the UK and the US. Coincidentally, as I was surrounded by library books, I opened an email from *The New Yorker* entitled 'How Single Mothers are Coping during Covid-19 in New York City'. The short answer? They weren't. Once again, they lacked support, were overlooked and were nobody's priority, but they were also expected to do a truly superhuman amount: work and parent and homeschool and provide and live, totally alone.

When I was young, I didn't see the stuff in the papers – the headlines, the MPs and columnists who mocked and shamed lone parents and condemned their children to a lifetime of crime. I was only seven when John Redwood, the Secretary of State for Wales, said single parent families were 'one of the biggest social problems of the day'.[35] I was only ten when, in a column for the *Spectator*, Boris Johnson wrote that children of single mothers were 'ill-raised, ignorant, aggressive and illegitimate'.[36]

Historians Ruth Thane and Tanya Evans have written that 'the 1980s and early 1990s saw the most outspoken and persistent attack on lone mothers by representatives of any government of the century.'[37] And it started with Thatcher. When she suggested young girls got pregnant because they wanted to skip housing queues, it became a stereotype that stuck like superglue for decades. She slashed nursery care for 3– to 5- year olds, alongside a universal maternity grant and single payments for select items to mothers on income support.[38] The year I was born, 1985, the Inland Revenue decided a workplace nursery, something which would have been a godsend to my mum had it been available, was a 'perk' and therefore parents would need to pay tax on it. This hit middle-earners who were working full-time.

For working-class and low-income single mothers, it was a much harder situation; the attacks were more vicious and dehumanizing, smeared with classism. But all lone parents were outcast in some way and it was a lose-lose situation. Lone mothers who relied on the state for help were lazy. Lone parents who went to work were selfish. This was not a new idea – at least for the middle classes. While working-class mothers have long worked endless hours in unsafe conditions, nobody gave them much of a second thought. But following the Second World War, during which many middle-class women had joined the workforce, men wanted to turn back the tide and working mothers were deemed dangerous. A report from the World Health Organization in 1951, written by a man, concluded that 'working mothers are one of the causes of children's mental illness'.[39]

Yet even against this backdrop, my mum's faith in our little family of three powered on. I believe that becoming a civil servant and joining the Metropolitan police after my father left shows she still had faith in herself to pursue an interesting and exciting career, despite the challenges that lay ahead. Though, unsurprisingly, it turned out that lone, working mothers weren't exactly a hit there either.

When she joined the Met, she was the only working mother in her department. My mum's old colleague Nick tells me that in the early 1990s, equality in the workplace meant treating women like men and expecting women to do everything that men did, including acting like they had no parental or domestic responsibility. Which, in turn, meant that when either my brother or I were sick, my mum would have to phone in claiming she was unwell. Admitting she needed to stay at home with us would confirm the long-held suspicion that women couldn't and shouldn't be working. It also meant she rarely took a sick day for herself as she used them all on us. One year, on Mother's Day, we were having lunch with my gran when my mum was called into work. I remember standing in the car park of the restaurant crying my heart out, desperate for her not to leave. When she arrived in central London a few hours later she realized there was no emergency, just an exercise in power play from one of her male bosses who thought she had something to prove.

Her faith was, in part, rewarded with the arrival of New

Labour in 1997. The morning after Tony Blair was elected, she woke me up with the news, having stayed up all night, tears in her eyes, her smile as wide as the Mississippi river, overcome with disbelief and joy that eighteen years of Conservative government had come to end. Blair's government immediately set about reforming childcare and family policies, including significant benefits for lone parents. Society's dial had shifted once more and working mothers and single parents were no longer an enemy of the state. For the first time in a long time, my mum found hope in the changing culture around her.

Her determination to keep going never faded: commuting, driving me to ballet lessons, helping me with spellings, washing our PE kits, cooking dinner, doing the weekly shop, making Halloween outfits from bin bags (I was a vampire; that was my cape), all while tackling a highly challenging job that went well beyond the nine-to-five. Looking back, I wonder if it was because she was a single parent that her antennae for potential problems went into overdrive, as if overcompensating for the fact that it was all on her to protect us. I'll never forget the time she cornered my year eight French teacher about his 'strategy' should war break out during our trip to Le Touquet during the Balkan conflict. To say he looked surprised is putting it mildly but there was nothing she hadn't thought of.

Yet her parenting didn't just involve the military logistics of organizing our time, our dinner and our geopolitical safety. One of the things I remember most was her faith in us, a boundless faith in the kind of people we could be in the world. Which is how my brother and I sometimes found ourselves sitting in Lambeth town hall in Brixton on a weekday evening next to my mum, her work pass hanging from her neck, her Blackberry buzzing, as she scribbled notes while pushing her ringlets out of her face. Having finished a day at work, at this time temporarily based in south London, she'd drive home, a forty-minute commute, pick us up and then head back into the city. This wasn't childcare. This was an education.

This was the time of the MacPherson report, an examination of the Met's handling of the investigation into the murder of Stephen Lawrence, which had found the police force to be institutionally racist. Part of my mum's job was to attend meetings between the Met police, local government and the community, and she insisted we come with her. The 'stop and search' tactic was rife on London streets, targeting Black men and boys. As naive as I was to the reality of that situation, I could feel the air in those meetings was electric.

My mum and I were particularly taken with a smartly dressed elderly Jamaican man who'd slowly rise every week to ask what was to be done about the 'ladies of the night' outside his house and occasionally mention that he was under surveillance by the FBI. Yet other than this gentleman, the room was hostile. A wall of mothers would stand at the back, crossed arms, steady and precise, demanding to know why their innocent teenage boy had been stopped yet again. I remember one woman, whose fury propelled her into the aisle, her arms outstretched in desperation at the racism, injustice, her voice filling the high ceilings of the old building. Embarrassed white men sat behind a trestle table at the front of the room, shuffling through papers, looking for something to say, anything but the truth.

This was a new world to me and my brother. In our Guildford state school of 2,000 pupils, for a few years there were only two Black pupils and they were brothers. One evening, as we filed out after another heated round of questions and debate, a local councillor came up to me, eyed me suspiciously and said, 'You've seen the other side of the coin now, love.' Of course, that was precisely my mum's point: know more, understand more, understand your privilege, understand how this world really works, see a world far bigger than your own.

As I've got older, I've come to see her insistence on us attending those meetings not just as an education, to break through our home county bubble, but as a type of faith. Her faith was in the mothers holding the police to account and in the community standing up for themselves. And her faith was in us, that we would learn something from these meetings and take it with us.

It's a warm Friday night in Indianapolis and I head up to a restaurant a couple of blocks from Ted's B&B. It's busy but they squeeze me in at a bar, the last spot, where a friendly barman in a red plaid shirt and a mop of black hair is mixing drinks. He looks intrigued when I order a glass of wine. 'Are you Australian?' he asks. I explain I'm British and I tell him I'm making a trip across the Midwest. He tells me his name is Nick and then says, 'Don't bother going anywhere else in Indiana unless you like guns.' We chat on and off for the rest of the evening, that Midwestern hospitality making me feel like I'm an old regular. At one point, I ask him who is famous from the state. Suddenly, like a scripted flash mob, everyone at the bar chimes in. The guy next to me with dreadlocks down his back and big chains around his neck, turns and says, 'You don't know *Mike* was from here?' I shake my head, unsure who

Mike is. Nick helps me out: 'You didn't know *Michael Jackson* was born here?' his disbelief almost sounding like offence. A waiter serving the table behind me mentions Larry Bird, the basketball player, over my shoulder. Across the bar, a couple in their forties lean forward, 'Oh, David Letterman! And Cole Porter! Oh, and that writer, er, Kurt Vonnegut!' they yell, as if taking part in a TV game show. My British inclination to talk to no one evaporated.

Nick has started making me cocktails I haven't asked for but I don't refuse them. The young guys next to me leave and are replaced by an elderly man who everyone knows and Nick introduces as Gino. He's Italian-American, smart in a cream jacket and slacks. 'She's from England, not Australia, and she's writing a book,' Nick explains as he smiles at me across the bar. Gino's face lights up. 'You are? How wonderful.' We talk for a bit after he orders a glass of red wine and a bowl of pasta. He tells me he ended up in the Midwest after his family migrated to New York and he wouldn't change it for the world. 'The people – they're so kind,' he says. Gino slides a napkin across with a pen and asks me to write down the name of the book. He says he'll buy a copy. I decide it's time to leave and when I ask for the bill, I see Nick hasn't added the drinks. 'On me,' he says, coyly. 'Sure I can't get you another?' he asks, his look heavy on me. I blush and decline politely. 'Well good night, Marisa.'

When I get back to the B&B, Ted is baking. It's just after 11 p.m. Drinking at a bar with strangers makes for a wonderful time but is perhaps not ideal for accurate late night reportage. Nevertheless, I decide this is my moment: 'Are you still involved in politics?' I ask.

He chuckles. 'I'm too old,' he says.

'I see you're friends with Mike Pence,' I say.

He nods and speaks warmly of both Pence and his wife; his company has made jewellery for her at the request of Pence – a duck because of a convoluted story my cocktail brain can't quite keep up with. My questions have made him curious. 'And what are you doing here, Marisa?' he asks, even though I'd initially told him I was just travelling post pandemic.

'I'm writing a book about women's rights in the Midwest,' I say, laying my cards on the table.

He folds his arms and leans against the counter. 'Mike Pence is a great man,' he says. 'And like him, I'm pro-life, pro-family. And I love this part of the world. This here is the heartland.'

I wasn't short on women with impressive resumes but, unlike Ann DeLaney, not many of them were in their eighties and still working. Ann DeLaney is a lawyer with her own firm, which she runs with her daughter in downtown Indianapolis. She is also a trailblazing Democrat in the state. In 1984, she was the first woman in Indiana to run for the position of lieutenant governor. In 1993, she became the first woman in the state to lead a political party when she became the chair of the Indiana Democratic Party – 'a truly thankless job' she mutters. And in 2001, Bill Clinton appointed DeLaney to be the standing trustee for Chapter 13 Bankruptcy in the Southern District of Indiana. Today, she remains a long-running political pundit on local TV current affair shows. And in between all of this, she has spent fifteen years running a domestic abuse shelter.

When I meet Ann at her office downtown, she's glamorous,

all in black with a beautiful turquoise necklace. She gives me a firm handshake and we take the lift to her shiny glass office with views of the city. Framed pictures of grandkids and family line the window. I ask her what it's like to be a long-time Democrat in a red state. Indiana has turned blue only twice in the last sixty years: under Lyndon B. Johnson in 1964 and in 2008, under Barack Obama. 'That was wonderful, absolutely wonderful,' she beams. 'We were so excited about that.' Yet most of the time, 'It's like being in the Catholic church,' she says. 'I can't stand our archbishop – a reactionary who's anti-gay and other such nonsense like that. And some of my friends have stopped going to church because of him. But I said, "If you pull out, you leave it to the bastards!".'

Ann reminds me of my mother: tough, with a severe intolerance of useless, self-serving men and delightfully without filter. During our conversation, Mike Pence, who she has known for thirty years, is referred to as 'dumb Mike', Republican minority leader Mitch McConnell is 'the devil incarnate' and she hopes Donald Trump 'has a heart attack before the next election'.

Ann knows a thing or two about holding onto faith, especially when that faith is challenged. Her commitment to the Democrats and their never-ending uphill battle, especially in Indiana, is just one example. Another is her work as a female lawyer in the field of sex crimes in the 1970s. After she graduated, Ann joined the county prosecutor's officer in the Felony Sex Offense and Child Abuse Unit. 'Back then, male judges believed the victim somehow invited the abuse. Or often, it was seen as a "crime of passion". They just didn't get it.' And often, people didn't get her, a working mother, either. 'When I ran for lieutenant governor in 1984, I kept being asked, "What about your children?". I'd say, "Well, we still feed them, they still go to school." Those attitudes have changed, I think, in the sense that people may think it, but they won't say it anymore.' Back then, male colleagues were quick to doubt her, too. 'You needed to be tough, otherwise men would walk right over you.'

Her persistence in difficult arenas over such a long period of time has given her a different outlook to many of the other women I've spoken to – and indeed my own. For the most part, Ann is very positive. 'We've made great progress. When I graduated from law school, I think there was one woman trial court judge in the state. OK, now, if we're not half, we're damn close to it. And in fact, in terms of higher education and enrolment, a majority is female in this country. These are certain things [Republicans] can't change.'

I think of Gloria Steinem reminding the crowd at the Washington Women's March in 2017 that she was 'old enough to remember a time when it was even worse'. When I ask Ann how things have changed for women since she's been working, her answer was simple: 'Things have got better – there's better representation, there are more female judges, there's more success in civil rights and LGBTQ rights cases. Biden is taking a leaf out of the GOP playbook, stacking the courts with more diverse and liberal judges.' Ann shows me that a longer lens can offer a different framing of history – things can seem more hopeful.

But that's not to say she isn't incensed by what is happening now. She's rattled by America's biggest internal threat yet – 'The Big Lie', the idea that the 2020 election was stolen. Like other older women I've spoken to, Ann believes there is something novel about this time in American history. 'This just isn't more conservative, this is crazy! How can you have, as we have in this state, *four* elected congressmen who don't believe that Joe Biden is president?'

Conspiracies aren't new, Ann says. 'I still remember the debate about fluoride being a communist plot. Some of this stuff has existed for a long time, among a fringe of people.' But, she says, 'This stuff now is crazy. How do you deal with somebody who thinks you can't get the vaccine because the government's implanting a transmitter in your brain?'

Alongside the anti-vaxxers, the allegiance to Trump is, for Ann, shocking new ground. 'This is who we picked to lead this country. *This!* I mean, he's filed bankruptcy, what, four or five times?[40] He lies. He cheats. He steals. *And he was the president?* When Trump was in, I stopped watching the news. I could not stand to see his face or listen to him. It would make me physically ill to see that. He's like Boris Johnson in that regard.' The apex of her astoundment came on 6 January: 'I'm really worried about democracy.' Really? 'I never, ever thought I'd live to see what happened on January 6. Ever. And then to see people defending it?'

Her list of complaints against Trump are long: 'He's contemptuous of women. He was contemptuous of anybody with disabilities. He was just absolutely an abomination. And the fact that he got elected president shows me how much of a backlash there is against women who are assertive. I think Hillary had her problems. But I think the main problem she had was that she was female.'

When Ann worked to get Pamela Carter elected as the state's attorney general in the 1990s, the first African American woman to hold the role, Carter's Republican opponent, a white man, 'a total jerk', took two life-size cardboard cutouts of her with him when he went campaigning. 'He'd go to each one of the ninety-two counties to make sure everybody understood she was Black.' I think of the bullying and explicit racism towards Ketanji Brown Jackson, Anita Hill and Faye Wattleton. And there it is again: white American men consistently furious at Black women claiming power.

Ann recognizes what Laura Kaplan called the 'last cry of the white males'. Speaking of the far-right Republicans, she says, 'They know they're not expanding. They're against gays. They are anti-women in many regards. They're anti-immigrants. So there's no real potential for them. The number of white males is going down as a percentage of the population and they can't expand with the ideas that they've got. So, when it comes to elections, they've got to claim foul play. They are frightened and they should be. I mean, they lost by seven million votes. They don't have any agenda. They don't have anything they want to do. They just want to hold office and hate. And they're really good at it'.

We move on to her time running the domestic abuse shelter. 'When I joined, I thought I'd be there for a year; I wound up staying fifteen,' she smiles, a testament to a project she had so clearly found faith in. Ann arrived at the shelter in 1996. There were thirty-five women and their children, crammed into a six-bedroom former nunnery with just one large bathroom. She got to work raising money for a new building. She trialled and tested new ideas she'd learned about in other parts of the country, such as including the city's police force. When they moved to a bigger shelter, Ann persuaded the police unit for domestic abuse to set up an office on site. The dozen or so police cars parked outside at any one time made the women at the refuge safer and it gave police a much better understanding of their lives. Ann points out another positive: 'Nobody talked about domestic abuse thirty or forty years ago. Nobody. Now they do.'

Yet while awareness may be on the up, incidences of male violence doesn't seem to be going anywhere. The stats in the US mirror the UK: young women are the most common victims and one in four women experience intimate partner violence. [41] In the UK, domestic violence accounts for 16 per cent of violent crimes; it is 15 per cent in the US. America is much bigger and US police receive, on average, 20,000 calls a day relating to domestic abuse. And then there are the guns. Guns increase the chance of homicide by 500 per cent. 'The gun issue has a huge impact on women,' Ann tells me. 'Not that we carry weapons, but in terms of women's safety. It's like the Wild West.' A paper published in the *British Medical Journal* in October 2022, found that, 'Women in the US are more likely to be murdered during pregnancy or soon after childbirth than to die from the three leading obstetric causes of maternal mortality (hypertensive disorders, haemorrhage or sepsis). These pregnancy-associated homicides are preventable and most are linked to the lethal combination of intimate partner violence and firearms.'[42]

There is some good news, however. Recent and radical gun legislation has significantly narrowed 'the boyfriend loophole', which now stops anyone convicted of domestic abuse or stalking in a dating relationship from owning firearms for five years. The law previously only applied if the violent partner had been married to the victim, lived with them or had a child with them. In these cases, the prohibition of firearms is for life.

And then we move on to the common thread among the women I meet in the Midwest: Ann's faith in her faith, and how it led her to be a Catholic who is pro-abortion.

'My son's second child had a very severe health condition that was initially misdiagnosed and he and his wife felt their only option was termination. Eventually, my son found a doctor in Vancouver who offered a different diagnosis and they went ahead with the pregnancy after all.' Today, their child is a 'wonderful kid' with very serious physical disabilities. 'But the idea that the option of abortion wouldn't be available to somebody who was facing that situation is just crazy,' Ann says quietly. It's the only time I see her soften. 'I don't think God wants a child born to extreme pain and immediate death. I don't think that's part of the divine plan.'

Ann's convinced that the withdrawal of the right to abortion would cause a revolution: 'I think we could motivate women in the suburbs here to vote against the Republicans. The northernmost part of the city is Hamilton County. It's very wealthy and very Republican. And they almost went Democratic at the last election. They turned against Trump because of some of these social issues. The more educated women are, whether they work outside the home or not, the more liberal they tend to be.' She also has faith in local judges: 'Most of the abortions bans go to the federal court. And most of the federal district court judges here are either Democrats or moderate Republicans. Even one who's been here since Reagan, I think Reagan appointed her, and she's a pain in the ass to deal with but she blocked the last one.'

What we don't know on this warm October day in 2021 is that when the Supreme Court revokes the right to an abortion, Indiana will become the first state to pass a near total abortion ban. The only exceptions include abortions for a fatal foetal anomaly permitted up to twenty weeks and up to ten weeks for pregnancies due to rape or incest. Republican governor Eric Holcomb will praise the ban for 'protecting life' in a state that already ranks the third worst for maternal mortality rates in the country – and has some of the most relaxed gun laws across the US.[43]

However, as Ann predicts, a federal judge steps in. A week after the law comes into effect in September 2022, a Republican judge temporarily suspended the ban, ruling a woman's right to liberty and autonomy, including whether to carry a pregnancy to term. It will be a similar situation in states across the country. If a ban violates state constitutions, battles will slowly play out in front of judges, causing confusion for women and for health professionals, who are left to make difficult, real-time and sometimes life-or-death decisions while the war on what is or isn't legal rages on in the courts. As American feminist journalist Moira Donegan will write, 'The result [of overturning Roe] has been chaos, with so-called "trigger bans" blasting into enforcement in some states, long-dormant laws from before the era of women's suffrage being revived in others and still other states left in limbo, as abortion flickers in and out of legality, depending on the proclivities of whichever judge is determining whichever injunction.'[44]

But today, sitting in Ann's office, I realize that she has kept her faith: in her party, in her line of work, in federal judges and in her church, even when she was angry at homophobic archbishops or heartbroken over her son's predicament. For more decades than I have been alive, she has simply kept going, kept believing. It's what she still tells her husband to do. Ed

DeLaney is a Democratic state representative in Indiana. 'He gets so frustrated. They don't have the votes. And I say to him, "But you're up there speaking, and you're telling them why it's wrong. You're helping. You're not going to make it perfect but you're going to make it better."'

You're not going to make it perfect but you're going to make it better.

In both America's quest for a more perfect union and our personal own battles, isn't that all anyone can ask?

A few blocks down from Ted's B&B is an English pub-themed gay bar called the English Ivy. And that's where I decide to have dinner on my final night in Indiana. Inside, there are rainbow flags on every table, the ceiling is painted black, as is the furniture. In the separate restaurant section, offering bastardized versions of fish and chips and chicken tikka masala, there are a lot of men who look like they could be Marty Crane's pals – white hair, checked shirts, corduroy trousers, quietly minding their own business, as they nurse a beer. There are also a lot of mixed-sex couples and the pub website makes clear that everyone is welcome. I sit on the back wall. The TV ahead of me is showing a *60 Minutes* interview with Liz Cheney. She's discussing how she's been ousted from the Republican Party because she doesn't believe the election was stolen. I scroll through Twitter. The news tremors with hyperbole: a Virginian Republican says those who committed alleged election fraud against Trump should be 'executed'. Meanwhile, Vice President Kamala Harris likens images of Texan border patrol to slavery,[45] as white men on horses wearing cowboy hats are whipping Black Haitians trying to cross into the country.[46]

I order a glass of wine and look at the menu. Soon, a man and woman, who I presume to be a couple, walk in and sit at the table next to mine. I notice the thing on his belt that I know is everywhere in the US but have never seen – I see he is carrying a gun. Indiana is an open-carry state and a few months after I return to the UK, the state will vote to *repeal* a law requiring a permit to carry a gun in public. This reverse of laws is a nationwide problem and in June 2022, the Supreme Court will significantly repeal gun restrictions, giving Americans the right to carry a concealed weapon wherever they choose, despite the massacre in Uvalde – the mass shooting of 19 children – a month earlier.

As soon as I see the gun, I have an exceptionally strong urge to lean across the table and ask him why, on a Sunday evening, he's carried a gun to dinner at a gay bar and restaurant, not least because the 2016 Orlando shooting in a gay club comes to mind, an atrocity that saw forty-nine killed. But I already know the answer. It is his Second Amendment right and that is that. I couldn't know for sure but I'd guess it was less about safety and more about statement. In his world, for reasons I'll never understand, men, and specifically white men, could, and should, carry guns.

I wonder what others in the bar think. It feels perverse to me that everyone is behaving so normally while this man has a firearm on his hip. I can't see anyone else wearing a gun. Though that doesn't mean they never did. Or they think he shouldn't. All along the highways and in the small towns the Greyhound had taken me through, I've seen bumper stickers on cars celebrating guns, 'joking' about shooting anyone who took their guns away. At breakfast, another guest at the B&B

told the table a story about how he was play-wrestling with his 5-year-old nephew and dropped his gun. He said the little boy tried to reach for it, as if it was the punchline to a joke. There are accidental shootings by and of children every single day in the US. The man telling this story, who thought it a funny anecdote to share with strangers, turned out to be a police officer.

But I don't say anything. I eat up quickly and leave the pub. Not because I think anything dangerous would happen, although that wouldn't have been an entirely ludicrous concern, considering there are more shootings in America than days of the year. But because – to me, at least – it is unnerving. Seeing the gun on that man's belt, so brazen, so casual, so *relaxed*. It stopped me in my tracks. For a Brit, it is an entirely alien concept. It didn't help that I have just read that thirteen people had been shot dead at a Kroger supermarket in Tennessee that week.

I decide to take a walk. It is dusk and the light is a hint of dusty purple. The air is still warm. Pick-up trucks the size of Manhattan apartments crawl along the streets, their red lights like fireflies. American flags hanging from wide porches lightly sway in the breeze, slow breaths of patriotism that now seem sour. I can feel my heart race as I walk and do my best to not to hurry my step. At one point, I turn onto a road and find I am walking behind a young woman. She immediately crosses the street and then gives a quick backward glance, and I can see the fear isn't mine alone.

I chat with Ted a few more times during my stay. I hear him rise early and get breakfast ready. He always smiles warmly when he sees me, checking I have everything I need. He welcomes everyone to the morning breakfast table like an old friend, introducing guests to each other, offering a titbit here or there to get the conversation flowing. I am always one of the first ones at the long communal table and, over berries and tea, I tell him what I have planned for the day. We spoke about buses – he wasn't sure about them, a strange tic perhaps, or an indication of traditional America's stubborn love affairs with cars – and he briefly mentioned the time he'd visited the Soviet Union to teach 'American values'. I presume, when I'd come back after the cocktails, we may have got onto the question of cancel culture, although the haze of the alcohol means I don't quite recall. One morning, he gives me a newspaper article about university students no-platforming an author. 'You should read this,' he says. 'This stuff is crazy. Kids have got to be able to discuss ideas freely.' I am appreciative of the conversation he is trying to have with me. Or, perhaps more accurately, the way he is having it with me.

As I pay my bill, we talk about how different B&Bs are in England: sparser, colder, significantly fewer breakfast options. He loves the B&B but it isn't making him money. He can't compete with Airbnb, he says, especially after a pandemic.

As I leave, he tells me to read *The Splendid and the Vile*, a recent book on Churchill and the Blitz. 'It's very personal. I think you'll like it. He saved the world but, as with many people with power, he had difficulty getting off the stage.' In New York, Natalia had told me to read radical feminist Shulamith Firestone's famous polemic *The Dialectic of Sex*, and I smile to myself at the eclectic reading list I'm accumulating.

I stand at the back door, covered in stickers of American

flags with the words NEVER FORGET. Ted faux-cries, '*Oh Marisa*, you're leaving me! How could you! How could you!' We smile and say our goodbyes.

I text Ed in the Uber back to the bus station downtown. The strangest thing is that I like Ted.

People are complicated, he replies.

At first I think he's referring to Ted but, of course, he means us both.

In Indiana, I'd come across the holy trinity I'd heard about: Babies, Jesus and Guns. I'd been unnerved by the gun at dinner, I'd learned about Operation Rescue, who waged war on abortion clinics in the 1980s and 1990s in the name of Jesus, and I'd come surprisingly close to the state's governor (and former vice president) who thought aborted foetuses should have funerals and abortion should be banned across this unimaginably large nation. It is all here, here in the heartland.

But as I was discovering, the resistance is the fiercest, the most impressive, and the most committed the closer to the fight. The Midwestern states are nicknamed fly-over states because people literally fly over them, ignore them, write them off. But in Indiana, and in similar states, here is the work with the steepest climb, the work with the highest stakes. In a world without Roe, this will be truer than ever.

Ann, Sue and Dr McLennon-Wier are extremely committed to their own fights, and their determination to carry on despite the challenges and defeats which is powered, in part, by faith. Loud and headline-dominating Evangelicalism makes it easy for those of no faith to reject religious belief as a dangerous, harmful ideology. But I have been learning to ask better questions, keep an open mind, respect how faith helped these women.

My conversations have also made me consider a different type of faith – not a religious one, but something intangible nonetheless, something that comes from somewhere deep inside and powers you on, against the odds. Misogyny works to erode women's faith in themselves. It tells us to be quiet, that we are foolish, incorrect, ill-informed. The patriarchy deliberately fosters doubt – constantly reminding us to be small and silent till perhaps we wonder if we exist at all. But to have faith in ourselves rejects that premise. Faith in women – our choices, actions, desires, hopes and understanding – is the opposite of corrosive, controlling doubt. It is a form of power. And in a world laced with misogyny, women need some sort of faith to hand for when we encounter difficult times because it defies the very powers pushing against us. We need to believe in ourselves – and each other.

CHAPTER SEVEN

St Louis, Missouri: The joy of us

Still here

I arrive outside the Greyhound terminal and a young man, well over six foot with tattoos covering his entire face, is pacing in front of the only way in. As I approach, he moves closer to the door. We make eye contact. Suddenly, he pulls on the heavy handle and holds the glass door wide open for me. When I say thank you, he offers a shy smile and wishes me a 'safe trip, ma'am'.

Indiana's Greyhound station has a lot of the same features as the ones I'd already passed through. The homeless, the sleeping, the strip lighting, the timelessness. Many passengers have so much luggage you can only assume they're relocating to a new life. Here, a young woman in frayed denim hot pants with a pink mohawk is clutching a toy unicorn and standing next to three suitcases, two rucksacks and a giant IKEA bag, all her worldly belongings around her feet. I spot the Amish – men in wide brim hats, some black felt, some straw, always wearing braces. Women with their heads covered, wearing full-length dresses, with petticoats, in muted colours. A little girl near me asks her mother, 'Why are they dressed like that?' Even the devout have to adhere to wearing masks, a brush of modernity clashing with their traditional clothes.

I make my way to my line and instantly see the crowd is not happy. A sea of groans swirl around the woman at its centre. 'I SAID,' she yells, 'I will let you know when I have more information!' A turned over truck has been blocking the highway and this means our bus will be delayed but for how long she can't say. I message my Airbnb host and pull out my book. But then I see her.

A young white woman with a shaved head catches my eye. Her feet are covered in dirt and falling out of her slip-on shoes that are far too big. Her legs poke out of beige shorts that hang off her hips and a white tank top covers her pale, braless body. She is buzzing around the space, a pinball bouncing off the walls, running along the rows of seats, peeking into bins, darting in and out of my view. Suddenly, she is in the line next to mine. She holds up a kid's rucksack to the man in front of her. 'Do you like my satchel?' she asks, like a child. 'I found it in a dumpster.' And then she's gone again. Now she is at the kiosk, asking what she could get for one dollar. She bounces off again. I catch a glimpse of her face, her small features, a few freckles, inquisitiveness, eyes searching for something. As I see her head on for the first time, I realize she is pregnant.

She has a ticket and is clutching it tight, an anchor in the storm of her existence. Her vulnerability is acute, as exposed as broken skin, as lethal as ice. In an instant, she is Fantine from *Les Miserables*, but with a child-like resolve against her own predicament. I keep thinking, *Where is she going? Where will she go when she has a baby? Who will help them?* As she boards a bus to Chicago, I begin to berate myself. Why didn't

I give her $20? $50? Why didn't I offer to buy her something at the kiosk? I'm deeply ashamed of my own inaction.

I'd lost count of the number of homeless men I'd seen on my journey. Yet I'd never seen a homeless pregnant woman, certainly not one who moved around a room like a small bird who has flown inside a building and is now panicking because they can't find their way out. I wanted to know her story but she was gone. She clearly needed mental health support, maternity support, access to healthcare, nutritious food, somewhere safe and warm to sleep. She needed so many things and I wondered how on earth she'd ever get them in America – an America that still treats poverty as a personal failing, an America devoid of universal healthcare, an America in which the UN has declared that millions 'live in Third World conditions of absolute poverty'.[47] In the context of this woman, hope and resilience took on a different quality altogether; something less fleeting and ideological, something more urgent and essential, the rattling bones of survival. The romance of the Greyhound and the Americana I'd been inhaling quickly disappeared. Under the strip lights, and among those sleeping on metal chairs, there was just life. Unrelenting, unforgiving, life.

For the second time in thirty-six years, an Uber driver asks me if I'd like him to wait with me. It is shortly after 4 p.m. the sun is still in the sky and I have arrived at my Airbnb in St Louis, Missouri, a state underneath Iowa, above Arkansas and in between Kansas and Tennessee. 'This isn't a great neighbourhood sweetie,' the driver, an old guy with a flat cap and crooked teeth, says over his shoulder. Once again, I say

I'll be fine and make my way into the apartment, irritated at the world reminding me I wasn't safe. My mum used to tell me I looked like a 'target'. I was never sure what she meant but I was beginning to suspect she meant that I look like a woman.

Still, it got to me. I message my Airbnb host. 'Do I need to take extra safety precautions?'

'No,' he wrote back. 'There's the occasional carjacking so you'll be fine.' For once safer, I smirked, without a car than with one.

A couple of days later yet *another* Uber driver relays his concern. 'I don't want to scare you or nothin',' he says, 'but St Louis is not a safe city. It has the most homicides in the country. I'm getting out as soon as I can.' It's particularly striking coming from a man who tells me he served in Iraq. I try to calm myself by reminding myself that I had lived in dangerous neighbourhoods in London for years. And I melt my nerves into anger, thinking of all the conversations Ed wouldn't be having with Uber drivers if he was doing the very same trip.

Yet, as much as I hadn't expected to be made so acutely aware of my own safety here – or lack of it – I had, in some ways, come to the city because it is on the verge of becoming a lot less safe for women. In 2021, it is home to the last remaining Planned Parenthood clinic in the state of over six million people. The clinic has been locked in a legal battle for a few years, as Republican state legislators try to find ways to close it down and make Missouri the country's first abortion-free state. This is the fight for women's bodily autonomy in real time. A giant banner hangs on the front of the building and tall blue letters proudly affirm: 'STILL HERE'. When I see the sign in person, from across the street, I am overcome with emotion, surprised to find red-hot tears push at the back of my eyes. After all the conversations I'd had over the last few weeks, those small words summarize so much of what I've heard: refusal to give up, resistance, persistence, day in, day out.

In Missouri, I'm in the state of congresswoman Cori Bush, the Black pastor and single mother of two who went from sleeping in her car with her children to the White House, fighting against eviction on behalf of families everywhere. It is also the state of Josh Hawley – a far-right Republican senator who, among many things, wants to overturn Roe, believes American masculinity is 'under attack' and used the QAnon dog-whistle of child abuse to target Ketanji Brown Jackson at her Supreme Court nomination. The battle lines here, like so many purple cities in the Midwest, are starkly drawn.

Still here. I take a picture, cross the street, and then, without much thought, I introduce myself to Kevin. Kevin is standing on the sidewalk by himself. A slim man, 72, in khaki shorts and a blue T-shirt with slight silver-framed glasses, he stands patiently with a placard around his neck that reads 'PRAY TO END ABORTION'. I'm not quite sure what has made me stop and talk to him, other than our proximity and our shared interest in the building behind us. I was looking for the stories of women, not the men who make their lives harder, but, as I'd explored in my own family, sometimes it is hard to have one without the other. And so there I was, asking him questions, spending a minute in the September sun trying to figure out why an educated man – a former Boeing engineer – spent his retirement intimidating women he'd never met.

For Kevin, it came down to his Catholicism and a video he'd seen that alleged the doctors that supported Roe v. Wade had done so under duress. When I ask him where he found this video, he replies unabashedly 'the internet', as if it is a famously trustworthy place. He uses words like 'human rights' and 'choice'. I find it perplexing. And I find it galling that this softly spoken man, tangled in a web of lies and faith that had blinded him into believing everything he saw and heard but never thinking to question any of it, or caring to learn about the lived experiences of the women who may visit the clinic, is so set in his convictions.

'What about the human rights of women?' I ask repeatedly. 'What about *their* choice?'

'Don't punish the baby for the father's crimes,' he says matter-of-factly. 'How is that fair?' He looks at me as if the cruelty is all mine.

Kevin is a true believer, not a political schemester, a man who is convinced that ending abortion is his life's work to ensure himself a spot in heaven. The righteousness of the church is his shield, the internet is his evidence and women are simply the collateral damage in his mission, certainly not to be entrusted with agency, self-determination, basic autonomy or dignity. It occurs to me that men like Kevin are *still here* and always will be, and then something snaps. I'm suddenly done.

I thank him for his time and he shrugs. 'Often people drive past and give me the finger.'

I bet they do, I thought, wondering if that's precisely what I should have done.

Despite all the warnings from the male Uber drivers, I like the neighbourhood I'm staying in here in St Louis. Nearby is a café with a picture of a young Michelle and Barack Obama on the wall, rainbow flags and posters supporting women's rights. Hipsters hover over MacBooks and staff join in on a particularly loud rendition of 'Take Me Home, Country Roads', a song that reminds me of American road trips with Ed, singing at the top of our lungs on endless highways. I'm wearing the same Topshop T-shirt as one of the staff, which is noted with much fanfare when I make my way to the till to order breakfast. In this corner of the city, the display of support for LGBTQ rights, women's rights and for the BLM movement borders on the aggressive. Shop windows are plastered in signs making it plain you're not welcome if you don't agree. All this messaging of love and acceptance comes across like a growling dog, determined to protect his owner and giving some indication of just how close the threat is.

Over a coffee, I take stock of the day ahead and it proves to be quite a day. In the UK, the sentencing of Metropolitan police officer Wayne Couzens had taken place in London, six hours ahead, and I start to catch up on the harrowing details. It is the first time the general public has learned what actually happened to Sarah Everard after she was kidnapped by Couzens in early 2021 and it's nothing short of a sadistic nightmare. It's hard to process by myself – the rage, the horror spreads across me like a rash. The cheery café starts to feel removed and distant, a different universe, out of sync with what I'm feeling. I check my email and an editor from London asks: 'Can you write something?'

I continue scrolling through the day's news and see three US representatives, all women of colour – Cori Bush of Missouri, Barbara Lee of California and Pramila Jayapal of Washington – are publicly discussing their abortions, including experiences of rape, at a committee on reproductive rights in the face of the recent Texan anti-abortion law. Gloria Steinem will also speak at this committee – all these years after she first did in the Methodist Church in 1969 in New York City. Women are, yet again, *still here*, enduring the personal agony of telling their stories. I start to wonder: how many times we can keep asking women to resurrect yesterday's trauma?

It is hard not to feel furious – at Kevin; at what befell Sarah Everard, a woman from London just a few years younger than me; at the chief of the Met police, Cressida Dick, insisting the man who murdered her was 'a bad un'; at the very recent murder of Sabina Nessa, a young woman walking to meet a friend on a Friday night, killed by a male stranger, just as Nicole Smallman and Bibaa Henry had been, in a London park, a year before, their deaths overlooked and under investigated because, their mother claimed, they were two women of colour. It is hard not to feel furious at a political system that has done so much to curtail women's rights, despite brave women sharing their most intimate stories. It's hard not to feel furious at constantly feeling unsafe on streets simply because I'm a woman. They are all squares in the same patchwork, continuing generation after generation after generation.

And as I sit in front of my laptop and coffee, trying to process the news, it strikes me that it's still so hard to be a woman. On both sides of the Atlantic. In the 'progressive', Western world. Old battles, ones women were fighting for when my mum made her trip across this part of the world, that have been raging against for decades, that perhaps we thought we'd won, are still taking place. Those battles are *still here*. And today it feels like we're losing.

Which is why, I think, that, for the first time on my trip,

I reach a roadblock. Something inside of me is punctured: *Has anything changed at all?* It's hard in this moment to remember Dean Williams' lessons of hope or Ann DeLaney's observations of progress or the persistence of women like Giovanna or Keea or Sue. Instead, all I can think about is how fifty-two years ago, Gloria Steinem and others shared their illegal abortion stories in a church in New York City. Now, *fifty-two years later,* I'm watching Steinem on my laptop screen fighting for the same thing again. But somehow it's worse because she's not demanding the creation of a right, she's demanding the protection of an existing one. And just as my mum had found herself in a history-making moment for women in the early 1970s, here I am too. But for all the wrong reasons.

Agitated, I head back to my Airbnb and channel my rage into 800 words before my deadline. The murder of Sarah Everard and abortion rights in the US are two very different situations but, ultimately, it's the same story. It all comes down to the same thing: the universal right for a woman's body to be safe from harm and free from control – and the refusal of far too many men to let this happen.

I spend the rest of the day at my Airbnb, trying to shake the feeling – or, perhaps, hiding away from the world. I spend time in the courtyard with a neighbourhood cat. I wash clothes that dry instantly in the insane heat. I try to catch up on some reading but can't focus. I meet my deadline, furiously banging away at a laptop for a few hours. I send some angry tweets about Couzens, chomping down on M&Ms, resisting the trendy cans of wine I'd found in Wholefoods until I feel calmer.

Eventually, I decide to head out to a smart Mexican restaurant I'd spotted a couple of blocks away. It's just past 7 p.m. and already pitch-dark but still so warm, the humid air against my skin like a blanket and a surreal contrast to the Halloween decorations that adorn every house on the street. The walk will take all of six minutes but that evening it feels far longer. The day has been a difficult one; I am furious and also afraid.

As I walk, I find myself in a position that millions of women do every day and have simply learned to accept as part of our reality. I'm looking over my shoulder, walking as fast as I can, one hand gripped around my phone in my pocket, my nails pressed into the palm of the other. There's hardly anyone around, the occasional crawling headlights putting me even more on edge. Despite my thudding heartbeat it is an uneventful walk. I make it to the restaurant and a woman pouring a glass of wine behind the bar looks up at me.

'I'll be right with you,' she smiles.

Instantly, my heart begins to slow down and I climb up onto a bar-stool.

'What can I get you?' she asks

'Erm . . .'

I'm hesitating and I can see she's looking at me as if she sees something she doesn't quite understand. 'Are you OK?' she asks.

'Yes,' I say, 'thank you.' I pause. 'Is this a safe neighbour-hood?'

A look of recognition spreads across her face. 'Sure. I live a fifteen-minute walk away.'

'Do you walk home from work?'

'I drive,' she says, awkwardly.

'Have you heard of Sarah Everard over here?'

As we're talking, the hostess comes up to me and interrupts. 'I just love your skirt! Wait, *where* are you from?!'

As she chats away, beaming at me, I wonder if they can tell, if they can see my fear, smell it? Are they always this kind and friendly? Maybe, but I feel something else. I feel an understanding, a circling of a sisterhood that says: 'We get it. We know. You're safe here.'

In St Louis, I learn about the sisterhood and not just from my new friends at the fancy Mexican restaurant. It is Saturday and rallies and marches are taking place across the country to protest the new Texas SB8 law, which bans abortion after the detection of a foetal heartbeat at six weeks, as well as ongoing erosion of abortion rights across the US, and the collective fear of what fate might befall Roe.

I make my way downtown. It's muggy; rain is in the air. By the time I arrive, stalls have been set up selling posters and pin badges. Volunteers are asking attendees to sign petitions. A small stage has been erected and women are milling around with homemade placards. Some are older, sitting down. 'We Are Ruthless' a banner reads, a reference to the death of Ruth Bader Ginsburg and a conservative Supreme Court that now has an anti-abortion majority. Nearby, three 20-year-olds with straight hair and painted nails stand together looking excited. It's their first rally, they tell me. They are chatty and giggly. We pose for a selfie together. There's a festival spirit as music is blaring and I spot a fantastic amount of eye glitter. This burst of positivity and optimism among the protesters is infectious, instantly reminding me of the hope – and the fight – that lies among these women.

The crowd starts to swell and spills over the other side of the road, then onto the steps of the old courthouse. Chants have started and anti-abortion protesters begin to arrive. One man is holding a placard with a particularly gruesome and offensive picture of what I assume is a dead foetus. Pretty soon, he's surrounded. Like a predator swallowing its prey to the narration of David Attenborough, in an impressively well-rehearsed manoeuvre, pro-abortion activists circle him, lifting up their banners and singing over him. Suddenly, he is completely hidden. State troopers patrol the area but seemed removed. The only time I see any action from them is when one trooper takes off his felt hat as it starts to rain to cover it in what I can only describe as a shower cap.

Speeches commence from local officials, activists and poets, as well as a representative from Planned Parenthood. The speakers today are all women of colour – a statement of intent, showing a deliberate reclaiming within the movement itself to reflect those who are most impacted. I'm particularly taken by a young Native American woman who speaks of her own abortion – a decision she believed was in the best interest of her family. Applause and whoops and whistles follow each speech, and the message is the same: *this is the fight of our lives.* Only later on would I realize how right they were.

There's a David and Goliath feel to the rally. This group of women, and some men, are up against the power and money of the Republican Party in an extremely red state, defending their last city under siege, surrounded on all fronts. In Missouri, there's one abortion clinic to the seventy-five so-called 'pregnancy clinics'. These 'clinics' purport to offer unbiased counselling to anyone facing an unplanned pregnancy but that is a cruel lie. The sites are used to lure vulnerable women, often via the offer of free services and provisions, such as nappies for their children or mental health support, only to dissuade them from terminations. They are built and paid for by the anti-abortion lobby and have an extremely strong online presence, catching the attention of girls and women googling for help and support via sophisticated and well-funded search engine optimisation (SEO) capabilities.

This Saturday morning, I can feel the commitment of the speakers and the crowds, however, I'd be lying if I said I couldn't sense a wariness, a tiredness. Here they are, again, fighting, fighting, fighting, against mostly white men and women whose laws disproportionately impact the most marginalized and the most vulnerable. Many have been in this fight for most of their adult lives, aware of both the inefficiency and precarity of the ruling of Roe v. Wade. They rallied for Planned Parenthood v. Casey in the 1990s. They marched against the Republican myth of 'partial-birth abortion' in the 2000s – a cynical, political spin on a medical study regarding a form of procedure for late-term termination. Once again, the right effectively used emotive language, suggesting it was an inhumane and horrific process, painting it as an insight into what the pro-abortion movement was truly capable of. The Partial-Birth Abortion Ban Act was decades in the making but held at bay under President Clinton, until, in 2003, President Bush, a staunch anti-abortion advocate, signed the Act, from which medical terminology was glaringly absent. It was upheld by the Supreme Court four years later, in 2007, and, for the first time in the thirty years since the passing of Roe, the court ruled to support the ban without any exception, including the mother's health. Abortion has been under attack consistently since it was recognized as a right in the 1970s and many of these women had been fighting for just as long. They have made these speeches before. They have held the same placards. They have turned out to protest more times than they can remember.

I mingle in the crowd as music plays, selfies are taken and young men and women dance. And then the rain comes. The prepared pull out raincoats and umbrellas. The efforts to hide the anti-abortion protests continue. As cars drive past, they honk their horns and we all cheer. Older women, in their sixties and seventies, tell me how long they've been doing this, tell me about their abortions. 'It saved my life,' one woman shouts into my ear over the music, her hood pulled tightly over her ears. She has tears in her eyes when I look at her.

The rain comes down harder, there's a rumble of thunder. Some leave but the determined stay. Young women are dancing like they are in the Glastonbury mud, joyous in the chaos, and I see there is hope and it is defiant. Despite the rain, despite the restrictions, despite the inevitable end of Roe. I might have lost my hope the day before but it doesn't matter because it is all still here, with or without me. In this moment, hope is dancing in the rain with new friends; hope is the belief that small efforts are worth it; hope is turning out on a Saturday with a couple of hundred strangers because *it is better to do than not do.*

Watching those women sing and shout and chant, I realize that this sort of rally is as much for them as it is for their opponents. In such a tough battle, moments of joy, of communion, of coming together with others who believe what you believe, is essential to keep going. The joy and the hope work in tandem; the women feed off each other. *We're still here. We*

– powerful, restorative, hopeful, encouraging, a never-ending well of resilience. *We*.

Soon the rain is too heavy and most call it a day, me included. I run into a place for shelter and grab some lunch. Unlike yesterday, I feel celebratory. Tomorrow, I think to myself, is always another day – a phrase my mum used to say to get me through a difficult time, and surely to herself too. Once the rain has eased off, I walk around downtown. I follow the tourist loop and pass under the city's landmark giant arch, down by the Mississippi and pass the first church in the city, on the banks of the river, before ending up back outside the old courthouse.

Later, I discover that this building, on whose steps protestors had stood hours before, bore witness to the very beginnings of two of the biggest social movements of the twentieth century. In 1875, Virginia Minor went in front of the state's Supreme Court here after she'd illegally voted in a St Louis election and had been arrested. It was also here, nearly thirty years earlier, in 1846, that Dred Scott argued for his and his wife's freedom as they had been held as slaves in free states. As it was for Minor, the Supreme Court did not rule in the Scott's favour when it heard the case in 1857, a decision which would in part spark the Civil War. While I was in awe of the history those walls contained, it was not a good omen for times to come – and a warning of just how long some battles take.

I've booked an Uber to take me back to the Airbnb and as I wait, I see that on the steps of the courthouse, a few people remain, nearly two hours since the crowds left. On the right of the steps, three anti-abortion protestors mingle, holding their vile banners, once more exposed to the world. And on the left, a single woman remains, drenched but determined. Every time the anti-abortion protestors chant, she chants louder. When cars honk or a passerby crosses the street, the woman yells 'STAND UP FOR WOMEN'S RIGHTS!'. Even from a distance I can see she is angry, tearful, frustrated, trapped in a painful limbo where anger and desperation merge and stubbornness is all that is left.

But she is still here. She is refusing to leave. I stand and watch, amazed at her persistence, getting the sense that she will not leave until her opponents have, that she'll be there till midnight if needs be, that by refusing to leave those steps, the right outcome will happen, somehow, that her commitment will win out, that her faith is ironclad, that this whole fight boils down to her and those three morons with their offensive placards. Just then my Uber pulls up. 'THANK YOU!' I yell from across the street raising my hand in a peace sign. She mirrors my action back and, for a moment, our eyes meet. For the second time in St Louis, I swallow back my tears.

All we need is each other, my mum would tell us when we were little. But she was wrong; we needed more. How would have things been if we'd had a sisterhood, a community?

Women don't abandon women

The next day, I meet Caroline Fan in the city's beautiful horticultural gardens. When Caroline arrives, she's finishing a phone call. She's talking about a launch meeting. Next she mentions dates and names. Then she suggests making a helpful introduction – all at lightning speed. There's something purposeful and on point in her tone, as if she is resourceful of every moment.

I will come to see that the phone call is a pretty good insight into who Caroline is.

Alongside consultancy for political campaigns, non-profits and entrepreneurial start-ups, Caroline is an avid volunteer and community organizer, regularly working with Heather Booth at the Midwest Academy – 'a national training institute committed to advancing the struggle for social, economic, and racial justice'.[48] Booth, the founder of Jane, came up in my first conversation with Laura Kaplan at the start of this trip and I take some small joy in the connection. Caroline also sits on numerous committees for the Democrats and leads community organizing efforts for the party (the process of educating and mobilizing others to help influence and support policy or culture change). Most recently, she was a core team member of the AAPI (Asian American and Pacific Islander) for the Biden team, mobilizing volunteer teams across the US to translate Biden's messaging into multiple Asian languages.

Organizing is something Caroline became involved in at college, interning with organizations that introduced her to trade unions, to politics and to how organizing works, and sent her to communities across the country that needed support in standing up against exploitation and injustice. She was most moved when she took part in an immigrant workers freedom ride in 2003. Buses carrying 900 immigrants and allies like Caroline set out from nine US cities. They went first to Washington DC, to lobby congress, and then to New York for one of the largest immigrant rallies in US history. As part of her work during this time, Caroline spent time in Oregon 'because I spoke a little Spanish. And I remember talking to these workers. One said she'd been a garment worker for twenty years and in that whole time, she only received a total combined raise of 50 cents per hour.'

Born to Taiwanese immigrant parents who wished for her to be a doctor, Caroline ignored their direct and specific pleas *not* to be an activist and has never looked back. Most recently, Caroline founded and become president of the Missouri Asian American Youth (MAAY) Foundation, the first state-wide AAPI non-profit to focus on civic engagement and youth leadership development. She also works to drive voter registration and support local independent business, and is passionate about representation, bringing AAPI congressmen and women to the state to show young people what is possible. With so many irons in the fire, it's easy to see why her phone calls have the urgency of Jerry Maguire's – but it's not money she's after. It's change.

Not only does she clearly possess time management skills I could only dream of, Caroline's commitment to public service and to building the sorts of communities she wants to see goes beyond a full-time job, or even overtime. The commitment is total and it is extremely impressive. Speaking and listening to Caroline is yet another moment on the trip when the efforts of the women I meet become an uncomfortable mirror: What, I wonder, am I doing? Where is my commitment?

When Caroline first arrived in Missouri from New York in 2014, she immediately got involved in the aftermath of the nearby Ferguson Uprising, the anti-police and racism protests that followed the murder of Michael Brown by a police officer. Caroline set to work, bringing AAPI and Black communities together, as well as helping locals rebuild their lives in the wake of damage to property and businesses. Her work can be ambitious, involving large numbers of people and powerful state leaders, building pipelines and lobbying for governmental reform. Or it can be small but just as transformative. In one case, she set up an elderly man in Ferguson with his first ever email address so she could connect him to pro-bono lawyers.

Caroline's work is the other side of the same coin of the rally I saw downtown the day before. If rallies are the fun part, the restorative part, the joy, then the work Caroline does is the graft: the showing up every day, not just when it's easy but when it's hard, painstakingly untangling a knot of regulations, laws, bureaucracy, and cultural and social prejudices that work against people who need the most help. But like the rally, it's always about building something better for others. This is what links the Carolines of today with the Laura Kaplans of yesterday; it is what Dean Williams believes is missing from today's social movements and it represents the commitment to community, to each other, that Keea is trying to protect.

Much has been written about the individualism of today's society – a neoliberalism born in the 1980s that has slowly eroded the notion of community. My mum, on behalf of Boomers everywhere, is forever complaining about 'Me-Me-Me-Millennials'. This criticism has been particularly lobbed at fourth wave feminism.

At first, after the backlash of the 1980s, and following the resurgence of a feminist movement in the 1990s with things like Riot Grrrl music scene, known as the Third Wave, the Fourth Wave of feminism was hopeful and promising – an online project that sought to awaken a new generation. Soon, there was momentum. But when that momentum tipped into full-blown mainstream acceptance, crystalized by Beyoncé performing in front of six-foot letters spelling out 'feminism' something shifted. Soon, a political movement with its roots in collective action and a community focus became about the celebration – and commercialization – of the self. Wealthy white women making mountains of money were hailed as feminist heroes simply for being rich. And it's not just feminism, either. Dean Williams' criticism holds true that much – though of course not all – social action has become about being a successful individual with a large social media following, increasingly divorced from the original issue they were allegedly fighting for.

But Caroline, Laura Kaplan and so many of the women I've met are different. There's no glory, no brand deals, no millions of social media followers. Instead, there is strategy, planning, agenda and the slog of door knocking or phone banking or frustrating local council meetings.

Caroline's drive comes from a personal place. Her parents emigrated to America in the early 1970s and she always felt an outsider. Growing up in Chicago, she was sent to a Catholic school – her family aren't Catholic – where she was bullied constantly. The school sent her to speech therapy lessons because of her accent. During high school, she worked in a branch of Baskin-Robbins when one day, she learned a white supremacist with a gun was on the loose. The realization hit her: she might not be safe simply because of who she was.

That awareness hasn't gone away. After 2016, Caroline noticed things changing. Going through security at an airport, she was 'manhandled' by a woman in such a way she felt violated and was taken into a separate room to be interrogated. When she tried to vote in a local election, Caroline faced an elderly white man who wouldn't accept her driver's licence as ID, despite the fact it was within the rules – and as a keen organizer of voter registration drives, Caroline knew this well. The man asked Caroline how he 'could really know where she was from'.

During the pandemic, hate crimes against the Asian American community soared. Caroline also points to the vicious anti-science, anti-vax sentiment stirred up by Trump and his supporters – especially in red states like Missouri. She felt her husband, an Asian American doctor, became a particular target and feared for his safety.

Caroline makes it clear that being an Asian American woman in the Midwest has never been easy. When she began her involvement with unions, she realized, for the first time, her own mother, a nutritionist in a hospital working 60–80-hour weeks, had been exploited, with no one to protect her or advocate for her. Despite her mother's fear of an activist life for her daughter, she was the motivation to try to make things better. Here I notice for the first time some similarities between Caroline and myself: seeing what our mothers experienced made us angry, and we want change. The difference is that Caroline is making that change. She's bridge-building, organizing, helping to register votes and now, in Missouri, working with anyone she can. 'In New York, at dinner parties over debates, they'd perhaps be 5 per cent of the discussion that you didn't agree on. Here, I start the other way round. I say to people, "Right, what's the 10 per cent we do agree on?"'

On my way back to the Airbnb, I think of Caroline disobeying her mother and following her own path in her early twenties, young and headstrong. Like my mum was. In contrast, I always wanted to please my mum and to some extent I had – I became a writer, like she'd once wanted to be. She's often told me I should be in 'harder news' or politics because that's her passion, and I've spent many hours thinking I've disappointed her, but still I've forged a career in journalism, meeting MPs, writing about hard-hitting issues from time to time and knowing that, for the most part, she's exceptionally proud of my career.

But through Caroline, I saw things differently. Caroline's mother had raised a daughter who felt a strong moral obligation to do what she believed was right, and that was to help other people. Her mother's ideal of a middle-class profession for her meant being safe, steady, respectable. But perhaps diverting or pulling away from our mothers is its own kind of compliment. Because these women have raised daughters who know their own minds, who follow their own paths. Our mothers can inspire and inform us, but perhaps the best gift of all they can give us is the courage to choose our own journeys, to write our own stories. The irony is not lost on me that I'm just figuring this out now, while following in my mum's footsteps.

When I first told my mum about the trip, she said, 'Couldn't you just do it on Zoom?' That was her fear, the protective mother, putting out a hand in front of me, keeping me from harm. But when I called her from the departure lounge at the airport in London, she was full of excitement for me, in awe at my undertaking. Breaking away from our mothers is progression, a move forward. And sometimes it's precisely because of a mother's love that it is possible. My mother broke away from hers and it changed her life. It was essential she did so to find the freedom she was chasing. I have always stayed close to my mother, under her wing, and to go against her like Caroline went against hers has, for most of my adult life, felt like a betrayal. But now I see that perhaps I'd got things the wrong way round. Now I see in some ways that would have been the biggest tribute of all.

I'm still in the city when I get a text from Caroline:

'Wanna meet Phyllis Schlafly's granddaughter?'

I re-read the message in disbelief and instantly reply: 'YES PLEASE'.

Phyllis Schlafly is a huge name in the fight against American women's rights in the twentieth century but not one really known in the UK, unless you saw Cate Blanchett's portrayal of her in *Mrs America* on BBC 2. I also suspect a fair amount of sexism has stopped Schlafly from having the historical weighting that some of her male contemporaries have received. But this is certainly not something that she'd ever admit.

Phyllis Schlafly, who first came to national attention in the mid-1960s, was one of the most outspoken opponents of the women's lib movement of her generation, famous for going to head-to-head with leading feminists, cracking 'jokes' about her husband 'letting her out' to 'wind up the women's libbers'. According to one former Republican activist, Ilyse Hogue writes, Schlafly 'unearthed the political gold of misogyny'.[49] In 1972, Schlafly founded the Eagle Forum – a conservative group she remained the head of until she died in 2016 that worked to push her agenda. She was a conservative Christian opposed to communism, abortion and homosexuality, and joined forces with the likes of Jerry Falwell to see Reagan in the White House. Her views were extreme, such as denying the existence of marital rape because marriage was consent enough, yet her main focus was stopping the Equal Rights

Amendment (ERA) from being ratified, something she is single-handedly credited with. Most states had signed on to the bill that would protect equality in the US constitution – and previous Republican presidents had been on board with it too. It was tantalizingly close. And then Schlafly got involved and slammed on the brakes. To this day, the ERA remains unratified.

Like a lot of persuasive leaders, Schlafly preyed on fears – if men and women are equal, she warned, women will be signed up for war and sent off to places like Vietnam. They will be unisex bathrooms – heaven forbid. Women, she said, should be in the home, raising children, being good wives. If equality came along, they wouldn't be allowed to do that. She spoke to white, Christian women from the rural and suburban middle and upper classes. Much like those Falwell was courting, her audience had something to lose as America was changing. And she was remarkably effective. After the wild success of her first self-published book, *A Choice Not an Echo*, in 1964, which sold three million copies, Schlafly went on to secure white women voters for Reagan, joining the union of Evangelicals and conservatives who spoke of traditional 'American values' in the face of the emerging liberal attitudes of the era.

A wife and mother of six herself, she was a political powerhouse and, just like Margaret Thatcher, the inconvenient exception to her own rules about how women should live her lives. Schlafly was a contradiction in many ways – while she advocated women being in the home, she was out working. Though she advocated being a good wife, she was outspoken, political, ambitious and married to her career. She believed women should stay in the home but her mother had worked to support the family when her father lost his job in the Great Depression.

It's probably obvious that I am no fan of Schlafly but as someone interested in the lives of American women, I was extremely intrigued to meet her granddaughter – especially as I had been thinking so much about what gets passed down over generations. Would her granddaughter, Sarah, be like her? Would she agree with her grandmother's politics?

Over a short Zoom call, Sarah Schlafly is quiet but friendly and polite. And she's happy to talk about her grandmother, offering a perspective none of the books or articles I'd read could give me.

'I first realized my grandmother was different when I saw her in one of my eighth grade textbooks when I was about 13, but I didn't give it that much thought, to be honest. I was at a conservative school and the portrayal of her was kind. It was when I attended a liberal college that I began to realize my grandmother's notoriety. That's when I went back and did more reading and research. It was shocking at first. I didn't agree with her on a lot of things.' For example, her grandmother's stand on women's rights or her blind support of Donald Trump, who Schlafly described in her twenty-seventh and final book as an 'old-fashioned man', a complimentary nod to the traditional values she believed he upheld. According to Schlafly, Trump, a man with as nearly as many allegations of sexual harassment against him as the number of books penned by Schlafly, really only cared about two things: 'hard work and family'.

Although she remained politically at odds with her grand-mother, Sarah's feelings towards her began to change when

Sarah went out into the world. 'Starting my own business at 21 drove me to be a lot more fond of my grandmother,' she tells me. 'That really changed my perspective on her and gave me mad respect for her because to spark a movement like that is very, very difficult. How she got things done, how she managed to persuade so many people, how influential she was – it was incredible. It's definitely something I try to learn from.' Sarah's grandmother also had a more liberal attitude towards her granddaughter than the one she transmitted to her thousands of followers. Sarah's first investor in her sustainable protein company? Phyllis. And, Sarah believes, she has inherited some of her grandmother's ambition to be successful and have a family. 'When my mom saw me taking my baby to my work meetings, she said, "You know, you're just like Phyllis."'

When her grandmother passed away, Sarah took from her desk a small plastic cube on which are the words 'It CAN be DONE'. 'Sometimes I go to YouTube to remind myself of her and how effective she was. It's something I try to apply to my own work,' she says. A few days before her death, Schlafly was telling Sarah she was too busy and had more books to finish writing. Three days later, she was holding Sarah's hand when she died.

Sarah, like me, is looking at the women who came before her to figure out her path forward. She tells sweet anecdotes about time spent with Schlafly and, I sense, avoids saying anything too negative about her grandmother. She doesn't touch on the impact Schlafly had on women's progress, instead praising Schlafly the individual. She talks of a kindly grandmother, not the face of a movement that did its best to keep women in the home, tied to domesticity and warned of the 'horrors of homosexual marriage'.[50] But I don't push Sarah; I'm not expecting her to answer on behalf of Schlafly, to speak for what many would consider the hate, the discrimination and the rejection of the progress of women that her grandmother embodied. I'm not convinced that we are answerable for the crimes of our family members. Instead, in this instance, I am far more interested in *how* her granddaughter chooses to tell the story of both her grandmother *and* Phyllis Schlafly, to me, a stranger. How she constructs the narrative, joins the dots.

Sarah is most animated when she points out how many things the FX/BBC 2 drama got wrong about Schlafly, details about family life that don't fit family memories. A fierce criticism is that the programme's researchers and producers failed to speak to Schlafly's family members directly, instead building their own narrative of Phyllis. And I get that: Sarah is one of the guardians of the story of Phyllis Schlafly and that, I guess, is why she agreed to speak with me – to set a record 'straight', to offer the approved family narrative. Sarah, after all, will feel ownership over the story of Phyllis, both her personal and public persona. I have learned on this trip that family stories are hard to reach but they can also be hard to tell. Doing so under the glare of the spotlight, and when that family member exerted such national influence, must be even more complicated.

In St Louis, where Phyllis lived, Sarah says the Schlafly name still opens doors for her, a mark of the ongoing loyalty to a famous resident in a Republican state. But the local celebrity status is not what Sarah appreciates about her grandmother, she tells me. It was her commitment, dedication, drive and belief – all the qualities I admire in the women I've met on my travels and, however much I disagree with her, can't deny were in Schlafly.

It's easy to feel a particular scorn for women like Schlafly – and Thatcher – because their anti-feminist agenda feels like an even greater betrayal than if coming from a man, as not only were they women but working mothers with big, lofty ambitions. It's not just the refusal to acknowledge this blatant contradiction – and the hypocrisy – it is the sting of the attack coming from someone who should, in theory, be on your side. Madeleine Albright's famous words about hell and women who don't help other women ring loudly whenever I think of either of them.

I'm reluctant to offer up internalized misogyny as an answer to the riddle of them even if that is partly true because it feels like an easy excuse. And, as ever, I'm sure the bible and their faith is a reliable alibi for those who chose to see it that way. I also have no doubt there are some compelling arguments that women of their generation – they were born a year apart, Schlafly in 1924, Thatcher in 1925 – who wanted to lead, especially in a political arena, felt pressure to behave 'like men', distancing themselves from the women they spoke to. To be listened to, they arguably needed to be perceived as different from other women; they had to be the exception in order to be permitted so much power and influence. But these possible reasons don't feel like they go all the way to explaining the enthusiasm these two women had for denying others rights and opportunities. Part of me is very willing to accept that Schlafly and Thatcher were women who simply didn't like women.

During my time in St Louis, I had been thinking about sisterhood. In my opinion, Schlafly held millions of women back but she indisputably created her own loyal community.

Women don't abandon women, Laura Kaplan had told me. Fascinatingly, I'm sure Schlafly would have said the same.

In St Louis, I walk into a feminist eutopia.

The low, brick building with tall windows in a run-down part of town is unremarkable, other than a small silver sign that reads 'Rung for Women'. I walk through the car park past a small vegetable garden and into an ice-cool air-conditioned reception. Once inside, I feel like I've entered a tech HQ in Silicon Valley – new furnishings, murals on the wall, exposed brick, low chairs and glass doors. But unlike at a tech HQ in Silicon Valley, I see exclusively women, coming and going.

I'm met by Ali Hogan and Leslie Gill, respectively the founder and president of Rung for Women, an organization built to help women earn over $50,000 a year (around £40,000), a figure that is seen as a significant baseline in the US, a threshold over the poverty line that can move them up the socio-economic ladder. Rung offers places to women who have a stable history of employment, who have secure housing and who are committed to months of self-development and applying themselves in order to access better pay and better opportunities. Most of their applicants are women of colour and single parents and all are keen to improve their lot, to escape a low-income life and the stresses and strains that come with it. Women apply to Rung to obtain skills that can help propel them forward in an economic system that is historically known for holding back Black women and single mothers through low, conditional benefits that trap families in poverty and ingrained, systemic racism. In the US, Black women are typically paid just 64 cents for every dollar paid to white, non-Hispanic men.[51]

Rung begins with a six-month cohort-based programme and each member has their own personal coach. After that, the coach remains an accountability partner as the member navigates her own individualized path through the Rung program, which takes between a further six to eighteen months. Additionally, participants have access to a crèche, a gym, yoga, counselling, gardening, finance and healthy cooking lessons. This is all for free.

My British instincts take over and I don't ask the big question, the one I can't get past in my head: *who the hell is paying for all this?* Instead, I listen as they start to explain how the programme works. I slip up when I suggest that the women accepted to the course 'need help'. 'They don't need help. They have had a lifetime of handouts. They need to be *empowered*,' Leslie says, echoing Megan Jeyifo in Chicago. A lot of their applicants are survivors of domestic abuse and are slowly rebuilding their lives. Yet again, when having conversations about the lives of women, it seems I'm only ever a sentence or two away from male violence.

I am extremely taken by the focus on empowerment and sustainable economic independence, the ingredients so crucial to freedom. And, most impressively, everything offered here is in one place. This is a holistic one-stop shop where kids can be watched; mental health support can be accessed; women can work out, learn how to eat and cook healthily, and be coached towards better career and earning prospects. Its simplicity and its purpose feels revolutionary. That said, it's not without its challenges. The impact of social media seeps in everywhere.

'A lot of the women want to be influencers,' sighs Ali. 'I mean, where do you start with that?' I echo Ali's question back at her. 'We have to tell them it's not stable,' she replies.

Finally, my curiosity gets the better of me: 'Who has paid for all this?' I ask, expecting a long list of grants, fundraising, maybe even local businesses.

There's a pause.

'I did,' says Ali.

Ali inherited *a lot* of money from her philanthropist grandfather, who encouraged her to do something good with it. As a single mother herself, she knew instinctively who she wanted to help – and she knew she wanted to create something that allowed women to be self-sustaining. She employed Leslie to run the operation, knowing she wanted an African American woman at the helm.

I want to tell her that I am the daughter of a single mother and that's why I'm here, sitting across the boardroom table from her with a Dictaphone and notebook. I want her to know that I am in awe of someone, somewhere, finally, prioritizing single mothers, especially single mothers who have been through trauma, investing in them, believing in them, spending huge sums of their own money on them, putting them in buildings normally reserved for tech bros or others at the top of the corporate ladder. I can't help but wonder what such a place could have done for my mum and something tugs inside me, not for the first time. So many of the routine barriers have been overcome here: cost, time, childcare. When I was growing up, childcare was expensive; my mum was always driving from the station to the childminders, back home, to the supermarket, to school – always so busy. Here are women trying to make things easier for women. And because of that, there is a tenderness to it, a sisterhood.

A recent Pew study from 2022 showed American attitudes towards single mothers regressing, with nearly half of all Americans believing single mothers and their children are a problem, up from 7 per cent in 2018.[52] Yet, despite that, this building, in a run-down neighbourhood, houses boarded up across the street, is a temple to hope and progress. Inside, women's resilience is not only recognized but rewarded. The existence of Rung tells a very interesting American story about the absence of a solid welfare state, but it also tells another about human empathy and allyship. Ali tells me she is 'socially liberal and fiscally conservative'. Her act of philanthropy is one of Republican tradition, where the wealthy step in and help precisely because they don't believe it is the government's job to do so. This practice comes with its own problems of course, such as contributing to potentially problematic power dynamics – who pays and who is deemed worthy of investment. That is all a conversation that needs to be had and another reason why Ali put Leslie, a woman of colour with expertise in the field, in charge, not herself. Yet one thing is unmistakable: Ali has put her faith in these women; she has invested in them and there is no sense of pity. Just a quiet belief in all they could be if the world was fairer.

I once saw a journalist – a single mother – talk about her 'radical happiness'. I think of that in Rung. Here there is 'radical happiness': a happiness found where society tells you there is none.

That evening I head back to the Mexican bar; it's my third visit in four days. After almost a month on the road, I'm grateful for the familiar faces. The staff all squeal when I walk in, delighted to see me, like I'm part of their gang. Without asking, a beer is poured and tortillas are placed. The hostess, Nicola, comes up for a chat. She's skinny and cool, with a little pink heart tattoo on her collarbone and white-blonde hair that sits just on her shoulders. She asks about my day. The first couple of times we met, I just mentioned I was in town for work and not much else but as I'm leaving town soon, I tell her about the women I've met in St Louis, the rally, my journey following my mum's footsteps, the conversations I've had about women's rights. She looks intrigued and then she stands a little bit closer.

'I had abortion,' she says in a hushed, conspiratorial voice.

So much of my job as a journalist is persuading people to talk. But sometimes it's not really in what I say. Often it's creating a space in which women think they will be heard.

'Could you afford it?' I ask.

'Just about. It was $500. And then I missed two days of work, unpaid. And I felt pretty rough. The guy I was seeing didn't offer any support either. But you know, I'm privileged. I don't have kids. I could get the time off.' Her smile is sad, resigned. She looks away for a second before her face brightens again.

'Another drink?'

'Why not?' I give her the kindest smile I can. 'Thank you for sharing your story with me.'

'No problem,' she says. 'Time for margaritas.'

I eventually say goodbye to Nicola and the other kind staff who almost feel like friends, or who feel like they would become friends in the alternative ending where I stay in Missouri for good. Instead, I make the short walk back to my Airbnb, occasionally looking over my shoulder. I think about Nicola sharing her story with me and then about all the women's stories I've heard. I think about how, since I've been on this trip, the individual stories have morphed from a few hushed murmurs to something more like a choir, a collection of different voices singing one song – one of injustice and pain, but also resilience. Resilience and hope.

Yet in this choir of voices, I realize there is one voice missing: mine.

Despite my profound love of storytelling and my blind faith in all it can achieve, I have kept my own story untold. In all the thousands of words I've ever written in newspapers and magazines and online, my story has been omitted. But there was something in the way that Nicola told me about her abortion, straight out, like a hand outstretched, that finally reached something inside of me. I'd long suspected that in order to be faithful to storytelling, in order to tell this story as it deserves to be told, authentically and honestly and bravely, that one day it would be my turn.

On this trip I had collected stories from 20-year-olds to 80-year-olds. Women shared their stories, their mother's stories, their grandmother's stories, their daughter's stories. They offered them as a way to answer the questions I put to them, to explain the unravelling of women's rights, to find hope in the face of setbacks, to describe their own experiences of being dehumanized and disenfranchised. They told me their story – which often contained their deepest vulnerabilities – so that maybe it would help a woman somewhere further down the line or play a part in the bigger, broader picture so that womanhood can move forward, inch by inch.

Women's stories are powerful but they can be fragile and painful. They're not always easy to share; reliving forms of trauma is not always cathartic. Sometimes there is nothing to gain from giving away a piece of yourself, one you hadn't wanted the world to know. And that is why storytelling can take great courage, because if you take the most fragile and painful part of you, and you share it with the world, it is a gamble. You are gambling that it will help you and another woman, another person. It might. It might not. But either way, you are sharing your story in the belief that it might mean something, that it might matter, that you might matter. In the very act of storytelling, there is hope and there is resilience and there is sisterhood and community. And while it is a form of unpaid labour – something women know only too well – it can be a liberation. Because, perhaps, finally, you control the story, it doesn't control you. The story is yours.

So, here, in St Louis, Missouri, I finally accept that I need to tell my story. If I am going to be brave, if I am going to seek liberation, if I am going to do the work that I believe I should. And maybe now, after hours on Greyhound buses, it is the beginning of another journey. And in that hot October moment, a few weeks away from my thirty-sixth birthday, I know it is finally time.

'James!' my mother screams, 'Call the police, he has a knife!'

My brother and I are in the living room, in our pyjamas, feet bare. We must have been woken up by the noise and come downstairs. The kitchen door is almost closed. We are frozen to the spot.

We cut men out of photographs in my family. But I took things one step further. I wrote my stepfather clean out of my life. When

I started writing publicly, he simply didn't exist. I erased him. And for a time, I felt fraudulent. I was a champion of single parents but my mother had remarried. I wrote myself a story where he didn't exist.

They were married for twenty years. On her wedding day, I was 10 and wore a velvet navy blue dress that hovered just above my ankles, with white tights and black ballet pumps. I wanted to look like Aurora at the end of Sleeping Beauty as she dances and the fairy godmothers change the colour of her dress from blue to pink and back to blue. My hair was in ringlets. I was her only bridesmaid.

She was, of course, still a single mother; she had been for the first 10 years of my life, 14 years of my brother's, and she continued to be after he moved in. She paid for us entirely, she parented us entirely, she did everything: cooked, cleaned, everything. He just happened to be in the house, occasionally offering a lift to the station. And it would have been better if she had been a single parent in the traditional sense, alone in the house. But she wasn't. One time, on a cold Tuesday school night, we fled to a McDonalds for safety. My mother sat us in a corner, tucked away, in the upstairs of the restaurant, trying, I see now, to hide us as best she could. We caught our breaths, until he walked in. I learned never to underestimate the cunning of abusers.

In the 2020 Domestic Abuse Act, thanks to work of women like Labour MP Jess Phillips, children who witnessed domestic abuse growing up are recognized as victims in their own right. When this Act was passed, it felt like coming up for air. All those years, I'd often questioned if anything had ever really happened to me, holding myself together as if nothing had *happened at all. I had no bruises, no proof. But one study suggests that children who grow up in violent homes have the same levels of PTSD as soldiers returning from war.*

When she left him and pressed charges, the police told her there wasn't enough 'evidence'. Those words collapsed our lives into nothing. We are the evidence, I wanted to scream. Everything about who I am, everything I do, every step on this journey is the evidence. My existence and experiences had been invalidated. We didn't exist. How could we if there was no evidence of this world we lived in for twenty years?

The shadow of him and those years never leaves. It's there when I walk alone at night. When I wake up startled from a dream, jump nervously as a door slams, when I report on domestic abuse or rage against men controlling women's lives in any way they can. When I board a Greyhound bus, it is there. When I step into an Uber late at night, it is there. But so is her strength. Her survival. Her resilience. Her fierce and furious love.

I feel a deep sense of shame as these words come loose from some dark private place. This was the one story I took great pride in not telling, hiding my private wound, giving nothing away. I have been so proud of my thirty-year-long poker face. The thought of exposure is paralysing, almost. But the women of the Midwest have made me realize that we need to take our anger and turn it into action. That the time to do something is now. And so I offer up this wound of mine. And I say: I am the evidence. Here it all is. In me. In my mother's story, in all these women's stories. We are the evidence. As we always have been, for decades, for centuries.

CHAPTER EIGHT

Omaha, Nebraska:
Back to the future

Arrivals
June, 1974

She can't believe she's finally here: Omaha bus station. The heat feels suffocating as she stares at the men in their cowboy hats. She's tired and anxious that she can't see June, wondering if maybe she's gotten the date wrong or forgotten she's coming. But then, here she is, beaming as she walks through the door, a touch of home.

'Hi honey!'

'June, why didn't you tell me?' she gasps.

'If I'd told you, you wouldn't have come,' June says, giving her a sly smile. June is pregnant for the tenth time.

June drives them back to the house. On the way, Jacqui spots strange silver objects on long thin legs sitting on the lawns of all the houses they pass. 'What are they?' she asks, thinking they look like something from space. June looks. 'Those?' she laughs. 'That's a barbecue, honey.'

*

The next three weeks are a brilliant injection of pure suburban Americana under the cloudless blue skies of a Midwestern summer. June's small army of kids follow Jacqui around, in between splashing in the plunge pool in the garden to manage the 40°C heat. The little ones climb on her lap and hold her hand, enthralled by their pretty cousin with her English accent. The older ones take her to the local lido, where a boy called Richard carves her name in a gate and they tease her when she can't tell the difference between Pepsi and Coke. In the evenings, over the pool table, she gets drunk on bottles of American beer. One day, Joe, the eldest, takes her on a drive to show her how fast his car can go – a low and metallic 1960s muscle car. They go to a drive-in and see *The Poseidon Adventure*, starring Gene Hackman, and at night, she shares the basement with Vicky, the eldest daughter, that also doubles up as shelter when the tornadoes come. Vicky smokes in bed in the dark and it's the coolest thing Jacqui has ever seen.

But she especially loves spending time with June. They talk and talk and talk – delighted to see each other, June thrilled to have a piece of Essex in Nebraska. Sometimes at the beach, sometimes at the kitchen table after dinner over wine, but always talking for hours on end. Four hours waiting in an antenatal clinic passes without much notice because they're too busy chatting.

Jacqui is impressed by everything in Omaha; she loves it all, thrilled with every minute she spends – even despite the homesickness of missing her boyfriend, Tom. And she's particularly mesmerized by the hallmarks of American life: the drive-ins, the high school car park packed full of cars, the big gardens and big houses, the wide cars and even wider roads. But it's the endless plains that make her catch her breath. Driving out through the great plains is like nothing she's ever seen – the space, the sky that rolls on forever more, the horizon that looks like it can never be reached, the heat-scorched grass, the earth humbling her to America's impossible size. This is what she will remember. This is what she will think of when *OmahaNebraska* rolls off her tongue like a song when she tells her children about that trip decades later. It will be the endless plains that rejuvenate her and push her on. It will be this landscape, alien to anything she'd ever seen, but now forever alive in her imagination, that will become a calling to all that she could be. It is this idea of the plains, and all their unknown possibility, that she will pass on to me and my brother – the desire to explore a country that might, somehow, as it did for her, inspire, push us on and tell us something about ourselves.

One night, just before she's due to fly home, her cousin Danny takes her fishing. As they sit by the lake, the soft silence of the summer evening is punctured only by my mum inhaling a cigarette and remarking with delight as she watches fireflies. And here, in all this peace, drenched in a blue-pink light, she is content and happy with her great adventure. America is proving to be everything she hoped. In that moment, something opens up again inside her, something she thought she'd lost in the fog of being unsettled and unsure in London. Instead of feeling overwhelmed, she now feels excited and ready for what is coming next.

When I'm back in the UK, a few months after my trip, my mum messages me to say she's been clearing out old boxes in the attic and she's found the notebook she took with her to visit Aunt June in the 1970s.

'Can I see it?' I ask

'Maybe.'

A few weeks later, I try again and this time she agrees.

'Some of it will be redacted,' she says, and I laugh.

When she next visits she brings the small yellow pad. It's a legal pad, ruled and with two thin red lines running vertically down the left-hand side. There's a navy stripe across the top. She bought it in America. It has the price on (29 cents) and a Dayton, Ohio, business address printed in small letters in the top right-hand corner. Her handwriting is identical to now and the pad is bleached with age and time. The paper feels fragile, a few of the pages now loose.

I thought she'd been joking but parts of the notes really are redacted. Some of the pages are only two-thirds long, the last part neatly cut away, some missing entirely. Like with a government document threatening national security, clearly some thoughts were simply off limits – even to, or maybe especially to, her daughter. There are no clues given to even the themes of the redacted content. It's just erased. The women in my family are good at telling half stories and making them seem whole. This, I've learned, is the way we are. I have proved adept at it too. But it reminds me that when we go looking for people, there will simply be things they don't want us to know, and that we don't have the right to know. Even when I've asked my mum about her memories, and told her about this trip and what I've been looking for, there have been lines drawn I know I can't – and won't ever – be able to cross. There are places I can't access, questions I've never uttered, stories she's never told, even to her daughter, her close confidant. Perhaps some mothers and daughters don't have those lines. But I suspect most do. I suspect that, as humans, there are some things we simply cannot tell our children. We want to pass down some things to our daughters but not everything because life isn't always a lesson; sometimes it is just painful, or a mistake or misguided, or simply ours and ours alone. And as much as women's stories can save us, it should always come down to choice if they tell them or not.

October 2021

I step off the bus and, like my mum did, I can't believe I'm here. I've made it. I see no cowboy hats but I do spot a man in cowboy boots decorated with the American flag.

Omaha is slap bang in the middle of the country. It's also the place on my itinerary that raised the most eyebrows when I mentioned it. An elderly man I got chatting to in a coffee shop in St Louis told me, 'There's nothing there, just insurance companies. The only time I go there is to drive through it – and that's enough.' My American friend in London offered to make introductions to friends of hers in the states I was to visit. Her list was extensive until we got to Omaha: 'I've got nothing,' she said. When I told my friend in New York I would be finishing in Omaha, she looked surprised. 'Wow. Good luck.'

I'm thrilled to have reached my final destination and I'm extremely relieved to have stepped away from Gregg. My final Greyhound ride was the one part of my trip where I'd had to sit at the back of the bus. When it picked us up, it was already full of passengers and the only free seats were at the rear. I ignored the chorus of voices in my head that had previously warned me against sitting at the back, knowing this was a long journey and I wanted a seat.

Gregg was sat behind me. I'd first been alerted to him when he tapped me on the shoulder. I turned around and looked through the gap in the headrests. 'You dropped something, Miss.' I was pretty sure I hadn't and thought it was just an excuse to chat, though it did turn out that he was right – an earbud. I smiled and turned back around. A few minutes later, he tapped my shoulder again. My heart sunk. I turned around begrudgingly to find him holding up a bag of Reece's Pieces, smiling. I politely accept and said thank you. Gregg wanted to know where I was from. When I told him he christened me 'Miss England'. 'Take a couple, Miss England!'

Soon after, I heard him open a can and got a distinct smell of beer. My heart plunged another level down. I turned up my music and hoped that was the end of our exchange. But a short while later, his phone rang. He chatted away in a rich, deep drawl, using creatively explicit language, punctuated by a long, loud laugh.

I felt another tap on the shoulder. By this time, my heart was somewhere in the pit of my stomach. He hadn't been aggressive but I knew I didn't want to talk. Something felt . . . off. 'Hey, Miss English. Speak to my cousin, Davey.' And with that he held his mobile phone out to me, 'go on, take it.' He looked at me as if this was an entirely normal situation. Unsure of what else to do, I took the phone, holding it extremely carefully, timidly, like it was an alien object I'd never seen before. 'Erm, hello . . .?' And sure enough, Davey, Gregg's cousin, who I learned had recently been released from jail, asked me how

I was and if I was enjoying my trip. We chatted politely for a few minutes before I handed the phone back over. Gregg nodded, giving me a look that suggested he was happy to do me the favour.

At first I was confused by my encounter with Gregg and his cousin. Then amused. And now I'm really not. I'm aware that this man sitting behind me on the bus, in his fifties, with cans of beer and oceans of confidence, was intimidating. I had played along out of a mild fear of what could have happened if I hadn't. I felt the precarity of my position, the power of his. I went along with his game as a strategy to keep safe, to keep Gregg – a man I'd never met – happy, however minor or innocent his demands were. I see the ambiguity of friendliness and it has left me on edge.

As I collect my luggage from the hold, I wonder if I am overthinking the encounter but the feeling won't shake. I'm aware that my whole body feels huge relief to be away from him. At least it will make a good story, I tell myself. And haven't we all got so many 'good' stories like that? Stories that exist in the grey, that men might find funny, but women will catch that look in your eye and find in it something else entirely. Stories that we'll never truly understand but we'll always remember exactly how they made us feel.

I'm only in the city for a couple of days and I'm staying downtown. My hotel appears empty, aside from a teenager wearing a T-shirt with 'Jesus' written across in a graffiti font and who wishes me a blessed day whenever I see her. Omaha looks similar to a lot of the other Midwestern cities I've seen – especially downtown: office blocks, Starbucks, wide boulevards. The old town has been turned into a collection of hip shops selling vintage furniture and expensive coffee. But there is an empty feeling here that I didn't notice elsewhere, as if it's partially deserted.

I'm well aware that being car-less in this part of the world means I can see very little. And, despite what I've heard, I'm looking at this city through the filter of my own personal wonder. After all, this is the place my mum always made sound mythical and otherworldly, that sounded and felt so far away when she told me about it, that had a transformative effect on her. It was where she'd passed through the looking glass or the wardrobe or some other portal into a different world. Yes, it is unmistakably middle America but it was something else, too. It was the start of it all.

Crawling forward

I meet the embodiment of the city's future while I'm there. Or at least, that's the impression Morgann Freeman leaves me with. We meet in a café and sit on the pavement, making the most of the early evening sun. The café, I notice, is covered with stickers decrying fascism, supporting local Democratic candidates and championing human rights issues. It's as I've seen before in these Midwestern cities: pockets of liberals sticking together, loudly and proudly defending their beliefs, almost aggressively, to the Trump voters around them. Nebraska is a mostly red state, especially in the rural areas, but the nearby city of Lincoln and parts of Omaha showed support for Barack Obama in 2008 and most recently for Joe Biden in 2020.

Morgann is extremely impressive. At 30, she's confident, astute and outspoken. She's progressive, political, an activist and a community organizer. At 28, she ran as the first Black woman candidate for Congress in the state's 153-year history, which not only reflects her ambition but gives telling insight into the state of Nebraska.

Morgann and her husband, a doctor, are settled here, to some extent. Her husband loves his job, they have a nice house and she's running a campaign for her friend who wants to be mayor. But she is at fundamental odds with so much about the city. During a Black Lives Matter (BLM) protest, which Morgann helped organize after the murder of George Floyd, demonstrators found themselves being attacked as police mobilized SWAT teams. 'There were families present, my pregnant friends were there, there were elderly people there. There were disabled people there. And then they were tear gassing people without warning.' Morgann livestreamed the whole thing, as the police used flashing canisters and pepper bullets against the protestors. Morgann was hit with the tear gas and collapsed, unable to breathe. 'It was absolutely terrifying. I started choking. I was retching. I burst blood cells in my eyes. I couldn't find my husband. In the end, I passed out. Luckily I was pulled to safety.' What impact did that experience have on you? I ask. 'I no longer feel safe here,' she says.

Do you ever think of leaving, I ask. 'All the time. We're ready to go. But where is there a safe place for someone like me?' To be an outspoken and progressive young Black woman comes at the high price of not feeling safe, especially in red states. 'Although, to be fair, I cause trouble wherever I go,' she says. The feeling of attack is on two fronts: being non-white in America and being an activist.

When Morgann was campaigning for Congress she found herself talking to constituents who kept Confederate flags in their house. But in 2020, a lot of people, she said, were open to conversation, to have their minds changed. 'One man said to me, "What about those liberals trying to take away my guns?" I said, "Hold on, sir. I'm a liberal. I don't want to take your guns. In fact, I come from a military family, my military family would be pissed. That's not what this is at all. We're just saying, we want to stop the mass shootings. Don't you want to stop those too?"

'When I was running, I started to see the other side of people, people as a whole. And I started having conversations as a candidate, where I was sitting down in people's living rooms or in their kitchens, talking about what kind of changes that they wanted to see in their community. I was sitting down with everyone. I wanted to talk to everyone, at least in the beginning, because, at the end of the day, I'm going to represent everyone. And I wanted to make sure that everyone felt seen. I recognize that, once we get past partisanship, once we actually build up the issues, we're not as far apart as we think we are. We all want to have safe, healthy communities; we all want our families to have an opportunity to thrive economically, socially and politically. It's about having some real conversations about the things that we need, that our families need, our neighbourhoods need. And I was sitting down and talking to people I would have never expected to talk to, people from the hard right.'

But now, just a year and a bit later, she says it feels impossible;

division has buried too deep. 'So much has changed. The racial tension, the brainwashing of so many people on the right, like conservatives, as well as moderates. And it's been like a slow progression towards radical Eurocentric white supremacy for fifteen years.'

This division, if left unchecked, will have big consequences. Morgann believes we're 'two election cycles away from revolution' unless something changes. And it's not impossible to see why she thinks that, in light of 6 January, the 'Big Lie' and police brutality, in such a divided nation where facts and science can't be agreed on. The one constant refrain I've heard over the last month is the line in the sand caused by 6 January. I suspect it's too soon, too recent, to understand the full ramifications, but for the women I've spoken to in their seventies and eighties, to the young women I've met in their twenties and thirties, and all those in between, the storming of the capitol upended America, shifted something. And young people in particular don't feel safe.

In St Louis, I met Hannah, a student at Washington University. After an incident on campus when a student had demolished a 9/11 memorial in protest of how little respect the lives of those killed by American military in the Middle East receive, the university's Republican group filmed the act of demolition and sent it to Fox News who aired the video. The next day, Hannah and the rest of the university received an email from the FBI warning them not to go to campus because the Proud Boys had threatened to come and cause trouble. This misogynistic and racist militia group has a history of violence and hate. Hannah, from a Jewish family, was nervous about going to her own university.

Morgann is a young woman who wants to change the world she lives in but, unlike many in the generations before her, the hope is buried, harder to access, not encased in a blind belief of what can be achieved. 'To be honest,' she says, 'I have no clue where we're going to be in a year, where me and my husband will be, where this community will be. I don't know where the United States will be, or even the world, unless something starts to change.'

I sense Morgann doesn't have faith that social movements can change the world, that it's all theirs for the taking, in the same way Natalia and Laura spoke about being young in the 1970s. Instead, in Morgann, I see anger, agitation, struggle and fear.

'I'm consulting on a campaign right now for a Black woman running for district attorney and I'm a police abolitionist activist, and that's a really uncomfortable place to be, but I think we've allowed people to remain incapable of having tough conversations about the full landscape of our realities. Just look at the military. Both of my parents are veterans. And I am very much against increasing our defence budget, I'm very much against American imperialism. So many of our troops are terrible people. Especially after 9/11. And now we're twenty years into a conflict that has completely destabilized that entire region. And we've literally created not just our own worst enemy, we've created the world's worst enemy. It's bullshit.'

'I'm really terrified of what would happen if America goes towards a civil war,' she tells me, the threat of 6 January and the police brutality she experienced hanging over her. 'And I think everyone should be. Because if America had a sort of civil war, if we get to the point of an American nationalist, white supremacist regime, there's going to be millions of people that are waiting to die. And I will be one of them.' Morgann is not overreacting, nor is she alone in wondering about the chances of another civil war after the Capitol insurrection; in the months to come, I will listen to David Remnick on *The New Yorker* podcast ask historians and academics just how likely this is.

I think of all those hopeful, radical beginnings in New York fifty years ago I learned about just a few weeks back. Here in Nebraska, I see a young person who is already tired of what she's up against. 'I went through a period recently of feeling like I might have to stop activism and campaigning because I couldn't see a way forward. I truly thought I would just have to set it aside and try to focus on something else.'

But, for Morgann, as for Laura Kaplan, it is better to do than to not to, even in the face of fear and despair. 'When I get connected to campaigns, I am able to reconnect with the work. And it feels like a really great affirmation, "No, you're on the right track, this is exactly where you need to be." And if I can't do it, then what is the purpose of me? The thing that keeps me going is that there's always another moment where someone I meet says, "I heard you speak at the women's march back in 2017 where you talked about being a sexual assault survivor and that empowered me to tell my truth and start my journey." Or somebody that's learned so much from a conversation that we had about race and gender. It's everything, it's the whole reason why I'm still here. Because in the moments when I'm at my lowest, feeling overwhelmed or useless, when someone out there sees me, or appreciates I'm doing something good, that is my purpose to me.'

I sense that for Morgann, this isn't just the work of hope, but rather, the stakes are too high to simply not try. It is a similar attitude to the one I've seen in young people organizing for gun control in America. There is no idealism; there is a desperate need for something else. 'America was never constructed for people like me,' Morgann continues. 'But America could become the kind of reality where people like me and my children one day will have an opportunity to thrive. And not just an opportunity, but opportunity upon opportunity. And that's the world that I want to build. And I see other people who think that they can do that. Because it's not just me; there are so many of us all across the United States that are doing it in their own communities. And we're all trying to work hard because we all believe in America and what it could be. But we're under no illusion – we all acknowledge what it has been, what it is now.'

While some of the issues, like police brutality and reproductive rights, aren't new, Morgann and Hannah are part of a generation that feels under attack in a whole host of ways: affordability to live, the right to housing, the rise of right-wing populism, the refusal to tackle climate change, the refusal of fact and science, the power of conspiracy, of undoing legal precedent. They are a generation that has known economic recession and a global pandemic, things which have happened during what's meant to be the most carefree moments of their lives. For them, Obama's presidency is a now distant memory and most of their adult lives have involved watching the reversal of rights, not the acceleration. How different the fight is when the winds are against you, when you can't see the hope and instead you have to find it, build it.

*

There is a set of peculiar photos from my mum's visit to Aunt June which show my mum, June, Bob and some of the children at a mall, sitting in front of life-size wax figures of Native Americans in full ceremonial dress. A bare-chested man is on top of a horse with a spear, plunging it into the back of a buffalo. A scene of stampeding buffalo is depicted on some sort of floor-to-ceiling backdrop. There's a wigwam and other men and women in ceremonial dress. In the foreground of the photographs, some of my mum's cousins smile for the camera. My mum looks distinctly awkward. She sat in the middle of the group, sticking out like a sore thumb in her denim hot pants and crop top, legs together and hands in her lap. Her face is cold, stern almost, like a teenager taken somewhere she doesn't want to be. When I asked my mum about these photos and what she remembers, she said maybe that this was some highly ill thought-out 'tribute', possibly because the mall was once on land that belonged to the Native Americans. As troubling as those photos are, they told me a different story of Omaha, one aside from June and Bob, first and second generation white European immigrants, and it is one I want to learn about while I am here.

But that isn't the only reason I am keen to speak to a member of the Indigenous community. In the story of women's rights over the last fifty years, it is Indigenous women, surely, who are most routinely overlooked, whose progress has been the most hindered, who have known the most violence – of every type.

Without doubt, the story of Native American women is the most extreme, persistent and unchecked version of the conversation I've been having with myself and with the women I've met throughout my journey across seven states. Native

American women are *ten times* more likely to be murdered than the national average. More than half have experienced domestic violence and more than half have experienced sexual violence. According to the FBI, 40 per cent of victims of sex trafficking are Native American women, even though they make up less than 10 per cent of the general population. Ninety-six per cent of those who commit violence against Indigenous women are non-native. And when they go missing, nobody looks for them – other than their own community.[53]

Native Americans also suffer the highest poverty rates and lowest labour force participation compared with any major racial group in the country, with those living on reservations particularly affected, left facing inadequate housing and poor access to healthcare. During the Covid pandemic, Native Americans on reservations died at a faster rate than any other community in the US.[54]

This is perhaps why my final conversation of the journey feels so important. At the end of this trip, I'm returning to the beginning of the story of the women of America. And it truly feels like an honour to speak to Colette Yellow Robe.

A member of the Northern Cheyenne Tribe, 45-year-old Colette Yellow Robe is a Native American Studies affiliate professor and academic retention specialist at the University of Nebraska-Lincoln, an hour from Omaha, where she is research-ing the impact of sex trafficking on native survivors. She is the chair of the Democratic National caucus for Nebraska and a member of the Native Women of Nebraska Taskforce that raises awareness around missing and murdered Indigenous women and girls, lobbying for governmental reform and design-ing policy change. This work is deeply personal for Colette.

It is about her community, her family, herself. Both her niece and nephew, who were in their twenties, have been declared missing and murdered and she describes herself to me as a 'a sexual assault and abuse survivor-thriver'.

The sexual violence against women 'goes back to when Columbus came over', Colette tells me. 'There was just an automatic assault upon Indigenous women's bodies, the concept being they wanted to conquer the land and so they conquered native women's bodies. We were to be owned and controlled. We were dehumanized right away.' Today, there are challenges specific to the state but the same problems remain, she says. 'In Nebraska, there are a couple of major interstates going through around the north, both latitude and longitude wise on the maps, and that contributes to a lot of sex trafficking.'

When Colette works to raise awareness, change policy or conduct research into the lives of Native American women, 'I have to remind colleagues that this goes beyond statistics or history lessons. Recently, a colleague emailed me wanting to organize a fundraiser. I reached out to the woman to tell her the story of my first cousin, who had been missing but was recently found in Montana, struggling with substance abuse issues, and having been taken advantage of. I said to my colleague, "This isn't a book or a CNN special. To some of us this is everyday life." I wanted to put it into perspective for her, why we have no choice but to do this work.'

The work takes a toll: 'Before I got into activism, I took a whole year to meditate. I believe in meditation and praying, to what we call my "Maheo" or creator, to prepare myself. I really had to take the time to become self-aware, do the work, do the healing.' It's plain to see that for Colette, as with many of the women I have met, helping others comes at a huge personal cost and it's not always possible to draw a line between that work and the self.

It's important to say that there have been some advances. In 2018, two Democratic candidates, Sharice Davids of Kansas and Deb Haaland of New Mexico, became the first Native American women elected to Congress. In 2021, Haaland also became the first Native American secretary of the interior. As American news outlet NPR noted, the appointment is 'symbolic as it is historic. For much of its history, the Interior Department was used as a tool of oppression against America's Indigenous peoples.' This is the first time that Native American tribes are working with the government leadership of a Native American.

Sharice Davids also become the first openly LGBQT member of congress from Kansas at the time. For Colette, the #MMIW (Missing and Murdered Indigenous Women) movement has to be inclusive on all fronts: 'Indigenous sovereignty is a solidarity movement. We stand by the LBGTQ members of the Native American community; we stand by missing men. The movement is linked to Black liberation. It has to be about solidarity with all.'

But while there is allyship with a host of communities, she is all too aware of how painful the shared experience of women across cultures and backgrounds is. 'This is the saddest part,' Colette says. 'What unites us is that assault upon our bodies and our womanhood – the misogyny. That's always so striking to me.' And her words sting. For all the different women I've met and for all the ones I haven't, for all the women's names I do know and all the ones I don't, the common ground we share is the violence we face – the physical, sexual, political, economic violence against us, the assault upon our bodies and our womanhood. I ask Colette how she carries on this work, knowing such a painful truth. 'There is a strength in being Northern Cheyenne which is fundamental. We refer to it as the soul. Northern Cheyenne women are treated pretty egalitarian in the society. And my mother did a great job of instilling that in us. Me and my sister are independent, strong women. Our mother taught us to be secure in that strength and that's a type of resilience. It's not a boastful, false sense of pride. It's a sense of security. And I will always credit my mother for that. Even at my age and as a mother myself, I have no idea how she pulled that off. She has always told me to go forward and not be afraid. To take risks. She'd say, "Do your career, go off and get your degrees." She was always saying, "Go, don't hold yourself back." And that gave me the solid foundation to deal with the reality of these hard issues and not shy away from them. Part of that strength is knowing who you are. Wherever I go on this planet, I am Northern Cheyenne. Wherever you go on this planet, you will be who you are. Don't give that up. That is resilience – to be proud and be purposeful in who you are.'

Now, Colette's lessons of the past have one direction: 'Growing up, my mother would always say that the next generation should always be two or three times better than you. Take the ego out, she'd say, this is not about you. This is about the grandchildren.'

Colette reinforces so much of what I'd seen in the Midwest: that where the battle is greatest, the resilience and the strength of women is the most inspiring. It is in the darkest corners of America's history and the greatest acts of injustice and misogyny where I have found the women who radiated the greatest fight, the greatest determination. It is a compelling and complicated space – the stories that broke my heart the most were often told to me by the very women who gave me the most hope that things could change, and who were often doing the most to bring about that change. Despite the emotional toll, the economic toll, the personal toll, it was these women, up against the most resistance, who were doing the work.

Colette crystallizes other lessons I've learned on my journey, too: how we take what's come before us and use it to build a better tomorrow. The importance of focusing on the community, not ourselves. The resilience of the Northern Cheyenne women is something I'll never understand but I can see the strength radiating from her. And, to some extent, I can understand what it's like to take strength from our mothers, knowing all they'd been through, and to carry that with us, both as a shield against whatever we may face and as a compass helping us choose which path to take – however different or similar it is from their own.

The relationships we have with our mothers, grandmothers and the women who help to guide us through life are so often complicated and knotty. And too often, on top of this, motherhood has been undermined and shrouded in derogatory, lazy stereotypes because it is the work of women. But Collette tells a different story. A story I know. That our relationships with our mothers, and the mother figures in our lives, can be some of the most important we'll ever have. And through Collette, the strength of women to overcome, again and again, feels ancient, born from a time long before and passed on from generation to generation.

Colette leaves me with a Northern Cheyenne proverb: *A nation is not conquered until the hearts of its women are on the ground. Then it's finished; no matter how brave its warriors or how strong their weapons.*

It's my last night in Omaha before I cheat and fly to London via Chicago. I opted out of taking the bus back to New York like my mum, which, now I'm here, I regret, thinking of how much I'd enjoy one long last leg on the bus, fields flashing past, a cast of characters waiting to reveal something about American life to me.

In the final few hours, I take a walk across the Bob Kerrey Pedestrian Bridge that crosses the Missouri river, just before the sun is setting. I stand with a foot either side of the state line where Nebraska meets Iowa and take a picture, enjoying being a tourist, trying to make these final moments count. And then I head to a restaurant near my hotel. I relax into the warmth of the October evening, sad my adventure is over but with a strong feeling of contentment, and excited to see Ed. I order a cold bottle of beer and some food.

In the small concrete outdoor patio area, there is a couple eating and three little Black girls playing together like meowing kittens, tumbling on the soft seating, running up to the couple at the table to see what they've got. When I sit down, suddenly, the eldest, who tells me she is eight years old, appears at my side.

'Wanna see my cartwheel?' she bursts, the words tumbling out of her mouth with a frenetic, infectious energy.

'Sure,' I smile.

Instantly, she flings her skinny legs in the air before landing back on the concrete.

'Wow! You should be a gymnast,' I say.

'I AM a gymnast,' she retorts.

'Oh yeah?'

'Yeah! Well, I was, but my mom can't afford it at the moment, so I can't go to classes.'

Just then, her smaller sisters appear and, without prompting, tell me they are five and six years old. One starts looking in my handbag. Another picks up my phone and sees Ed as my screensaver with his little niece and nephew.

'Who's that?' she asks inquisitively. Before I've answered, another sister asks, 'Where do you live?'

I tell them I live in England but I'm staying at that hotel just across the way.

'Does it have a pool?!' one asks. 'Can we go there now?!'

Just then, the woman who served me at the till comes out. 'Girls, don't bother the lady.'

And I realize who they belong to. Their mother is working. Their mother couldn't get childcare. It's late and it's a school night but this is just how things are. So here they are, charming me and others in the restaurant. They flit about, tripping each other up, giggling, practising handstands, playing tag in this small space. One climbs on the metal chair next to me and leans right over my plate.

'You want some?' I ask. She looks at her big sister.

'No. Go ask mom.'

In a few minutes, she comes out with a bowl of chips and a Fanta. Soon another table comes in and the little ones have lost their interest in me; there are new people to impress with cartwheels. They flit over and I can see this party of four are just as intrigued and confused by these little eager faces as I was, wondering who they belong to and what they are doing.

And as I watch them, I see another story. Behind the joy they bring everyone and each other, big smiles spread across pretty faces, behind all the squeals and pushes and shoves, and impromptu crabs revealing bare tummies, there's the story of a mother, doing whatever she can to give those girls whatever they need. And on that warm evening, the last of the sun fades into a pink sliver across the skyline, the light turning bluer and darker and thicker, I think how one day, in the not so distant future, they'll realize all their mother did for them, how hard she worked while they played on restaurant patios at 8 p.m. at night while their mother finished her shift. Maybe the elder one won't get back to her gymnastics class but, in time, she'll know her mother did everything she could, day in, day out. And it was all for her.

CHAPTER NINE

Somerset, England: All that we are

In less than nine months after I return from the US, Roe is dead.

On Friday 24 June 2022, in a 6–3 vote in a case called Dobbs v. Jackson Women's Health Organization, the US Supreme Court found that there is no constitutional right to an abortion. Through this decision, the court overruled Roe and reversed the constitutional right to privacy, the idea upon which Roe had been won. Now it will be up to individual states to decide the fate of the thirty-six million American women who look set to lose bodily autonomy.

The world instantly reacts. Activists celebrate and commiserate outside the Supreme Court. Tears of joy and popping champagne corks from self-declared 'pro-lifers' are met by hundreds of devastated and furious abortion supporters. Marches take place across numerous American and international cities protesting the ruling. Alexandria Ocasio-Cortez, the progressive Democrat, attends a rally that evening in Union Square in New York City. In front of hundreds of people and their recording iPhones, AOC tells her story of being raped in the city and her fear of pregnancy, but of knowing she had a choice – a choice millions now don't. It was in Union Square where I met Natalia all those weeks before as she warned me of this moment.

Red states begin to mobilize, including the thirteen who can now implement trigger laws, seven of which go into automatic bans, and the rest are expected to do so in a matter of weeks.[55] One of them is Missouri. The Supreme Court's decision came just before 9 a.m. By 9.22 a.m., abortion was outlawed, including in cases of rape and incest, the only exception being a medical emergency. Professionals who facilitate abortion can face up to fifteen years in prison.

Immediately, I think back to my time in the state. My mind turns to the lone young woman I saw on the steps of the old court house in St Louis, defiantly refusing to leave at the end of the rally. I wondered where she was when she heard the news. I think of the banner hanging from Planned Parenthood: *STILL HERE*. But not anymore – at least, not the part providing abortions. I think of the phone calls made there that afternoon to the women who had abortions scheduled, that will not now go ahead, and the infinite potential consequences they will be facing.

That evening, Ohio introduces the previously blocked 'heart-beat bill', which bans abortion after just six weeks, with an even more restrictive ban expected to follow. A story comes to light two weeks later of a 10-year-old rape victim who is pregnant and is forced to travel to Indiana, the neighbouring state, for an abortion because she is more than six weeks along.

In my own frazzled efforts to make sense of this moment, I listen to a podcast from the Chicago Women's Health Center featuring Terri Kapsalis, who I had met at the centre on my trip. Terri is discussing the roots of the feminist health movement. She explores the advent of the specialist gynaecology sector in the mid-nineteenth century, led by a famous American surgeon called J. Marion Sims, known as the 'father of gynaecology'. Sims learned by 'experimenting' and 'practising' on enslaved women. She mentions the forced sterilization of Native American women that took place in the 1960s and 1970s. Terri makes plain the historic links between male violence and women's reproductive health and freedoms – particularly with regards to women of colour. When a state refuses a raped child the right to reproductive healthcare, that is yet more violence, on top of what she has already suffered at the hands of the abuser. And it is a direct continuation of a long history of the brutal violation of women and girls' bodies – all in the name of health and life and faith.

In the coming days and weeks, other states will dissolve current injunctions or repeal laws found unconstitutional by Roe. At time of writing, up to twenty-six states are expected to ban abortion; in many states, the bans will be as severe as they are in Missouri. Anti-abortion politicians begin to discuss criminalizing abortion pills as well as out-of-state travel for the purpose of accessing abortion, while Mike Pence announces he supports a national ban. The goal is unmistakable: to make abortion impossible.

I think of all those who will now be forced to carry a foetus to term and the myriad of ways their lives will be forever transformed – emotionally, economically, physically, psychologically. I'm furious at the injustice. I'm heartbroken at the reality. I'm stunned at the audacious theft of women's freedoms.

The US is the most dangerous place in the industrialized world to have a baby – the fifty-fifth safest nation in the world. Its peers are countries 'who stone women', as law professor Michelle Goodwin, an expert commentator on issues of reproductive justice, has pointed out. In my mind's eye, I see the US now tumble even further down that cruel leader's table, the number of women's deaths rising on a tragic flicker board. In America, there is no paid maternity leave, no universal healthcare, minimal childcare benefits, frequent shootings in schools and enormous wealth disparity. Mothers will suffer and be forced to birth children into a world that is immediately hostile to their existence.

Of the six justices who voted to overturn Roe, two of them – Clarence Thomas and Brett Kavanaugh – have been accused of sexual assault.[56] All six justices are members of the Federalist Society, an organization set up in 1982 which became a pipeline for young conservative lawyers to stack the courts, a key move in the long-term game plan against abortion rights. Justice Samuel Alito, whose draft decision was leaked two months earlier, argued that because the original constitution of the 1800s didn't mention abortion, it shouldn't be protected by the constitution today – a terrifying suggestion that historical periods devoid of women's rights should dictate today's laws. In his concurring opinion, Clarence Thomas made it explicitly clear that in the light of the reversal of Roe, other established cases granted on the basis of privacy should now be revisited, specifically naming rulings pertaining to gay marriage and the right to contraception. Amy Coney Barrett, the only woman on the court who voted to overturn Roe, has previously publicly supported a religious group that believes life begins at fertilization. Consequently, that group believes that IVF should be criminalized because of the disposal of unfertilized eggs. Coney Barrett refused to answer if IVF is a constitutional right in her nominee hearings.

It is extremely hard to see this group of justices as anything other than a collective united in their hatred of women. And it's obvious that the forty-year battle leading to this decision by this Supreme Court was not about one medical procedure on one person's body. For the powerful minority, it is, and has always been, about curtailing and diminishing a woman's freedom, her democratic right as an equal citizen, her ability to live the life she chooses with dignity. The end of Roe will surely not be the end of this extremist crusade.

There have been some pretty loud warnings over the years, foreseeing this reality. But not many were as chillingly prescient as the one Nora Ephron delivered at her former college, Wellesley, in 1996:

> *Don't underestimate how much antagonism there is toward women and how many people wish we could turn the clock back. One of the things people always say to you if you get upset is, don't take it personally, but listen hard to what's going on and, please, I beg you, take it personally. Understand: every attack on Hillary Clinton for not knowing her place is an attack on you. Underneath almost all those attacks are the words: get back, get back to where you once belonged ... The acquittal of O J Simpson is an attack on you. Any move to limit abortion rights is an attack on you – whether or not you believe in abortion. The fact that Clarence Thomas is sitting on the Supreme Court today is an attack on you.*

Five months after my trip, I'm in a CVS in Tucson, Arizona, on holiday with Ed, never able to stay away from this beguiling place. I'm prowling the aisles, feeling shifty, almost like a thief. Sheepishly, in mild disbelief, I buy a pregnancy test and take it back to the hotel. Ed waits on the white sheets of the large bed. It's positive.

Once the news starts to sink in, the anger I've felt for most of my life towards men attempting to control women – their lives, their bodies – burns in a new, brighter, rawer way. I see abortion through a fresh lens. As I spend weeks nauseous and exhausted, with cramping so bad it wakes me up in the night, causes me to vomit and leaves Ed asking if he should call an ambulance, the thought of forced pregnancy and motherhood seems even more barbaric, even more of a violation of basic human rights. I didn't think I could be more furious. But here I am.

My pregnancy also puts another light on the conversations I had across the Midwest. I had been eager to understand what came before in order to help propel us forward. I wanted to learn from our grandmothers, our great-aunts, our mothers, our mentors. Now I am no longer at the end of that chain, simply absorbing the lessons of lives already lived, trying to put them into practice. I am no longer just a recipient. Soon, I will start passing something on to another generation and it starts to feel like a responsibility. I understand for the first time that the women in New York City, Ohio, Illinois, Indiana, Missouri and Nebraska who opened their doors and gave me their time did so not just as an act of generosity but because there is a responsibility to the ones who come after – to forewarn, to educate, to prepare, to guide, to push out further. Like Colette

Yellow Robe's mother told her, and she'd told me, the fight is for the future.

In my quieter and less angry moments, I wonder about what kind of mother I'll be. How I can possibly be everything my mother was to me? Can I replicate the joy and love, be someone's North Star, their biggest fan and fiercest advocate, their most loyal ally, their best example – like she has always been to me? I'm excited to see her as a grandmother, wildly fortunate that, once again, she'll be passing on her love, her strength, her stories, her laughter, her cynicism, her wild rage at injustice, her fearlessness, her passion for ABBA and Second World War planes and the Tour de France and power tools and art and literature and life. She's always said if she makes it to 80, she'll start smoking again. I hope my child grows up believing their grandmother is the coolest, most outrageous and most inspirational woman they've ever met. Just like I did.

I'm always taking lots of photos. On my phone and with a polaroid camera. Now I plan to recreate my mum's old school desk, full to the brim with memories, a record of all the time we'll share, a catalogue of evidence of all the things that have passed and a place for my child to one day explore when they are trying to understand who they are. And maybe who I am.

When my mum returned from Omaha, Nebraska, at the end of the summer in 1974, she was in a momentous period of change, both in terms of the culture and society she was living in and in the direction of her own life.

Now, on my return, destiny has seen fit to cast me in the same moment – forty-seven years later. I'm pregnant, my own period of momentous change. And there is an unmistakable shift happening in the culture and the society I'm living in as human rights are under a barrage of attacks. There is even an uncannily similar economic backdrop. Much like in the early 1970s, Britain is experiencing strikes again. There's another energy crisis – this time in terms of costs. There is inflation and a cost of living crisis. People are facing a lack of electricity, though not through an emergency government measure as under Ted Heath, but as a consequence of decades of austerity, a demolished welfare state and unaffordable energy prices brought about by war in Ukraine. Once more, we are a nation in which nothing works.

In an inverted mirror image, my mother and I have lived through extreme historical moments for women's rights just as our own lives are changing. As my mum's adventure was beginning, there was an expansion of women's rights, demanded by a generation of young people who expected a more inclusive and liberated world. My mum was a product of that moment: she was driven by a belief in new possibilities, riding a wave of ambition to realize opportunities previously denied, as social mobility shot her off to UEA and the BBC.

I too am a product of my age. I'm not married and have no plans to be. I'm a relatively older mother, due two months after my thirty-seventh birthday. I have put my career first – until now. But my exciting new journey begins with the end of Roe, caused by (mostly) old white men who want to remove rights, maintain political and patriarchal control, and live in accordance with extremist ideology.

This ruling, coming from one of the most powerful countries on earth, will embolden anti-choice nations, groups and activists around the world. Indeed, a week after the US Supreme Court's decision, British conservative MP Danny Kruger stood in the House of Commons and said that he didn't believe 'women hold full bodily autonomy' and the question of abortion should be up for 'political debate'. The ruling holds little hope for change in places like Poland and Malta where strict anti-abortion laws exist, or for Northern Ireland to actually provide the reproductive healthcare it promised after the referendum.

A roll back on abortion rights is not an isolated issue – it never has been. And the undermining of women's freedoms can be seen elsewhere. Just weeks before the 24 June Supreme Court ruling, Amber Heard lost her case against Johnny Depp.[57] Millions across social media interpreted the loss as a message that women who allege abuse should remain silent, otherwise they will be humiliated and bullied by the press and the public, as well as being financially devastated. In 2022, women's rights groups sounded the alarm in the UK over the formation of the Bill of Rights to replace the Human Rights Act. If the Bill is passed, the government will remove a vital democratic tool to hold institutions to account when they fail victims of abuse or sexual violence. No small thing when the country's largest police force – my mum's former employer – the Metropolitan police, has been repeatedly found guilty of misogyny and racism, as well as covering up a vast internal culture of domestic abuse.

On International Women's Day 2022, Amnesty International declared there had been an 'alarming assault on women's rights around the world'. Amnesty's secretary general, Agnès Callamard, wrote, 'Events in 2021 and in the early months of

2022 have conspired to crush the rights and dignity of millions of women and girls.' She pointed to the unequal fallout of Covid, the situation in Afghanistan, where the Taliban are inflicting medieval laws on women, and Turkey's withdrawal from the Istanbul Convention, a European human rights treaty against violence against women and domestic violence (something the UK was famously slow to sign onto, only doing so in November 2022).

'Each is a grave erosion of rights in its own terms,' she continues, 'but taken together?' Her unanswered question is an indication of the tsunami of damage happening and its unmeasurable toll.

In the aftermath of the overturning of Roe v. Wade, American journalist Rebecca Traister wrote in *New York Magazine* that the first response was 'doing the thing that people have always done on the arduous path to greater justice: Find the way to hope, not as feel-good anaesthetic but as tactical necessity.'

I went looking for hope in the American Midwest and I found it. I saw it take many forms. I saw it expressed in joy, in community. I saw it at its most quiet and unassuming; the private work of showing up time and time again, without fanfare or social media update. I saw it in the form of stubbornness and anger. I saw it as a wild belief, full of promise and excitement. I saw it born of wisdom and experience, rooted in a sense of purpose by those who categorically know that there is no way forward without it. And even when I saw hope dismissed, typically by younger people who were deeply frustrated, I watched them act as if it was there anyway, with a determined forward motion in their step, trying to make tomorrow better. In the Midwest, I learned that however it is deployed, wherever it is found, hope is, exactly as Traister says, a tactical necessity. Hope, I now understand, is like a renewable energy source that will power us through when everything else is gone, generating its own infinite momentum – as long as we invest in it. It is how women have fought these battles for so long, especially those with the most to fight for, who have only known struggle and resistance. Often, hope can be derided as hollow and whimsical but that's not what I saw. It was the graft, the action, the substance. It took people to marches, to stand outside trials of women they didn't know accused of foeticide, to train as lawyers, to perform illegal abortions, to organize, to write letters, to give voices to the marginalized, to achieve when the world told them they couldn't and wouldn't, to make the world a fairer and safer place. And even on the days where it was reduced to a whisper or a ghostly trace where conviction once stood, or when it felt like a cruel trick, hope always returned.

Hope has the connotation of something beautiful but fleeting, wonderful but problematic. Barack Obama spoke of the 'audacity of hope', of daring to dream of something better. The nerve of believing something could be different, the high-stakes gamble that we might just get what we want after all. In the Greek myth of Pandora, after she's opens the box and lets all the evils into the world, when she shuts the lid again, all that is left inside is hope. Hope hasn't escaped. The ambiguity of the myth's meaning speaks to how we can feel about hope, never quite sure if it's an ally or a foe. Some days, we can't get out of bed without it but at other times, we're too frightened to rely on it because of the bitter and crushing disappointment we might face. We may even feel deceived by hope, foolish that we allowed ourselves to follow its path straight into the mouth of heartbreak, left wondering if we are better off without it.

But that's not the sort of hope I saw in the Midwest. I saw something concrete, dependable. Something that wasn't a naive disillusion or an assumption that things will go our way simply because we want them to, without giving much thought or energy to how. Hope was to be relied on; in some cases, it was the only thing to be relied on. Hope – daring, courageous, committed, strategic, realistic, honest, painful, dogged and determined hope – was the foundation for the fight.

And hope *is* women. Women *are* hope. It was through the women I met – their tenacity, their commitment, their efforts – that I discovered the stuff of hope. Seventy-four-year-old Laura Kaplan refused to give up her fight. Thirty-year-old Chelsie Walter refused to leave her state. Thousands of women across America are refusing to adhere to the Supreme Court's ruling and are providing abortion care regardless. History has shown us, time and time again, there will always be a group of women who come together to fight, persist, regardless of the potential prosecutions. The work is always happening, even when we can't see it. After the ban on abortion in Missouri, the CEO of Missouri Planned Parenthood announced they had stealthy built a clinic just fifteen minutes away from the existing clinic, over the water and crucially in Illinois, a state where abortion remains legal. Many states won't have such a luxury and those trapped in a desert of red will have to travel for thousands of miles to seek an abortion. But the new Illinois clinic demonstrates Laura Kaplan's adage: *women don't abandon women.*

Hope drives the resilience – the ability to fight and fight and fight. To get back up time and time again. The friction of pain and hope lights a spark, fuelling women, moving them forward despite the ferocity of the winds against them. Hope is a type of faith that provides an armour against incoming attacks and defeats and disappointment. Hope isn't whimsical when it provides the strength to carry on, regardless, day after day. In fact, it's the opposite. In her essay, Rebecca Traister quotes the prison abolitionist Mariame Kaba, who said, 'It's less about "how you feel" and more about the practice of making a decision every day that you're still gonna put one foot in front of the other, that you're still going to get up in the morning. And you're still going to struggle … It's work to be hopeful.' [58]

In my new understanding of the sustenance and substance of hope, I realize I had gravely misunderstood something. I began this journey asking where the wild hope that danced across my mother's face in that picture had gone. But my premise was off. Because it didn't go anywhere. It was there all along. My mum never gave up her wild hope, despite what came her way. And her hope truly was a discipline: an alarm clock that rang just after 5 a.m., a 7.15 a.m. train, a spelling test after dinner, a few lines of *Huckleberry Finn* before bed. Her hope was the same commute for thirty years, a walk over the same bridge, a weekend of the same commitments, years of saving money and making it to the end of the month. It was the fierce love for her two children. Her hope was her joy. It was in the way she'd pretend to be *Sesame Street*'s Count as she washed our hair in the bath, counting bowls of water as she threw them over our giggling heads. The way she'd play Pulp as loud as she could on the CD player in the kitchen and dance. The way she'd drive us to the coast every Christmas morning, whatever the weather, and even if we were trapped in the car, unable to face the lashing rain and howling winds, she'd be laughing. There were no bad moods, no complaining that things weren't fair. Not a shred of self-pity. Just joy, just love. There was always her hope.

And so in many ways, the woman in the picture from the school desk was the woman I knew all along. I just didn't understand that hope can have many faces and not all of them are the freedom of a 22-year-old in hot pants in a hot Nebraska summer. That young woman in the polaroid, the one determined to find her happiness and pave her way, was the same woman I saw growing up. It might not have been the path she thought she would take but she pursued a career in current affairs, a huge passion, in a job that was demanding but also exciting and challenging, that had her working alongside mayors and ministers. She found time for the things she loved, like our little adventures across France and Italy, packing Marmite for the warm French bread in the mornings. And as life brought her more and more challenges, her resilience only became fiercer. My mother's ability to put one foot in front of another for so many years, through such unspeakably harrowing times, is nothing short of a miracle. But she did. And plenty of women do. Colette Yellow Robe spoke of the assault on our womanhood. And that is unquestionable and something I understand profoundly. But our ability to keep going, in spite of those attacks, makes being a woman even more miraculous.

So perhaps I always knew what hope and resilience was made of because I'd seen it every day of my life. I always knew that it is born of all the things that my American women told me it was: fight, faith, enduring hard work, a commitment to something other than yourself. But perhaps I had to go out into the world and hear that truth from others to appreciate my mother in a way I hadn't before, that I hadn't been able to see when I assumed that she and the woman in the polaroid were two different people. Everything that young woman was becoming would serve her for everything she would face – her restlessness, her faith in herself, her wonder of the world and the people in it, her belief in the stories of others and the importance of what is just, her tenacity to push on, her sheer resilience and survival, her ability to inspire in the face of so many things trying to drag her down. And while systems and society and men may have laid traps, none of things I first saw in that tiny picture have ever left her. That's the woman in the polaroid and that's my mother. And today, after one hell of a journey, she still has a face full of freedom.

On my trip, I put into practice the lessons I was learning in real time.

Looking back towards my mother truly paved a way forward for me. It was that polaroid that set me off in pursuit of so many wonderful adventures: solo trips to a Blues bar in a Chicago suburb, sitting underneath the wind chimes on Laura's Kaplan's porch, taking the elevator to an ex-Republican's Manhattan penthouse, making friends at a Mexican bar in St Louis. It was my mother's courage that inspired me to push through doubt and book a flight. I was doing what both my parents had done, and in many regards my brother, too: searching America for stories to tell – about others, about ourselves. And I realized, just as many of the women I spoke to had done, that I too made sense of the world we live in through stories of those I am closest to.

I have come to understand how the communion of women leads to hope – something more important than ever. I was constantly met with generosity and kindness. I cherish a moment in the Columbus bus terminal when an elderly Black lady and I entered the toilets at the same time. She'd come to freshen up but I was desperate and the toilets were an abomination, almost comically so. Except for one clean cubicle right at the end – which had no door. 'I'll stand watch,' she said. 'Go on.' And so she stood by the sinks while I weed in privacy. I heard her stop a woman from entering as she splashed the cold water on her chest and neck, humming to herself. After I'd finished, I washed my hands next to her and I offered her some of my posh lavender hand sanitizer. She rubbed it into her wrinkled hands as if it was cashmere. She closed her eyes and smelt them. 'Thank you, my dear,' she smiled. And in this small, fleeting exchange, over in a few minutes, I felt it all: the solidarity, the kindness and the care of women for one another – something often found in the privacy of a women's bathroom.

I practised my faith in storytelling not just with the women I'd arranged to meet but the ones I happened to encounter along the way, like the hostess at the Mexican bar with the pink love heart tattoo on her collarbone or Sarah Schlafly's stories of her grandmother's final days. I found a voice I never had before – the one shared in this book. Going in search of women's stories – and telling my own – really has been a liberation. I was living out the advice I was collecting.

But, in the spirit of Laura Kaplan, I refuse to paint an exclusively misty-eyed Hollywood version of a dreamy road trip, disappearing into the sunset with hair blowing in the wind as a Simon and Garfunkel song plays over the credits, masking the horrors of what is happening. As Rebecca Solnit has written, 'Grief and hope can coexist.' During my journey, I also witnessed first hand the darker side to what these women were warning of: the vulnerability of women's lives and the refusal of a society to make them safe was evident at every turn. The threat of male violence was an ever-present refrain in my conversations, even the ones when I wasn't expecting it. The story of Gabby Petito on CNN played out like a sinister soundtrack from hotel to hotel room, the dreamy American road trip morphing into a nightmare. Her body was discovered on 19 September in Wyoming. This time, the violence had come not from the stranger on the street – the place where women are taught to be fearful and have good reason to be – but from the man in her home, in her bed – the place where women are statistically least safe and have the hardest time escaping, but whose dangers are most overlooked and ignored. Gaby's story, narrated by Cuomo's dramatic patter, was a chilling reminder of the relentless male violence in our lives. It also reminded me, night after night, whose stories get airtime and whose don't – not the Black women Keea told me about in Pittsburgh, or the women Giovanna will know of, or the members of Colette Yellow Robe's family and tribe. We're not even telling the whole story yet, so far we are from accepting the scale of the problem. When you also consider relaxed guns laws and illegal abortion, it's not hard to make the case that American women's right to life is now on the line.

The women I met all predicted the fall of Roe. Dean Williams spoke of the inevitability of backlashes – something that was evident in the laws of each state I passed through, alongside efforts to crack down on human rights, curtailment of voting rights through racist redistricting and elected officials who believe the election was stolen and the 'Great Replacement Theory' is true. The women warned of a crumbling democracy in light of 6 January and, in time, congressional committee hearings will reveal just how close the United States government came to being violently overthrown. The chaos of 6 January and the reversal of women's rights are part of the same story – one which is a sharp move away from democracy towards something that bears the hallmarks of fascism.

I saw the truth in their warnings with stories of Proud Boys threatening a university campus and police launching attacks on BLM protests. Since my return to the UK, the states I passed through have now granted guns more protected rights than women. And so, however enriching these lessons were to me personally, they were vital in reminding me just how much is on the line.

This is also how my journey helped me to understand that I'd got something else wrong, too. I began by asking how hard-won rights unravel. But I see now that a right isn't a trophy we put on a shelf, job done, on to the next. No matter how grave the institution that grants them, rights are vulnerable, fragile and under attack from the minute they are fought for. They need constant protection, defence, surveillance. They are not won and written in stone; they are etched in the sand, exposed to the winds of political change and social uprising. We need to be reminded why we have those rights and what's at stake if we don't. And if we rest our world and identities upon them, then we have the responsibility to keep them robust and safe. We can never forget that someone, somewhere, is always chipping away. However slight the damage may seem, relentless undermining from all angles can lead to erosion, until one day, we wake up and they are simply not there anymore. This all happens within the rules of the game, slowly prised away from us in broad daylight. We have to drown out all those who roll their eyes, smirk and say that 'it will never happen'. Because that's what so many said about Roe.

The morning I flew to New York City in September 2021, Ed dropped me off at Heathrow. The last thing he said to me as we kissed goodbye at the lifts to the departures lounge was 'You are braver than you realize.'

This trip was never meant to be about me. In fact, I was warned relentlessly by the women I met that we all need to spend a hell of a lot less time thinking about ourselves and think about others instead. But I was naive to assume a journey, a pilgrimage, to my mother wouldn't also be about me in some way. It just wasn't the way I'd expected.

To grow up with fear in the house, in the next room, at the dinner table, sharing the same bathroom, on the same holidays with you, driving the car you're in, cooking in the kitchen, watching the TV, means to grow up believing that danger can be found anywhere, everywhere. But that fear doesn't necessarily mean you're stuck at home with the doors locked and curtains closed. Sometimes that fear shapeshifts into doubt – a fear of your own failing, incompetence and inability. Low self-esteem is a common by-product of abuse. It is something I have known intimately and profoundly.

When I got home, Ed and I laid on the living room floor as I told him about my adventures and that I'd found another version of myself in the Midwest – the brave one he could see but I never could. As I was pushing on into unknown places to hear the stories of women, I felt like I was exactly where I was meant to be. I was alive with the mission I was on. For a month or so, I had been gloriously without doubt. I felt physically lighter. I hadn't just been smelling the breezes, I'd felt like I was floating on them.

I once had a moment on a treadmill in Deptford. Possibly the only time I've experienced a runner's high. As I ran, it was as if I'd taken off from the ground and was ascending higher and higher into a blue sky among fluffy white clouds. As I lifted, I realized that I was getting away from the men that have impacted me: my father, my stepfather, the man I was seeing at the time who was unkind. I ran and ran and ran away from them, and for a moment, left them all behind.

Riding the Greyhound gave me that same feeling: I could leave behind a heavy weight. My sadness, something I've always carried around like a rucksack, had vanished. I'd almost forgotten I had it. I was in a mode of perpetual adventure and discovery. Possibility grew on trees; this feeling of magic – life moving along as effortlessly as a bus down an interstate – is a life without the weight of men's decisions. In my own technicolour American dream, I left all my darkness behind and I felt free.

My journey to find a version of my mother actually led me to discovering a picture of myself. I hadn't realized that by asking *who are you?* I would in fact be asking *who are you and, therefore, who am I?* But what are our parents if not distorted mirrors that we're sometimes blind to or that are too painful to look at, so painful we cut them out of photographs? On my trip the answer came, even though I didn't know I'd posed the question. For too long, I had been buried, hidden away, in a dark and safe place, suffocatingly wrapped up in a perverse comfort blanket, an inner voice of doubt reminding me there was no point in even trying, there was no hope in me succeeding, I should just stay exactly where I was – a message echoed by the society I live in. Stay inside, it's safe. Stay quiet, it's safe. Stay still, it's safe.

But I left that behind when I made the trip across the Midwest. I uncovered a version of myself, bringing her out into the bright American sunlight – the person who had been there all along, just like 22-year-old Jacqui had been. The wisdom and stories and the struggle and joy of my mother, of the women I met, is oxygen, an engine, a firelighter. Those stories collected together become a book of faith. And I finally found the courage to see myself and all that I could be, all I could fight for, all that I could do, just as my mother had once done, one hot summer in Omaha, Nebraska.

ACKNOWLEDGEMENTS

A sincere thank you to all the women who feature in this book. Thank you for inviting me into your homes and offices, or to share a coffee, offering me time and insight. Meeting you all was an experience I will never forget. I was deeply inspired and fascinated by each of you and will carry our conversations with me.

Thank you to June, Brooke and all the family for letting me share part of your story. It is a privilege to know you, and to be a distant branch of your broad and beautiful family.

I spoke to many brilliant women on background, particularly Sara Love, Elizabeth Earle Beske and Elizabeth Yukins. Your experience and expertise were extremely helpful, and I am very grateful.

I would like to thank Richard Pike at C&W for taking my disjointed A4 document of an idea and believing it could be transformed into 80,000 words of non-fiction. Big thanks to Kate Fox, formerly of HQ, and Lisa Milton, who made space for the stories of these remarkable women. Thank you to Nira Begum for sensitive and thoughtful editing. Thank you to all those who helped bring these women's voices to readers.

A huge thank you to my dear friend, Jane Hunter. Your

belief in and enthusiasm for this book has been unwavering, and your introductions to women across the Midwest was invaluable. As ever, you made all the difference.

A huge thank you to another dear friend, Ben McCluskey. You were my very first reader, and your edits and insights were extremely helpful. My Swiss army knife: your constant advice, guidance and encouragement on everything from PR strategy to sentence structure has truly been a gift. Mostly though, thank you for the best book title that never was.

Thank you to Natasha Lunn. Yet again you have believed in me, and this project, when I was at my most doubtful. How lucky I am to have a friend who is as kind and compassionate as she is shrewd and wise. Our friendship is in every one of these pages and it is one of my most precious treasures.

Thank you to my family for letting me write my story, which of course, is your story too. I am fortunate and proud to be from a tribe of artists and storytellers.

To my mum, the most remarkable woman of them all, I hope I've made it plain, but just in case: Thank you. A million times thank you. I love you.

And to Ed. From the very first day your faith in me has burned brightly and fiercely, lighting up my darkest skies, patiently showing me a way forward, encouraging me to fight harder, encouraging me to smell the breezes. Thank you for filling our lives with your love, brilliance and adventures. It all feels possible next to you.

REFERENCES

1   Jenny Diski, *Stranger on a Train: Daydreaming and Smoking Around America with Interruptions* (London: Virago, 2002), 99

2   Kavanaugh 'categorically and unequivocally' denied he ever was involved in such an assault.

3   Clarence Thomas 'vehemently' denied Hill's allegations.

4   In 1970, The Boston Women's Health Collective self-published *Our Bodies, Ourselves*, a pioneering feminist project to inform and educate women about their health and sexuality – information that women could often not otherwise access. The book became a word of mouth sensation and was published until 2011

5   Rewire News Group, '"It's Time to Raise Hell": Activists Today Are Shouting About Abortion Pills', 1 December 2022

6   Tony Michels, *Uprising of 20,000 (1909)*, Jewish Women's Archive, https://jwa.org/encyclopedia/article/uprising-of-20000-1909

7   Susan Bevan and Susan Cullman, 'Why We Are Leaving the G.O.P', *The New York Times*, 24 June 2018 www.nytimes.com/2018/06/24/opinion/abortion-rights-republican-party-women.html

8   *Pittsburgh Inequality Across Gender and Race 2019*, City of Pittsburgh's Equality Commission

9   Tereneh Idia, *The Pittsburgh area has stark racial inequalities. Black Pittsburghers face a key question: Should they leave?* 4 November 2019, www.publicsource.org

10 Statistia.com, 'Number of NCIC missing persons files in the United States in 2021, by age and gender' www.statista.com/statistics/240387/number-of-missing-persons-files-in-the-us-by-age/?

11 ONS (2019) *Families and households*, Table 1

12 Susan Faludi, *Backlash: The Undeclared War Against Women*, (London: Vintage, 1992), 62

13 Faludi, *Backlash*, 62

14 Faludi, *Backlash*, 48

15 Nora Ephron, extract taken from *Time Magazine*, Monday, Apr. 11, 1983

16 Shelia Rowbotham, *A Century of Women: The History of Women in Britain and the United States* (London: Penguin Books, 1999), 432

17 Rowbotham, *A Century of Women*, 45

18 Pat Thane and Tanya Evans, *Sinners? Scroungers? Saints? Unmarried Motherhood in Twentieth Century England*, (Oxford: Oxford University Press, 2012), 171

19 Clarence Thomas vehemently denied these allegations.

20 The Reconstruction Era is the name given to the period after the American Civil War when America attempted to integrate freed Black slaves into society and was met with considerable resistance. After civil rights legislation in the 1960s, including desegregation in schools, this became known as the 'Second Reconstruction'.

21 Fabiola Cineas, 'Black Women Will Suffer the Most Without Roe', Vox.com, 2022 www.vox.com/2022/6/29/23187002/black-women-abortion-access-roe

22 When deciding to set up a women's health clinic after Roe had been passed, the group split. Those who wanted to work with medical professionals set up the CWHC in 1975. Those who saw that as a betrayal of Jane's original spirit and an introduction of hierarchy founded the Emma Goldman clinic, named after the anarchist midwife and birth control advocate.

23 Rebecca Solnit, *Hope is the Embrace of the Unknown* (London: Canongate, 2016)

24 Sylvia Plath, *The Unabridged Journals of Sylvia Plath* (Anchor Books, 2000)

25 Aron Blake, 'Mike Pence doesn't dine alone with other women and we're all shocked', *Washington Post*, 30 March 2017, https://www.washington-post.com/news/the-fix/wp/2017/03/30/mike-pence-doesnt-dine-alone-with-other-women-and-were-all-shocked/

26 Edwin Rios, 'US schools remain highly segregated by race and class, analysis shows', *Guardian*, 15 July 2022, https://www.theguardian.com/education/2022/jul/15/us-schools-segregated-race-class-analysis; Sarah Carr, 'In Southern Towns, "Segregation Academies" Are Still Going Strong, *The Atlantic*, 13 December 2012, www.theatlantic.com/national/archive/2012/12/in-southern-towns-segregation-academies-are-still-going-strong/266207/

27 Ilyse Hogue and Ellie Langford, *The Lie That Binds* (Washington DC: Strong Arm Press, 2000) 15

28 Hogue and Langford, *The Lie That Binds*, 17–28

29 Hogue and Langford, *The Lie That Binds*, 22

30 Ewan MacAskill, 'Woman who attempted suicide while pregnant is accused of murder', *Guardian*, 15 April 2011 https://www.theguardian.com/world/2011/apr/15/woman-attempted-suicide-pregnant-accused. For more on Bei Bei Shuai's story, you can purchase *Bei Bei: A Documentary* on Vimeo at https://vimeo.com/ondemand/beibeifilm

31 Michael H. Keller and David D. Kirkpatrick, 'Their America Is Vanishing. Like Trump, They Insist They Were Cheated, *The New York Times*, 23 October 2002 www.nytimes.com/2022/10/23/us/politics/republican-election-objectors-demographics.html

32 Francis Wilkinson, 'The Gospel According to Randall Terry', Rolling Stone, 5 October 1989 www.rollingstone.com/culture/culture-news/the-gospel-according-to-randall-terry-47951/

33 *Reversing Roe,* directed by Ricki Stern and Anne Sundberg, 2018

34 Andy Campbell and Alanna Vagianos, 'Truck Driver Rams into Abortion Rights Demonstrators at Roe Rally in Iowa', *Huffington Post*, 25 June 2022 www.huffingtonpost.co.uk/entry/truck-driver-rams-into-protesters-roe-demonstration-in-iowa_n_62b66490e4b0cdccbe6b9399

35 Pat Thane and Tanya Evans, *Sinners? Scroungers? Saints? Unmarried Motherhood in Twentieth Century England*, (Oxford: Oxford University Press, 2012), 187

36 Jon Sharman, 'Boris Johnson said children of single mothers were "ill-raised, ignorant, aggressive and illegitimate" in newly unearthed column, *Independent*, 28 November 2019 www.independent.co.uk/news/uk/politics/election-boris-johnson-articles-women-women-journalist-spectator-labour-a9222036.html

37 Thane and Evans, *Sinners? Scroungers? Saints?* 169

38 Rowbotham, *A Century of Women*, 498

39 Rowbotham, *A Century of Women*, 292

40 Trump has never filed for personal bankruptcy, but he has reportedly filed for business bankruptcy at least four times.

41 National Coalition Against Domestic Violence, ncadv.org/STATISTICS

42 Rebecca B Lawn and Karestan C Koenen, 'Homicide is the leading cause of death for pregnant women in the US', *British Medical Journal*, October 2022

43 Indiana University Health, 'Addressing Indiana's Maternal Mortality Rate', 26 July 2022 iuhealth.org/thrive/addressing-indianas-maternal-mortality-rate

44 Moira Donegan, 'The US made women second-class citizens. Now we must give a stinging rebuke', *Guardian*, 8 November, 2022 www.theguardian.com/commentisfree/2022/nov/08/the-us-made-women-second-class-citizens-now-we-must-give-a-stinging-rebuke?

45 Katie Balevic, 'Vice President Kamala Harris said images at the border of offices chasing Haitian refugees reminded her of "times of slavery", September 2021, www.insider.com/kamala-harris-images-border-haitians-officers-horses-times-of-slavery-2021-9

46 Bernd Debusmann Jr, 'Grim echoes of history in images of Haitian at US–Mexico border', BBC News, September 2021, www.bbc.co.uk/news/world-us-canada-58654351

47 United Nations General Assembly, *Report of the Special Rapporteur on extreme poverty and human rights on his mission to the United States of America*, 2018, 3

48 www.midwestacademy.com/heather-booth-changing-world/

49 Ilyse Hogue and Ellie Langford, *The Lie That Binds* (Washington DC: Strong Arm Press, 2000), 23

50 Hogue and Langford, *The Lie That Binds*, 25

51 National Partnership for Women & Families, 'Black Women and Wage Gap Fact Sheet', October 2022 www.nationalpartnership. org/our-work/resources/economic-justice/fair-pay/african-american-women-wage-gap.pdf

52 Pew Research Center, 'Rising share of Americans see women raising children on their own, cohabitation as bad for society', 2022 www. pewresearch.org/fact-tank/2022/03/11/rising-share-of-americans-see-women-raising-children-on-their-own-cohabitation-as-bad-for-society/

53 National Congress of American Indians, 'Research Policy Update: Violence Against American Indian and Alaska Native Women', February 2018 www.ncai.org/policy-research-center/research-data/ prc-publications/VAWA_Data_Brief__FINAL_2_1_2018.pdf

54 Nina Lakhani, 'Indigenous Americans dying from Covid at twice the rate of white Americans', *Guardian*, 4 February 2021 www.theguardian.com/us-news/2021 /feb/04/native-americans-coronavirus-covid-death-rate

55 In the coming weeks, some federal judges start to place bans on the trigger laws, claiming they are not constitutional within the laws of the individual states. This temporary measure is a short-term relief but causes chaos and confusion among clinic staff and clients.

56 Both men deny the allegations against them.

57 Depp always denied the allegations of abuse, and Heard's case was almost wholly dismissed by the jury.

58 Mariame Kaba on the podcast *Intercepted with Jeremy Scahill; Hope is a Discipline: Mariame Kaba on Dismantling the Carceral State*, 17 March 2021

ONE PLACE. MANY STORIES

Bold, innovative and
empowering publishing.

FOLLOW US ON:

@HQStories